The ICSA Company Secretary's Checklists

THE ICSA COMPANY SECRETARY'S CHECKLISTS

Tenth edition

Douglas Armour FCIS

icsa

The Governance
Institute

Published by
ICSA Publishing Ltd
Saffron House,
6–10 Kirby Street
London EC1N 8TS

First published 1992
Second edition 1997
Third edition 2000
Fourth edition 2002
Fifth edition 2004
Sixth edition 2009, reprinted 2010
Seventh edition 2011
Eighth edition 2013
Ninth edition 2015

This edition published 2017

Typeset by Hands Fotoset, Bexhill, East Sussex

Printed and bound in Great Britain by
Lightning Source, Milton Keynes, Buckinghamshire

British Library Cataloguing in Publication Data
A catalogue record for this book is available from the British Library.

ISBN 978-1-86072-717-7

Table of Contents

About the author

Douglas Armour FCIS had a career spanning more than 31 years at David Venus & Company, including a period as managing director following the acquisition of the company by the Equiniti Group. Douglas was group company secretary at Equiniti Group PLC during its transition from private equity ownership through its IPO and Listing on the London Stock Exchange in 2015. Douglas left the Equiniti Group at the end of 2016 and after a short career break joined Intertrust's capital markets governance team as a senior manager.

Douglas has more than 30 years' experience in all aspects of company secretarial procedures for companies of all sizes from owner-managed private companies to FTSE 100 companies.

Over the course of those 30 years, Douglas has accumulated a wealth of practical experience and has drawn on this to include in this book those procedures that company secretaries, directors and practitioners will find most useful.

Preface

The ICSA Company Secretary's Checklists provides a handy, quick reference guide to the more common company secretarial procedures. The book is not intended to be a legal reference book, and accordingly little explanation of the relevant legislation is made. As more detailed information will often be required, the book has been cross-referenced to the relevant legislation, *The ICSA Company Secretary's Handbook* (11th edition) (H) and *Company Secretarial Practice: The Manual of the Institute of Chartered Secretaries and Administrators* (CSP), both of which are published by ICSA Publishing.

Each topic comprises a general commentary on the particular matter, a checklist of items to be considered, procedural steps to be taken, Companies House filing requirements, as well as general notes and cross-references.

The Companies House references are to their series of guidance booklets which are available on request by post or may be downloaded from the Companies House website (www.gov.uk/government/organisations/ companies-house).

These checklists should not be regarded as exhaustive, to be followed in all circumstances, but should serve as a guide to the reader indicating procedures that should be considered in the context of the matter at hand.

Although, overall, the checklists have been prepared with private or non-traded public companies in mind, many of the procedures are equally applicable, and in some cases only applicable, to public or listed companies.

The book will be of particular interest to the following:

▶ *Accountant/auditors.* Many private company directors will turn to their accountant for advice on company secretarial matters. This book sets out answers to the majority of procedural queries likely to be raised.

▶ *Solicitors/chartered secretary practices.* While most solicitors and chartered secretaries will have access to extensive libraries of legal reference books, these are often too detailed for quick reference. This book is intended to complement rather than duplicate existing reference sources.

▶ *Company secretaries/directors.* Company secretaries will find this book of particular use when advising their directors on particular matters, even if advice will ultimately be sought from the company's professional advisers. An understanding of the practical issues for any particular matter will

▶ facilitate proper discussion at board level, collation of relevant information and the issuing of coherent instructions to professional advisers.

At the time of writing, implementation of the Small Business, Enterprise and Employment Act 2015 is almost complete, with only the general prohibition on the appointment of corporate directors remaining to be implemented. Also at the time of writing, although the Department of Business, Energy and Industrial Strategy have confirmed their intention to implement the legislation, no implementation date has been published.

Douglas Armour

August 2017

Acronyms

ABI	Association of British Insurers
AGM	annual general meeting
BEIS	Department of Business, Energy and Industrial Strategy
CA2006	Companies Act 2006
CGC	UK Corporate Governance Code
CIC	Community Interest Companies
EEA	European Economic Area
EEIG	European Economic Interest Grouping
EES	European Employment Strategy
EU	European Union
FCA	Financial Conduct Authority
FRC	Financial Reporting Council
FSMA2000	Financial Services and Markets Act 2000
HMRC	Her Majesty's Revenue & Customs
HR	human resources
ICSA	Institute of Chartered Secretaries and Administrators
LLP	limited liability partnership
LPA	lasting power of attorney
LPDTR	Listing, Prospectus, Disclosure and Transparency Rules
LTIP	Long-term Incentive Plan
MCA2005	Mental Capacity Act 2005
MiFID	Markets in Financial Instruments Directive
NAPF	National Association of Pension Funds
NEX	Growth Market Rules for Issuers
NI	National Insurance
OCR	Overseas Companies Regulations (2009)
PAYE	pay as you earn
PLC	public limited company
PROOF	PROtected Online Filing
PSC	person with significant control
RIS	Regulatory Inspection Service
SAIL	single alternative inspection location
SAYE	save as you earn
SBEE2015	Small Business Enterprise and Employment Act 2015
SIC	Standard Industrial Classification
UCITS	Undertakings for Collective Investment in Transferable Securities
UKLA	United Kingdom Listing Authority
VAT	value added tax

Accounting reference date

All companies, whether trading or not, must prepare accounts and file a copy with the Registrar of Companies. The accounts are prepared in respect of each accounting period. Accounting periods begin at the conclusion of the previous period, or the date of incorporation, and end on the accounting reference date. Companies may choose an accounting reference date. If no alternative date is chosen, the company's accounting reference date will default to the last day of the month of its incorporation.

A company may change its accounting reference date at any time, provided the filing date for the existing period has not expired. An accounting reference period may not exceed 18 months and, except in the circumstances set out below, a company may not extend its accounting period twice in any five-year period.

A company may only extend its accounting period more than once in any five-year period if it is changing to fall in line with the accounting reference date of a holding or subsidiary company, or if the company is in administration.

Provided the filing date for the period being shortened has not expired, a company may shorten its accounting period as often as it wishes and there is no minimum period. Where the accounting period is shortened, the new filing date will be nine months (private company) or six months (public company) from the end of the accounting period or, if later, three months after the notice to shorten.

Checklist

▶ The filing period for the financial year being changed must not have expired.

▶ The filing period for the proposed new period must not have expired.

▶ The new period must not be longer than 18 months, unless an administration order is in force.

▶ If extending the period, the company must not previously have extended its accounting year end in the previous five years, or if it has, can the change be justified?

▶ If the new year-end has already passed, can accounts to that date be prepared (e.g. stocktakes, asset valuation)?

▶ Directors' resolution is required either at a meeting or by written resolution.

▶ File form AA01.   s.392(1)

Procedure

▶ Convene a directors' meeting to authorise the change in accounting year.

▶ Form AA01 must be filed at Companies House.

Filing requirement

▶ Form AA01.

Notes

▶ The company's first accounting period must be longer than six months, but not longer than 18 months, starting from the date of incorporation. The first accounting period begins with the date of incorporation even if the company does not immediately commence trading.   s.391(5) s.390(2)

▶ The second and subsequent accounting periods may be as short as the directors wish, but may not exceed 18 months.   s.392(5)

▶ A company can extend its accounting year only once in any five-year period, unless the accounting period is being changed to coincide with that of its holding company or any subsidiary. The accounting period can be shortened as many times as required.   s.392(3)

▶ The length of any accounting period, even one that has ended, can be altered, provided that the relevant form is received by the Registrar before the end of the period in which the accounts for that the current or proposed period must be filed. The change in year-end will become effective once the Registrar of Companies has received the appropriate form.   s.392(1)

▶ Directors wishing to extend the accounting period must first confirm that the accounting year-end has not been extended in the previous five years.

▶ The date by which accounts must be submitted to the Registrar may be lengthened when the accounting period is for a period of less than 12 months, as the filing period is the usual period after the accounting reference date or three months after the date of receipt of the form AA01, if longer (see page 12).

▶ Normally a private company has nine months from its accounting reference date to file its accounts; for a public company the period is six months.   s.442(4) s.442

▶ Companies can make their accounts up to any date within seven days of the actual accounting reference date. This is to enable companies to undertake a stocktake outside normal business hours without needing to change their year-end.

s.390(2)(b)

▶ Companies may apply for an extension to the filing deadline provided this is received by the Registrar prior to the filing deadline; however, there need to be exceptional circumstances in order to be granted an extension.

s.442(5)

▶ In addition to notifying the Registrar of Companies, the directors may also consider notifying the following: bankers, auditors, accountants, HM Revenue & Customs, subsidiaries, joint venture partners, London Stock Exchange (if listed).

▶ The change in accounting reference date is only effective once the form AA01 is accepted and registered by Companies House.

More information

 Chapter 11    Chapter 15   Guidance
Filing accounts

Accounts – approval

Accounts, whether audited or not, must be prepared and approved by the board of directors and issued to the company's members, any debenture holders and anyone else entitled to receive notice of general meetings.   ss.394,414,423

Although members of a public company consider and receive the accounts in general meetings and can vote on whether or not to accept them, they do not, strictly speaking, approve them. If the members reject them, the directors are not obliged to amend the accounts unless they contain a factual error. However, non-acceptance of accounts will be regarded as a vote of no confidence in the board.   s.437

Checklist

▶ Convene a directors' meeting for directors to approve the accounts. Ensure valid quorum present.   s.414(1)

▶ The strategic report and directors' report must be signed by a director or by the company secretary.   ss.414D(1),419(1) s.433

▶ Quoted companies must prepare a directors' remuneration report which must be signed by a director or the company secretary (see page 7).   ss.420,422

▶ The balance sheet must be signed by at least one director.   s.414(2)

▶ The name of the person(s) signing the directors' report, strategic report, remuneration report (if any) and balance sheet must be stated.   s.433

▶ If audited, the audit report must be signed by the auditor, if an individual, or by the senior statutory auditor, in the case of a firm, and the person's name and the date of approval shown.   ss.503–505

▶ The name of the senior statutory auditor may be omitted if there are concerns over safety.   s.506

▶ Small companies must issue to their members the accounts in the same format as those placed on the public record. In the case of a private company it must send out its accounts to members before the end of the period allowed for filing the accounts (usually nine months (see page 12)). In the case of a public company, the accounts must be sent out at least 21 days before the date of the meeting to receive them.   ss.423,424,444

▶ In the case of a public company, the accounts must be sent out at least   **ss.441,442**
21 days before the date of the meeting to receive them.

▶ Full or abridged accounts must be filed at Companies House by the
due date (see page 12).

Procedure

▶ Convene a directors' meeting to consider the accounts and to convene
a general meeting. Ensure valid quorum present.

▶ Final draft of the accounts to be approved by the directors.

▶ The directors' report, strategic report and the balance sheet must be
signed. The directors' report and strategic report can be signed by the
company secretary or a director; however, the balance sheet must be
signed by at least one director. The published accounts must include
the names of the director and/or company secretary who have signed
the balance sheet and directors' report.

▶ A quoted company must prepare a directors' remuneration report,
which must be signed by a director or the company secretary.

▶ The same director can sign the directors' report, strategic report,
directors' remuneration report (if any) and the balance sheet.

▶ If the accounts are audited, signed copies must be returned to the
auditors so that the audit report can be signed.

▶ Once signed, a copy of the accounts must be filed with the Registrar
of Companies within the appropriate period (see below).

▶ Copies of the accounts must be sent to the members and public   **s.442**
companies must convene a general meeting of the members, for the
shareholders to consider the accounts, within six months. Private
companies are exempted from the obligation to convene a members'
meeting unless required to do so by their articles of association.

▶ Companies, if authorised to do so by individual members, may issue   **s.426**
the strategic report and supplemental material to the members in
place of the full accounts, provided that the full accounts are made
available on request. This replaces the option to issue a summary
financial statement which has been withdrawn.

▶ Certain companies may file abridged accounts with the Registrar of   **s.441**
Companies (see pages 17 and 21).

▶ Full accounts will be required for submission to HM Revenue &
Customs.

▶ Additional copies will normally be sent to the company's bankers.

▶ The usual period for delivery of accounts to the Registrar is nine   **s.442**
months from the end of the accounting period for a private company,
and six months for a public company. However, if the accounts are
the first accounts and are for a period of more than 12 months, the

accounts must be submitted no later than nine months (six months for a public company) from the first anniversary of incorporation, or three months from the end of the period – whichever expires later.

s. 442(3)

▶ Where the accounting period has been shortened, the period for delivery of the accounts is nine months for private companies and six months for public companies from the end of the period, or three months from the date of notice – whichever expires later.

s. 442(4)

▶ The Registrar of Companies imposes penalties for late submission of accounts. When setting the accounting reference date, care must be taken to ensure that the accounts can be prepared in time to submit them to the Registrar of Companies (see page 12).

s. 453

Filing requirement

▶ Full or abridged copy of the accounts within 21 months of the start of the accounting period for a private company (usually nine months after the year-end) and within 18 months of the start of the accounting period for a public company (usually six months after the year-end).

Notes

▶ Accounts must have original signatures on the directors' report, strategic report, directors' remuneration report, audit report (if audited) and balance sheet.

s. 414(1)

▶ The name of the person signing must be shown.

▶ The company registration number must be shown on the first page.

▶ As the Registrar will unbind and discard any folder, an unbound copy of the accounts should be filed.

▶ The accounts must be legible and be capable of being digitally scanned. Accordingly, it is best to file typed accounts printed on plain paper. Accounts printed on coloured or glossy paper or with graphics are likely to be rejected as illegible.

▶ As the accounts are not subject to member approval, it is not necessary to wait until after the general meeting at which the accounts are received by members before filing a copy of the accounts with the Registrar of Companies.

More information

Accounts – directors' remuneration report

Directors of listed companies are required to include a remuneration report in the annual report and accounts. The report must also comply with the Listing Rules and the UK Corporate Governance Code. Where the provisions of the UK Corporate Governance Code are not complied with, a statement of those provisions not complied with and the explanation for such departure must be included.

The requirements of the Large and Medium-sized Companies and Groups (Accounts and Reports) (Amendment) Regulations 2013 came into force on 1 October 2013 and, in particular, replaced schedule 8 of the Large and Medium-sized Companies and Groups (Accounts and Reports) Regulations 2008. References here to schedule 8 are to the 2008 regulations as amended by the 2013 regulations and as further amended by the Companies, Partnerships and Groups (Accounts and Reports) Regulations 2015.

In addition to these regulations, provisions of the Enterprise and Regulatory Reform Act 2013 ss. 79–82 made changes to the Companies Act 2006 regarding the payments to directors of quoted companies, and these will also need to be considered.

The Directors' Remuneration Report now comprises two parts: an annual Statement and Report on Remuneration (the Implementation Report) and the Directors' Remuneration Policy (the Remuneration Policy).

s.420(1)

Checklist

Annual statement

Para.3 sch.8, SI 2008/410 (as amended)

▶ Annual statement by the chairperson of the committee of any major decisions or substantial changes on directors' remuneration during the year.

Remuneration

Para.4–12 sch.8, SI 2008/410 (as amended)

▶ Single total figure of remuneration for each director, broken down into:

  ▷ salary and fees;

- ▷ all taxable benefits;
- ▷ money or other assets received/receivable for more than one financial year;
- ▷ pension-related benefits; and
- ▷ total (aggregate of the above).

▶ Total pension entitlements.

▶ Scheme interests awarded during the financial year.

▶ Payments to past directors.

▶ Payments for loss of office.

▶ Statement of directors' shareholding and share interests.

▶ Performance graph and table.

▶ Percentage change in remuneration of CEO.

▶ Relative importance of spend on pay.

▶ Statement of implementation of remuneration policy in the following financial year.

▶ Consideration by the directors of matters relating to directors' remuneration.

▶ Statement of voting at general meeting.

▶ Details of the unexpired term of any service contract of a director proposed for election or re-election at the AGM, and if any director does not have a directors' service contract, a statement to that effect.

Para. 13 sch. 8, SI 2008/410 (as amended)
Para. 14 sch. 8, SI 2008/410 (as amended)
Para. 15 sch. 8, SI 2008/410 (as amended)
Para. 16 sch. 8, SI 2008/410 (as amended)
Para. 17 sch. 8, SI 2008/410 (as amended)
Para. 18 sch. 8, SI 2008/410 (as amended)
Para. 19 sch. 8, SI 2008/410 (as amended)
Para. 20 sch. 8, SI 2008/410 (as amended)
Para. 21 sch. 8, SI 2008/410 (as amended)
Para. 22 sch. 8, SI 2008/410 (as amended)
Para. 23 sch. 8, SI 2008/410 (as amended)

Procedure

s. 422

▶ The contents of the remuneration report must be approved by the board at a board meeting.

s. 439

▶ A resolution to approve the remuneration report (advisory, not binding) must be put to shareholders at the same meeting at which the accounts are received.

More information

 Chapter 10    Chapter 16   **FCA Listing Rules**

Accounts – exemption from audit

Small private companies and dormant public companies qualify for exemption from audit if they satisfy certain criteria. These companies do not need to apply for the exemption; they are automatically exempt if they qualify.

ss. 477, 480, 482

For accounting years beginning on or after 1 January 2016, qualifying subsidiary companies can claim exemption from audit. Subsidiary companies that are public (unless they are dormant), regulated under FSMA and members of ineligible groups cannot take advantage of the new exemption.

s.476

Shareholders holding between them at least 10% of the company's issued share capital, or 10% of the members in the case of a company without share capital, may give notice to the company requiring that the accounts be audited, provided that the notice is given no later than one month prior to the end of the financial year.

s.477

Checklist

- Total exemption is available to companies:
    - that qualify as a small company in relation to that year (see page 21) by meeting any two of the following: **s.480**
        - whose turnover does not exceed £10.2 million in that year; or **s.478**
        - whose balance sheet total for that year does not exceed £5.1 million; or
        - whose average number of employees is not more than 50.
- A company is not entitled to exemption from audit if at any time during the financial year:
    - it was a public company, unless it was dormant; or
    - it was a banking or insurance company, e-money issuer, a MiFID investment firm, a UCITS management company or carried on insurance market activities; or
    - it was a special register body or an employers' association as defined in the Trade Union and Labour Relations (Consolidation) Act 1992 or the Industrial Relations (Northern Ireland) Order 1992.

▶ A company that is a parent or subsidiary undertaking at any time during the financial year is not entitled to exemption from audit unless:

   ▷ the group qualifies as small (see page 21) and was not at any time during that year an ineligible group (see below);

   ▷ turnover of the whole group does not exceed £10.2 million net or £12.2 million gross; and

   ▷ the group's continued balance sheet total does not exceed £5.1 million net or £6.1 million gross.

            s. 479

▶ A company that is a dormant subsidiary throughout the period is not excluded from qualifying as small under s. 479(2).

            s. 479(3)

▶ A group is ineligible if any member of the group is:

            s. 384

   ▷ a traded company;

   ▷ a corporate body whose shares are admitted to trading on a regulated market in an EES State;

   ▷ a person authorised under FSMA2000 to carry on a regulated activity;

   ▷ a small company that is an authorised insurance company, banking company, e-money issuer, MiFID investment firm or a UCITS management company; or

   ▷ a person who carries on insurance market activity.

Procedure

▶ There is no procedure; exemption is automatic if the criteria are met.

▶ To qualify for the subsidiary company exemption, the following must be filed prior to the expiry of the period allowed for filing accounts. In practice these are usually submitted at the same time as the subsidiary's accounts are filed at Companies House:

   ▷ Written notice that all members agree to the exemption.

   ▷ Form AA06 – statement from parent undertaking that it guarantees the subsidiary.

            s. 479C

   ▷ Copy of parent undertaking's consolidated accounts, including a copy of the auditor's report and annual report on these accounts.

Filing requirement

▶ Copy of the accounts within the appropriate timescale, usually six months for a public company or nine months for a private company (see page 12).

            s. 442

▶ Copies of the accounts are still required to be circulated to members within the appropriate timescale: six months for a public company and nine months for a private company.

            s. 423

For subsidiary exemption

▶ Written notice that all members agree to the exemption.

▶ Form AA06 – statement from parent undertaking that it guarantees the subsidiary.

▶ Copy of parent undertaking's consolidated accounts, including a copy of the auditor's report and annual report on these accounts.

Notes

▶ A company that qualifies for exemption from audit is also exempt from the obligation to appoint auditors.

ss. 475, 485

More information

 Chapter 10    Chapter 16   Guidance
Filing accounts

Accounts – filing period

All companies, whether trading or not, must prepare accounts and file a copy with the Registrar of Companies. The accounts are prepared in respect of each accounting period. Accounting periods begin at the conclusion of the previous period, or the date of incorporation, and end on the accounting reference date.

s.390

There are strict timescales for the filing of accounts and financial penalties imposed when accounts are filed late (see page 14).

s.390(2)

Accounts must be filed even where the company does not or has never traded.

Checklist

▶ Accounts for a private company must be filed within nine months of the accounting reference period ending, unless:

s.442(2)(a)

▷ it is the first accounting period and is for a period of greater than 12 months – the deadline is three months after the period end or 21 months from the date of incorporation, whichever is later; or

s.442(3)

▷ the company has shortened its accounting period – the deadline is nine months from the end of the new period or three months after the change was registered at Companies House, whichever expires last.

s.442(4)

▶ Accounts for a public company must be filed within six months of the accounting reference period ending, unless:

s.442(2)(b)

▷ it is the first accounting period and is for a period of greater than 12 months – the deadline is three months after the period end or 18 months from the date of incorporation, whichever is later; or

s.442(3)

▷ the company has shortened its accounting period – the deadline is six months from the end of the new period or three months after the change was registered at Companies House, whichever expires last.

s.442(4)

▶ Whether the filing period follows the period allowed for a private or public company is determined by the company's status immediately before the end of the relevant period.

s.442(6)

▶ When calculating the filing deadline, it should be noted that the date of the month is the same date in the appropriate month corresponding to the accounting reference date. Thus a private company with an accounting reference date of 10 January must file its accounts no later than 10 October following. **s. 443(2)**

▶ If the accounting reference date is the last date of the month, the filing period ends on the last day of the appropriate month. Thus a private company with an accounting reference date of 30 April must file its accounts no later than 31 January. **s. 443(3)**

▶ If the accounting reference date is the 29th or 30th (and not the last day of that month) and the appropriate deadline month is February, the filing period ends on the last day of February in that year. **s. 443(4)**

More information

 Chapter 10    Chapter 16   Guidance
Filing accounts

Accounts – late filing penalties

If accounts, whether audited or dormant, are received by the Registrar of Companies after the due date for filing has passed, the company will be fined according to a sliding scale.

s.453

It should be noted that the onus is on directors to deliver accounts to the Registrar of Companies within the specified time. It is not sufficient to show that they were posted within the specified time. Late filing penalties do not apply to annual returns.

s.441(1)

The scale of penalties is as follows:

	Private companies	**Public companies**
Up to one month late	£150	£750
Up to three months late	£375	£1,500
Up to six months late	£750	£3,000
More than six months late	£1,500	£7,500

Notes

▶ The penalties are imposed on the company, not the directors, and are a civil matter. However, under certain circumstances, the directors may also be prosecuted for failure to submit accounts on time. This is a criminal offence, and on conviction a maximum fine of £2,000 may be imposed by the court for each separate offence.

s.453
s.451

s.448

▶ Unlimited companies do not need to file copies of their accounts with the Registrar of Companies.

▶ The penalties are doubled if a company files its accounts late in two successive financial years beginning on or after 6 April 2008.

More information

Chapter 10

Chapter 16

Guidance
Filing accounts

Accounts – medium-sized companies

Companies qualifying as medium-sized can prepare accounts under special provisions applicable to medium-sized companies and can choose to submit reduced information to Companies House.

ss.441(1),445

Checklist

▶ In order to qualify or to be treated as qualifying as a medium-sized company in respect of any particular financial year, the company must be or have been medium-sized during one or more of the following periods:

s.465(1)

s.465(2)(a)

▷ in its first financial year;

s.465(2)(b)

▷ in that year and in the year before;

▷ in that year and if the company qualified in the year before; or

s.465(2)(c)

▷ in the preceding year and if the company qualified as medium-sized in respect of that year.

s.465(3)

▶ A medium-sized company is one that meets at least two of the following requirements:

▷ turnover not exceeding £36 million;

s.467(1)

▷ balance sheet total not exceeding £18 million; and

▷ average number of employees not exceeding 250.

s.467(2)

▶ A company does not qualify if at any time during the financial year it was:

▷ a public company;

s.467(1)

▷ authorised under Part 4 FSMA2000 to carry on a regulated activity or carry on insurance market activities; or

▷ a member of an ineligible group.

▶ A group is ineligible if any of its members is:

▷ a public company;

▷ a corporate body whose shares are admitted to trading on a regulated market in an EES State;

▷ a person (other than a small company) authorised under FSMA2000 to carry on a regulated activity;

▷ a small company that is an authorised insurance company, banking company, e-money issuer, MiFID investment firm or a UCITS management company; or

▷ a person who carries on insurance market activity.

Procedure

▶ The information required for medium-sized accounts must include:

▷ full balance sheet;

▷ profit and loss account;

▷ special auditors' report unless exempt from audit;

▷ directors' report; and

▷ full notes.

s.445(1)

s.445(3)(a)

ss.449(2),(5)

s.445(1)

Filing requirement

▶ Copy of the medium-sized accounts within the appropriate timescale, usually six months for a public company and nine months for a private company (see page 12).

s.442

Notes

▶ As with the exception of the profit and loss account and the omission of an analysis of non-financial key performance, medium-sized accounts are the same as full accounts; there may be little practical benefit from utilising the exemption.

s.423

▶ Copies of the full statutory accounts, omitting, if desired, disclosures relating to compliance with accounting standards and related party transactions, are still required to be circulated to members within the appropriate timescale: six months for a public company and nine months for a private company.

More information

 Chapter 10  Chapter 16  Guidance
Filing accounts

Accounts – micro-sized companies

Within the category of small companies is a sub-set for extremely small or micro companies.

s.384A

Checklist

▶ In order to qualify or to be treated as qualifying as a micro-sized company in respect of any particular financial year, the company must be or have been micro-sized during one or more of the following periods:

▷ in its first financial year;

s.384A(1)

▷ in that year and in the year before; or

s.384A(2)

▷ if it fails to qualify in that year but the company qualified in the year before.

s.384A(3)

▶ A micro-sized company is one that meets at least two of the following requirements:

▷ turnover not exceeding £632,000;

▷ balance sheet total not exceeding £316,000; and

s.384A(4)

▷ average number of employees not exceeding 10.

▶ A company does not qualify if at any time during the financial year it was:

▷ a company excluded from the small companies regime by virtue of s. 384;

▷ an investment undertaking;

s.384B(1)

▷ a financial holding undertaking;

▷ a credit or insurance institution; or

▷ a charity.

▶ A company does not qualify if:

▷ it is a parent company which prepared group accounts; or

▷ the company is not a parent but its accounts are included in consolidated group accounts for that year.

Procedure

▶ The information required for micro-sized accounts is:

   ▷ balance sheet;   **s. 444**

   ▷ abbreviated profit and loss account;

   ▷ special auditors' report unless exempt from audit;

   ▷ directors' report; and

   ▷ full notes.

▶ Additionally there must be the following note to the accounts: **s. 444**

   ▷ a statement above the director's signature on the balance sheet   **s. 442**
that the directors have relied on the exemptions the company is
entitled to benefit from as a micro-sized company.

Filing requirement

▶ Copy of the micro-entity accounts within the appropriate timescale,   **s. 444(3)**
usually six months for a public company and nine months for a
private company (see page 12).

Notes

▶ As with the exception of the profit and loss account, abbreviated
micro-sized accounts are the same as full accounts; there is little
practical benefit from utilising the exemption.

▶ Small companies must now place on public record the same set
of accounts and reports as circulated to its members. Previously,
companies circulated full accounts to their members and could
opt to file abbreviated accounts for the public record.

More information

 Chapter 10    Chapter 16    Guidance
Filing accounts

Accounts – overseas company

The obligation for an overseas company, registered in the UK, to file accounting information depends on whether it is required to prepare, disclose and deliver accounting information under its parent law and if it is, whether it is an EEA company.

reg. 34 SI 2009/1801

An EEA company that is required to prepare, disclose and deliver accounting documents under its parent law must deliver the same documents to Companies House within three months of the deadline for disclosure in its home country.

reg. 40 SI 2009/1801

An EEA company that is required to prepare and disclose but not deliver accounts under its parent law is not required to deliver accounts to Companies House.

A non-EEA overseas company that is required to prepare and disclose accounting documents under its parent law must deliver these to Companies House within three months of the deadline for disclosure in its home country.

A non-EEA company that is not required to prepare and disclose accounting documents under its parent law is required to prepare, sign and deliver accounts to Companies House. The accounting provisions are set out in the Overseas Companies Regulations 2009.

An overseas company that is not required to prepare and disclose accounts under its parent law is required to prepare accounts as if it were a company incorporated under the Companies Act, and ss. 390–392, 394–397, 399, 402–406, 441, 442, 451, 471–474 apply as modified by regs. 37–42 SI 2009/1801. The period allowed for filing those accounts is 13 months from the end of the relevant accounting reference period.

Checklist

▶ Is the company an EEA company?

▷ If yes and disclosure of accounts is required in its home state, file a copy of the same accounts within three months of the filing deadline in the parent country.

▷ If yes and disclosure of accounts is not required in its home state, no accounts need to be filed in the UK.

▶ If not an EEA company, does the legislation in its country of incorporation require the delivery of accounts? — **Regs. 36 and 37 SI 2009/1801**

  ▷ If yes, file a copy of the accounts under reg. 34 SI 2009/1801 within three months of publication together with certified translation if required; or reg. 31 SI 2009/1801.

  ▷ If no, prepare audited accounts in accordance with regs 37–42 SI 2009/1801. — **Reg 31 SI 2009/1801**

▶ Accounts must be for the whole company, not just the UK establishment.

Filing requirement

▶ Copy of accounts under reg. 34 SI 2009/1801 within three months of publication together with certified translation if required; or

▶ Copy of accounts under reg. 40 SI 2009/1801 within 13 months of year-end. These need not include directors' or auditors' reports, information relating to turnover, UK taxation, subsidiaries, directors' emoluments and loans to directors. — **Reg 40 SI 2009/1801**

▶ Filing fee £20.

Notes

▶ Different rules (not dealt with here) apply to overseas credit or financial institutions.

▶ The exemptions available to small- and medium-sized companies and dormant companies are not available to overseas companies.

▶ Although overseas companies that are required to prepare accounts are subject to the same rules regarding accounting reference dates (see page 1), as non-overseas companies they may extend their year-ends as many times as they wish.

More information

 Chapter 24    Chapter 16    Guidance booklet GP01

Accounts – small-sized companies

Companies qualifying as small-sized may file small company abridged accounts with the Registrar of Companies and circulate these to their members.

ss.441(1),444,444(a)

Checklist

▶ In order to qualify or to be treated as qualifying as a small-sized company in respect of any particular financial year, the company must be or have been small-sized during one or more of the following periods:

  ▷ in its first financial year;   **s.382(1)**

  ▷ in that year and in the year before;   **s.382(2)(a)**

  ▷ in that year and if the company qualified in the year before; or   **s.382(2)(b)**

  ▷ if the qualifying conditions were met in the preceding year and the company qualified as small-sized in respect of that year.   **s.382(2)(c)**

▶ A small-sized company is one that meets at least two of the following requirements: **s.382(3)**

  ▷ turnover not exceeding £10.2 million;

  ▷ balance sheet total not exceeding £5.1 million; and

  ▷ average number of employees not exceeding 50.   **s.384(1)**

▶ A company does not qualify if at any time during the financial year it was:

  ▷ a public company;

  ▷ an authorised insurance company, banking company, e-money issuer, MiFID investment firm or a UCITS management company; or   **s.384(1)**

  ▷ a member of an ineligible group.   **s.384(2)**

▶ A group is ineligible if any of its members is:

  ▷ a public company;

▷ a corporate body whose shares are admitted to trading on a regulated market in an EES State;

▷ a person (other than a small company) authorised under FSMA2000 to carry on a regulated activity;

▷ a small company that is an authorised insurance company, banking company, e-money issuer, MiFID investment firm or a UCITS management company; or

▷ a person who carries on insurance market activity.

Procedure

▶ The information required for abridged accounts of a small-sized company is:

▷ full balance sheet;

▷ a statement above the director's signature on the balance sheet that the accounts have been prepared in accordance with the special provisions applicable to companies subject to the small companies regime; and **s.444(5)**

▷ an audit report unless the company qualifies for and takes advantage of exemption from audit. **s.442(2)**

Filing requirement

▶ Copy of the abbreviated accounts within the appropriate timescale – usually six months for a public company and nine months for a private company (see page 12). **s.444(3)**

Notes

▶ Small companies must now place on public record the same set of accounts and reports as circulated to its members. Previously, companies circulated full accounts to their members and could opt to file abbreviated accounts for the public record.

More information

 Chapter 10    Chapter 16    Guidance Filing accounts

Acquisition of non-cash assets from members in initial period

Special requirements apply where a public company proposes to acquire non-cash assets from its subscribers within the period of two years commencing on the date of the issue of its trading certificate, or in circumstances where a private company is re-registered as a public company and the company wishes to acquire certain non-cash assets from the members of the company, either at that time or within a period of two years from the re-registration.

s.598

s.603

s.598(3)

In either circumstance the company may only acquire non-cash assets from its subscribers or members provided the assets are independently valued and approval is obtained from the members. These provisions do not apply where it is part of the company's ordinary business to acquire such assets and the transaction is entered into in the normal course of its business.

s.598(4)

These provisions should not be confused with the provisions relating to the issue of shares for non-cash consideration, which are subject to s. 593.

ss.598(1),603(a)

s.598(1)(c)

Checklist

▶ Is the asset being transferred from a subscriber or from a person who was a member at the date of re-registration as a public company?

ss.598(2),603(b)

▶ Is the value of the asset equal to 10% or more of the company's issued share capital?

s.599

s.600

▶ Is the transfer taking place within two years of issue of the company's s. 761 trading certificate for transfers from a subscriber or within two years of re-registration as a public company in respect of transfers from a member?

s.599(1)

▶ Appoint an independent valuer to value the asset being acquired in accordance with ss. 1150 and 1153 and any non-cash consideration issued by the company (usually shares credited as fully paid).

▶ Valuation must be within the six-month period prior to the date of transfer of the assets and must be circulated to members and the other party to the transfer.

▶ The transfer agreement is to be approved by members by ordinary resolution and a copy of the resolution must be forwarded to the other party involved in the transfer. **s.601**

▶ A copy of the ordinary resolution and the valuation report must be filed at Companies House within 15 days of the passing of the resolution. **s.602**

Procedure

▶ Convene a directors' meeting to appoint an independent valuer, usually the company's external accountant or auditor where appointed; recommend appropriate resolution(s) to members and to convene a general meeting. Ensure valid quorum present.

▶ A copy of the valuation report drawn up to a date not more than six months prior to the date of transfer must be received by the company. The valuation report must state those matters set out in s. 600(2). **s.599(1)(b)**

▶ Issue notice, signed by director or company secretary, together with a copy of the valuation report convening the general meeting on 14 clear days' notice for members to consider resolution to approve transfer agreement and valuation report. **ss.599(1)(c), 601(1)(a)**

▶ Enclose with the notice a form of proxy if desired. Listed companies must enclose a three-way form of proxy (see page 186). **LR9.3.6**

▶ Consider whether class meeting(s) also required.

▶ If the meeting is to be convened on short notice, the company secretary should arrange for agreement to short notice to be signed by each of the shareholders.

▶ Copy of valuation report and notice to be sent to the transferor of the assets if no longer a member. **ss.599(1)(c), 601(1)(c)**

▶ Hold general meeting. Ensure valid quorum is present. Resolution put to vote either by show of hands or by poll and to be passed by appropriate majority (ordinary resolution by 50% majority).

Filing requirement

▶ Signed copy of ordinary resolution and copy of the valuation report within 15 days of approval. **s.602(1)**

Notes

▶ The independent valuer's report must confirm that, in his or her opinion, the consideration to be received by the company is not less than the value of the consideration being paid (i.e. cash or shares).

▶ These provisions will apply even where the acquisition is only in part the acquisition of non-cash assets, provided that they exceed 10% in nominal value of the company's issued share capital.

▷ Transactions involving assets with an aggregate value representing less than 10% in nominal value of the company's issued share capital are exempt from these requirements. **s.598(1)(c)**

▷ If these provisions have not been followed, the company is entitled to reclaim any consideration paid to its subscribers or members, in which case the agreement shall be void. **s.604**

▷ If the consideration paid by the company is the allotment of shares credited as fully paid, the company shall be entitled to request from the allottee an amount equal to the nominal value of the shares together with any share premium. **s.604(3)**

More information

 Chapter 13    Chapter 2

Agreement to short notice

In most instances, members of private companies and small unquoted public companies can agree to accept shorter notice of a meeting than that prescribed by the Companies Act.

For any general meeting, other than an annual general meeting of a public company, a majority of the members holding between them at least 90% of the voting shares must agree to the meeting being held at short notice. This can be increased to not more than 95% by a provision contained in the company's articles of association.

s.307(6)

For an annual general meeting of a public company, all members must agree.

s.337(2)

It is not necessary for the members agreeing to the short notice to attend the meeting.

It is recommended that the agreement(s) to short notice are given in writing and that these are placed in the company's minute book, together with the minutes of the meeting.

If the meeting is being convened by a public company to consider the company accounts, the agreement to short notice must include agreement to accept receipt of the accounts less than 21 days prior to the meeting being held, if these are being sent with the notice convening the meeting.

s.424(4)

Although certain resolutions require that special notice be given, calling the meeting on short notice will not in itself invalidate the resolution.

However, caution must be taken when calling meetings on short notice of which special notice has been given.

Certain resolutions (e.g. purchase of own shares) require that documents be made available for inspection for a set period prior to the meeting. As a result, the option to convene the appropriate meeting on short notice is limited and for private companies, using the written resolution procedure may be an appropriate alternative (see page 240).

Checklist

▶ In addition to the requisite percentage of the issued share capital, is a majority of the members represented?

▶ Do any documents need to be made available for inspection for a minimum period prior to the meeting?

▶ Confirm consent to short notice verbally prior to issuing notice of meeting.

Procedure

▶ The company secretary circulates an agreement to short notice with the notice, and requests its signature and return.

Filing requirement

None.

More information

 Chapter 8    Chapter 14

Annual general meeting

Private companies do not need to hold an annual general meeting unless their articles of association require this. Where a company is required to hold an annual general meeting by their articles of association, the notice period, in the absence of any provisions of the articles of association, is the same as for any general meeting.

A public company must hold an annual general meeting within six months of its accounting reference date. Where a company's accounting reference period is shortened, the annual general meeting must be held within three months of the giving of the notice to shorten the accounting period.

s.336(1)

s.336(2)

As a consequence, a public company may not need to hold an annual general meeting in any particular calendar year if it has a financial year in excess of 12 months.

The normal or 'ordinary' business of the AGM is to receive the most recent accounts, consider the remuneration report (quoted companies only), confirm the declaration of a final dividend (where appropriate), approve the remuneration of the auditors and re-elect the auditors and retiring directors, if necessary. Any other business is deemed to be 'special' business.

Checklist

▶ The meeting must be held within six months of the company's accounting reference date.

s.336(1)

▶ If the directors propose payment of a final dividend, this must be approved at a general meeting.

art. 70 sch. 3, SI 2008/3229

▶ If the company is quoted, a resolution to approve the directors' remuneration report will be required.

s.439

▶ Check the articles of association to see if the directors are required to retire by rotation. Directors of FTSE 350 companies are recommended to retire and offer themselves for re-election every year. All other directors of listed companies should offer themselves for re-election at least once every three years.

CGC B7.1

▶ Check the articles of association to see if any new directors appointed by the directors during the year are required to retire at the next annual general meeting. If the company is a public company, each director offering themselves for re-election will require a separate resolution.

s.160

▶ Check the articles to see if there are any special requirements for the election or re-election of directors.

s.338

▶ Check to see if any members have validly proposed any resolutions required to be included in the notice.

ss.489,515

▶ Are the auditors to be reappointed, or are new auditors being appointed requiring special notice (see page 162)?

s.492

▶ The remuneration of the auditors must be fixed by the members or in such manner as they shall approve.

ss.549,551

▶ If appropriate, a resolution to extend or renew any authority (see page 256) to issue shares can be put as 'special business'.

ss.561,570, 571,573

▶ If appropriate, a resolution to extend or renew any waiver of pre-emption rights on allotment can be put as 'special business'.

▶ Consider whether there is any other business to be put before the members.

Procedure

▶ Convene a directors' meeting to recommend appropriate resolution(s) to members and to convene annual general meeting. Ensure valid quorum present.

▶ Only the directors may convene an AGM as members' right to requisition a meeting only applies to general meetings. The directors should formally convene the meeting and approve the contents of the notice and accompanying documents.

s.302

▶ Company secretary or director to give special notice to the company, if required (such as appointment of auditor other than retiring auditor).

s.312

▶ Issue notice, signed by director or company secretary, convening annual general meeting of a public company on 21 clear days' notice (20 clear working days, for a quoted company) for members to consider resolutions. Private companies holding an annual general meeting need only give 14 clear days' notice, subject to the articles of association.

s.337
CGC E2.4

s.307

▶ Notice must be given in hard copy, in electronic form (provided the person has agreed to accept documents and notice in this way) or by means of a website. Notice may be given partly by one such means and partly by another.

s.308

▶ If notice is given by placing it on a website, members must be notified where it may be viewed.

s.309

▶ Enclose with the notice a copy of any accounts and a form of proxy if desired. Where issued forms of proxy must be sent to all members entitled to vote at the meeting, listed companies must enclose a three-way form of proxy (see page 186).

s.326
LR 9.3.6

▶ Consider whether class meeting(s) also required.

▶ If the meeting is to be convened on short notice, the company secretary should arrange for agreement to short notice to be signed by each of the members (see page 26).

▶ Copy of notice to be sent to non-member directors and auditors. **s.502(2)**

▶ Hold annual general meeting. Ensure valid quorum is present.

▶ Resolutions put to vote either by show of hands or by poll and to be passed by appropriate majority (ordinary resolutions by 50% majority, special resolutions by 75% majority).

Filing requirement

▶ Copies of any special resolutions and those ordinary resolutions where notification required. **ss.29,30**

▶ Any appropriate forms relating to non-reappointment of directors or auditors. **ss.167,521**

Notes

▶ The company secretary should arrange a suitable venue for the meeting.

▶ Before the meeting the company secretary or, if appointed, the company's share registrars should check and count all the proxies received.

▶ At the meeting the company secretary should ensure that an attendance sheet is circulated.

▶ Arrangements should be made to ensure that members alone have access to the meeting; however, this is not always possible or desirable in practice.

▶ Unless waived by the meeting, the notice and the directors' report should be read to the meeting.

▶ There is no longer a statutory requirement for the audit report to be read to the meeting. However, if the auditor is present, it is common practice for him or her to read the audit opinion.

▶ For companies with a large number of shareholders, or at meetings where there may be questions from the floor, it is useful to prepare a chairman's script prior to the meeting. Additionally, the directors should meet before the meeting to discuss any matters that might be raised at the meeting and decide who will deal with certain queries.

▶ If a poll is likely, the company secretary should arrange for poll cards to be available. Companies that use registrars will normally use their services when conducting a poll. The directors should ensure that as many proxy forms as possible are received prior to the meeting. It is important that proxy forms are received at the registered office, or the office of the registrars, before the deadline for receipt of proxies. Most companies adopt the standard, and maximum, period prior to the meeting of 48 hours, but the articles of association must be checked as companies can adopt a shorter period up to the start of the meeting itself. Proxy forms arriving later than this cannot be accepted, and any proxy forms brought to the meeting are invalid.

▶ Additional copies of the latest audited accounts and directors' service contracts must be available at the meeting, together with a copy of the register of members and minutes of previous shareholder meetings.

More information

 Chapter 8    Chapter 14

Annual general meeting – best practice

This checklist sets out the main issues to be considered before, during and after an AGM.

In addition to the Companies Act requirements for general meetings, quoted companies must also comply with the provisions of the Listing Rules, Disclosure and Transparency Rules and the UK Corporate Governance Code. Finally, for most companies there will be provisions in the articles of association to be considered too.

Although this guidance is for AGMs, many of the requirements will apply equally to general meetings.

Checklist

Before the meeting

The venue

▶ Book a suitable venue with sufficient capacity for the expected number of attendees, suitable facilities for the disabled and presentation equipment.

▶ Confirm the date of the meeting with the board, registrars, advisers and others required to attend as early as possible.

▶ Companies with a large number of members and where the business is contentious should consider contingency plans in the event that attendees exceed the capacity of the room. Security arrangements should be considered.

▶ Arrangements may also need to be made to ensure that members alone have access to the meeting; however, this is not always possible or desirable in practice.

AGM notice – explanatory notes

While the core content of the notice is set out in the Act, it is good practice to provide additional information to clarify procedure or anticipate questions. This should include:

▷ the date and time not exceeding 48 hours by which members must be registered on the register of members to be entitled to attend and vote;

    ss.311(3)(b) & 360B and regs 41(1) & (6) USR2001

▷ a statement of a corporate members' right to appoint one or more corporate representatives;

    s.323

▷ a statement of the members' right to appoint one or more proxies and any more extensive rights conferred by the articles;

    ss.324 and 325

▷ instructions as to how and when the proxy appointment should be returned, and a statement that the return of a completed form of proxy does not prevent a member from attending the meeting in person;

▷ a statement of the order of priority for signing a form of proxy in the case of joint holdings;

▷ if relevant, that the chairman intends to call a poll on any or all resolutions; and

▷ an explanation of how the voting will take place at the meeting.

Proxies

▷ A proxy appointment should provide information on how to appoint a person or persons, other than the chairman, as proxy.

    s.324 and DTR 6.1.5

▷ If the company offers that a particular person, such as the chairman, will act as proxy, that offer must be made to all shareholders.

    s.326

▷ Include a note on how to change a proxy appointment and what happens if more than one proxy appointment is submitted.

▷ Provide details of how the proxy appointment should be completed and where it should be sent or delivered to and by when, which must not be more than 48 hours (excluding non-working days) before the meeting.

    s.327

▷ Proxy forms for quoted and traded companies should be worded to provide for three-way voting by including a 'vote withheld' option and a note explaining that a 'vote withheld' is not a vote in law and will not be counted.

    LR 9.3.6(2)

▷ Arrange regular updates on proxy voting totals. Where the chairman has been appointed proxy, ensure that he or she is aware of the number of votes cast for and against the resolutions so that on a show of hands or a poll, he or she will know how to cast his or her vote(s).

Preparing the chairman

▷ Brief the chairman on the main provisions in the articles governing the organisation and procedure of the meeting, voting procedure and his or her role and powers as chairman of the meeting.

▷ Prepare a script for the chairman to use.

▶ Familiarise the chairman with the process of taking questions from the floor. Prepare a questions and answers pack to anticipate questions, including any difficult issues which might be raised.

▶ Ensure that the chairmen of the board committees and the finance director will be present at the meeting and that they are fully briefed on possible questions that may be asked.

At the meeting

It may be useful to take the following items to the meeting:

▶ AGM notice and form of proxy;

▶ annual reports and accounts;

▶ the chairman's script;

▶ copies of presentations;

▶ questions and answers pack;

▶ the documents that need to go on display at the meeting;

▶ articles of association;

▶ contingency plan; and

▶ spare paper poll cards and pens.

Documents available for inspection

Listed companies must have the following documents on display for at least 15 minutes prior to the start of the AGM until it closes:

▶ non-executive directors' terms and conditions of appointment; and

▶ directors' service contracts.

Any documents to be approved or amended that were not circulated to the members with the notice must be on display for at least 15 minutes prior to the start of the AGM until it closes. They must also be available for inspection in the City of London (or another place agreed with the FCA) from the date the notice is sent until the close of the meeting.

All directors should attend the AGM and all the company's directors should be seated with the chairman, facing the shareholders.

The chairman

▶ Check the articles to confirm who will be the chairman of the meeting.

▶ Subject to the articles, a member, including a proxy, may be elected by resolution of the members present to be chairman of the meeting. **ss.319 & 328**

▶ If the chairman or chief executive is to give a presentation on the business, check that no inside information is being disclosed and that a copy is released to an RIS no later than the time the presentation is given to the meeting. **s.319A**

- The chairman should not propose their own election or re-election or propose any resolution in which they have an interest.

Dealing with the business of the meeting

- The resolution to receive or adopt the accounts should be separate from any resolution to approve the payment of the final dividend recommended by directors. It is also good practice generally to deal with different items of business by way of separate resolutions.

- Ensure that adequate time is allowed for shareholder questions.

Voting

- If a poll is likely, the company secretary should arrange for poll cards to be available.

- Before each resolution is put to the vote, the chairman should explain again its effect and purpose and, if necessary, elaborate on the information previously provided in the explanatory details circulated with the notice of the meeting. Shareholders may also be invited to speak.

- The chairman should indicate the number of proxy votes held.

- When announcing the decision on a poll, the total number of votes cast for and against and withheld for the resolutions should be disclosed. The information should then be made available as soon as possible on the company's website.

- If a significant proportion of votes have been cast against a resolution at a general meeting, the company should explain when announcing the results of voting what actions it intends to take to understand the reasons behind the result.

After the meeting

Following the AGM, the company secretary is responsible for ensuring that all minutes, forms and resolutions are prepared, signed and filed at Companies House and/or the FCA, and made available on the company's website.

Minutes and registers

- Prepare the minutes of the meeting. — **s.355(1)**

- Once agreed, the minutes should be signed by the chairman. — **s.356(4)**

- If appropriate, update the registers of directors, secretaries, members, charges or debenture holders. — **ss.113,876 & 743**

Statutory filings

- Any relevant Companies House forms. — **s.30(1)**

▶ For listed companies, arrange for two copies of all resolutions passed, other than resolutions concerning ordinary business passed at an AGM, to be forwarded to the FCA. In practice this requirement is met by forwarding a copy to the National Storage Mechanism. **LR 9.6.2**

▶ Listed companies should ensure that the appropriate announcements are made to an RIS as soon as possible.

Website

The company's website should be updated as quickly as practical and not later than 16 days after the meeting. **ss.341(1B) & 353(4)(a)**

Dividends

If a dividend has been approved at the meeting, the necessary arrangements for it to be paid should be made.

Articles of association (adoption or change)

The articles of association are the rules governing the company's internal affairs. SI 2008/3229 contains model sets of articles, appropriate for private companies limited by shares, private companies limited by guarantee and public companies.

s. 20

Under all previous Companies Acts, default articles of association were contained in Table A to the particular Companies Act in force when the company was incorporated.

Companies incorporated prior to 1 October 2009 will have as their default articles the version of Table A in force when the company was incorporated, and later versions do not apply unless specifically adopted by a company.

The model articles apply to any particular company, incorporated on or after 1 October 2009, to the extent that they are not excluded or varied by the company's articles.

s. 20(1)(b)

Alteration of any particular regulation or adoption of new articles requires a special resolution of the members in a general meeting.

s. 21

Articles may contain entrenched provisions. Amendment of entrenched provisions requires 100% consent from members entitled to vote or a court order.

s. 22

Checklist

▷ If the company has more than one class of shares, a separate class meeting may also be required.

▷ Check whether rights to be amended are entrenched.

▷ Consider whether amendment can be undertaken by amending existing clauses, by the adoption of new clauses in addition to or in substitution for existing clauses or by the adoption of a complete new set of articles.

Procedure

▷ Convene a directors' meeting to recommend resolutions to members and to convene a general meeting or, in the case of a private company, circulate a written resolution if appropriate (see page 240).

▶ Issue notice, signed by director or company secretary, convening general meeting on 14 clear days' notice, or circulate written resolution for members to consider special resolution to amend the articles.

s.21

▶ As a special resolution, the resolution must contain the full text of the proposed changes.

▶ Consider whether a class meeting is also required.

▶ If the meeting is to be convened on short notice (see page 26), the company secretary should arrange for agreement to short notice to be signed by each of the members.

▶ Hold a general meeting. Ensure valid quorum is present. Resolutions put to vote either by show of hands or by poll and to be passed by appropriate majority (special resolution by 75% majority).

s.283

▶ If the resolution is circulated by means of a written resolution, the resolution must receive approval of the holders of at least 75% of the members entitled to vote within 28 days of the circulation date of the resolution (see page 240).

Filing requirement

▶ Signed copy of special resolution within 15 days.

ss.29(1)(a),30(1)

▶ Amended copy of the articles of association with copy of resolution.

s.26

Notes

▶ Although it is not necessary to issue new copies of the articles of association to the members, the company should ensure that it has a supply for issue to those members who request a copy. In addition, a copy will normally be sent to the company's bankers and to their auditors.

▶ If a company files a copy of a resolution amending its articles but does not file a copy of the amended articles, Companies House may issue a notice requiring an amended copy of the articles be filed within a specified time. Failure to file the amended copy within the specified time will mean the company is liable to a £200 fine.

**s.27,
s.27(4)**

More information

 Chapter 3    Chapter 1    Guidance booklet GP3

Auditors – appointment to FTSE 350 company

Statutory Audit Services for Large Companies Market Investigation (Mandatory Use of Competitive Tender Processes and Audit Committee Responsibilities) Order 2014 came into force on 1 January 2015 and applies to financial periods of FTSE 350 companies beginning on or after that date.

- An auditor and a FTSE 350 company must not enter into or give effect to a Statutory Audit Services Agreement unless:
  - ▷ a competitive tender process has taken place in the previous nine years or the current engagement was subject to a competitive tender process; and
  - ▷ the terms of the Statutory Audit Services Agreement, including, to the extent permissible by law and regulations, the Statutory Audit fee and the scope of the Statutory Audit, have been negotiated and agreed only between the Audit Committee and the auditor.

Checklist

- Has a competitive audit process taken place in last five years? If not, a statement to be included in annual report giving details of the financial year in which a competitive audit process will take place and details of why that period is in the best interests of members.

- From 17 June 2020 an auditor may not be reappointed if they have been providing audit services to the company for 20 or more consecutive years at the date the regulations came into force.

- From 17 June 2023 an auditor may not be reappointed if they have been providing audit services to the company for 11 or more years but less than 20 consecutive years at the date the regulations came into force.

- The audit committee must be responsible for:
  - ▷ negotiating and agreeing the statutory audit fee;
  - ▷ initiation and supervision of the competitive tender process;
  - ▷ recommendations to the board of directors regarding the appointment of an auditor; and
  - ▷ authorising or establishing the policy for the provision of non-audit services by the auditor.

Procedure

▶ Convene an audit committee meeting to consider the appointment of an auditor and whether a competitive audit process is necessary. Ensure valid quorum present.

▶ A competitive tender process is required at least once in every ten-year period.

▶ A competitive tender process requires at least two auditors, which may include the current auditor, to compete for the provisions of Statutory Audit Services.

Filing requirement

▶ The appointment of auditors does not need to be notified to Companies House.

Notes

▶ The company may wish to notify its bankers, solicitors, subsidiaries, etc of the auditors' appointment.

More information

Auditors – appointment to private company

With the exception of private companies that are exempt from audit, dormant companies and non-profit-making companies subject to public sector audit, all companies must appoint auditors and prepare audited accounts. **s.475**

The members of a company which is exempt from audit may require it to appoint auditors, provided this request is made by members holding at least 10% in nominal value of its issued shares or 10% of the members for a company without shares. **s.476**

Directors will usually appoint auditors where they are being appointed for the first time or following a period where an audit was not required.

Directors may appoint auditors at any time before the company's first or next period for appointing auditors (see below) or to fill a casual vacancy. **s.485(3)**

If a company has no auditors, members may appoint auditors during a period for appointing auditors. **s.485(4)**

The period for appointing auditors is the period of 28 days beginning on the end of the period for sending out the accounts to members for the previous financial year or, if earlier, the day the accounts for the previous financial year were sent out. **s.485(2)**

If a company that is required to have its accounts audited fails to appoint auditors, notification of that must be sent to the Secretary of State and the Secretary of State may appoint auditors to fill the vacancy. **s.486**

An auditor is required to be registered as an auditor, and must not be an officer or a servant of the company, or a partner or employee of such officers or servants. An auditor may be an individual, a partnership or a limited company. **ss.1211–1215**

Checklist

▶ Does the company qualify for exemption from audit? **s.475**

▶ Has an audit been requested by members? **s.476**

▶ Does the person to be appointed meet the following eligibility criteria? **s.1211**

   ▷ Member of a recognised supervisory body **s.1212**

▷ Not an officer or employee of the company or partner or employee of an officer or employee of the company.   **s. 1214**

▷ Not connected with the company or an associated undertaking.   **s. 1215**

Procedure

▶ Convene a directors' meeting to consider the appointment of an auditor. Ensure valid quorum present.

▶ Where the appointment is to be by the members, this is by an ordinary resolution either at a general meeting convened by the directors or by written resolution of the members.

▶ A company that has no auditors may have auditors appointed by the Secretary of State.

Filing requirement

▶ The appointment of auditors does not need to be notified to Companies House.

Notes

▶ The company may wish to notify its bankers, solicitors, subsidiaries, etc of the auditors' appointment.

More information

 Chapter 11    Chapter 15

Auditors – appointment to public company

With the exception of dormant public companies that are exempt from audit, all public companies must appoint auditors and prepare audited accounts. **s.489(1)**

Directors may appoint auditors at any time before the company's first general meeting to receive audited accounts or to fill a casual vacancy. **s.489(3)**

Members may appoint auditors, by ordinary resolution, at a general meeting at which audited accounts have been laid or in circumstances when the company should have had auditors appointed but does not have auditors. **s.489(4)**

If a public company that is required to have its accounts audited fails to appoint auditors, notification of that must be sent to the Secretary of State and the Secretary of State may appoint auditors to fill the vacancy. **s.490**

An auditor is required to be registered as an auditor, and must not be an officer or a servant of the company, or a partner or employee of such officers or servants. An auditor may be an individual, a partnership or a limited company. **ss.1211–1215**

Checklist

▶ Does the company qualify for exemption from audit? **s.475**

▶ Does the person to be appointed meet the following eligibility criteria? **s.1211**

  ▷ Member of a recognised supervisory body. **s.1212**

  ▷ Not an officer or employee of the company or partner or employee of an officer or employee of the company. **s.1214**

  ▷ Not connected with the company or an associated undertaking. **s.1215**

Procedure

▶ Convene a directors' meeting to consider the appointment of an auditor. Ensure valid quorum present.

▶ Where the appointment is to be by the members, this is by an ordinary resolution either at a general meeting convened by the directors or by written resolution of the members.

▶ A public company that has no auditors may have auditors appointed by the Secretary of State.

▶ Auditors of a public company are appointed to hold office only until the conclusion of the next general meeting at which accounts are laid before the members, when they may be reappointed.

s.491

Filing requirement

▶ The appointment of auditors does not need to be notified to Companies House.

Notes

▶ The company may wish to notify its bankers, solicitors, subsidiaries, etc of the auditors' appointment.

More information

 Chapter 11    Chapter 15

Auditors – removal

The members of a company may remove the auditors from office by ordinary resolution. In practice the directors will normally invite the auditors to resign or will propose that the auditors are not reappointed at a general meeting at which accounts are to be laid.

s.510

Checklist

▶ Special notice must be given to the company of a proposed resolution to remove an auditor.

s.511

▶ A copy of the special notice must be sent to the auditor whose removal is proposed.

s.511(2)

▶ The auditor may make a written representation concerning their removal and request its notification to the members either by post or, if there is insufficient time, by reading it to the meeting.

s.511(3)

▶ The auditors' representation need not be notified to members if an application to the court is upheld.

s.511(6)

▶ On removal, notice of that removal must be filed at Companies House within 14 days.

s.512

Procedure

▶ Special notice given by a director to the company.

▶ Convene a directors' meeting to recommend resolution to members and to convene a general meeting. Ensure valid quorum is present.

▶ Copy of the special notice sent to the auditor.

▶ Issue notice, signed by director or company secretary, convening general meeting with 14 clear days' notice for members to consider.

▶ Ordinary resolution to remove auditor.

▶ Consider whether a class meeting is also required.

▶ If the meeting is to be convened on short notice, the company secretary should arrange for agreement to short notice to be signed by each of the shareholders.

- ▶ Representation of auditors circulated with notice, or separately.

- ▶ If appropriate, seek court order that representation need not be circulated or read out at meeting.

- ▶ If not circulated and no court order obtained, read auditors' representation to meeting.

- ▶ Hold general meeting. Ensure valid quorum is present. Resolutions put to vote either by show of hands or by poll and to be passed by appropriate majority (ordinary resolution by 50% majority).

- ▶ If removal approved, notify Companies House.

Filing requirement

- ▶ Form AA03 within 14 days.

Notes

- ▶ If a shareholder gives notice of their intention to propose the removal of the auditor, unless they also requisition an extraordinary general meeting, there is no requirement for the directors to convene a meeting. The resolution would, however, be required to be put at the next general meeting.

- ▶ The written resolution procedure cannot be used and the resolution must be put to a general meeting of the members.

More information

Auditors – resignation

Auditors may resign from office by giving notice in writing to the registered office of the company. If the company is a public interest company, the notice of resignation must be accompanied by a statement of any matters that they consider should be brought to the attention of members or, if there are no such circumstances, a statement to that effect.

s.516

s.516(2)

s.519

A resigning auditor of a non-public interest company may need to send a statement unless their resignation meets one of the conditions set out in s. 519(2A) or 2(B).

Checklist

▶ Auditors' resignation and statement, if any, received at the registered office.

▶ If there are circumstances to be notified to the members or creditors, the statement must be circulated to members within 14 days or an application be made to the court for an order that it need not do so.

s.520

▶ If court order sought, notify auditor.

s.520(3)

▶ Unless notice of application for court order received within 21 days, the auditors must file a copy of their statement with Companies House within 28 days of original notice of resignation.

s.521

▶ If court order not obtained, the company must circulate the statement to members within 14 days of the court's decision and notify the auditors, who shall file a copy of their statement at Companies House within the next seven days.

ss.520(5),521(2)

▶ Where the auditor resigns at any time other than, in the case of a private company, the end of the period for appointing auditors or, in the case of a public company, at the accounts meeting and a statement of circumstances has been issued by the auditor, the company must notify the appropriate audit authority.

s.523

Procedure

▶ Circulate statement of circumstances, if any, to members or apply to court for order not to circulate. If court order sought, notify auditor within 21 days of original notice being received.

▶ Unless exempt, notify appropriate audit authority within 28 days of receipt of auditor's resignation.

Filing requirement

▶ Copy of auditors' resignation letter within 14 days.

▶ Auditors to file statement of circumstances after 21 days but before 28 days, unless application to court made.

▶ If court upholds application, copy of that decision to be circulated to members.

▶ If application not upheld, statement to be circulated to members within 14 days and notify auditors, who must file their statement at Companies House within the next seven days.

More information

 Chapter 11    Chapter 15

Bank account

The company's bank account and banking matters generally are controlled by the board of directors.

All banks have a standard Form of Mandate and this is usually presented as a draft minute. Once the text of the authority and the instructions have been approved by the directors, a copy of the signed mandate should be inserted in the company's minute book as evidence of the appropriate decisions having been reached.

The majority of banks require security or collateral for overdraft facilities and care must be taken to ensure that the directors have authority to charge the company's assets.

Checklist

▶ Completed bank mandate form.

▶ Approved by the directors.

▶ Originals or certified copies of memorandum and articles of association, certificate of incorporation and any changes of name certificate to commence trading (public companies only).

▶ Money laundering verification of identity documents as advised by the bank. Often original or certified copies of passport or driving licence and a utility bill showing residential address will suffice.

Procedure

▶ Convene a directors' meeting to consider the terms of the bank mandate and approve the opening of the account. Ensure valid quorum present.

Filing requirement

None.

Notes

▶ The bank will note and return the original Certificates of Incorporation and any change-of-name certificates.

▶ Care must be taken to ensure that the signatories required for cheques are reasonable in the circumstances. Many companies empower an authorised signatory to sign cheques up to a certain limit, with directors (often two) required to sign cheques of larger amounts.

▶ The frequency with which the company is to receive bank statements should also be agreed.

▶ The banks prefer the mandate to be expressed in terms of the position held by the signatories rather than their names. If a named person is shown, when that person leaves the company it is necessary to complete a new mandate rather than merely change the signatory.

▶ It is normal practice to inform the bank whenever there are changes to the company's directors, company secretary, registered office, the company's accounting reference date or the company's auditors.

▶ The bank will often require a copy of the company's latest audited accounts for their records.

More information

None.

Boardroom – best practice

Reliance on unwritten boardroom procedures and practices is no longer acceptable in the modern business environment. While it is acknowledged that company law should not attempt to prescribe any particular style of boardroom management, certain basic principles of good boardroom practice can be considered to be universally applicable.

The following is intended to be a guide to the matters that should be addressed and, wherever applicable, accepted formally by boards of directors in recognition of a commitment to adhere to an overall concept of best practice. Although particularly relevant to public companies with external shareholders, all companies will benefit from striving to carry out generally accepted best practice. It of course recognised that all company boards are different and that exceptions and adaptions of best practice will be appropriate.

Boardroom procedures should be periodically reviewed to ensure their scope remains relevant and allow for the identification of additional matters that individual companies could advantageously bring within their scope.

Checklist

- Establish written procedures and policies:
  - Provide each director with a copy.
  - Monitor and review compliance (including risk) and report breaches to the board.
- All new directors to be given appropriate induction to enable them to perform their duties.
- Guidance for non-executive directors should include procedures for:
  - obtaining information; and
  - requisitioning a board meeting.
- In the conduct of board business, all directors should:
  - receive the same information at the same time; and
  - be given sufficient time to consider the information.

▶ Identify matters reserved to the board and lay down procedures when a decision is required before its next meeting.

▶ All material contracts, and especially those not in the ordinary course of business, should be referred to the board.

▶ The board should approve definitions of 'material' and 'not in the ordinary course of business'.

▶ Agenda for individual meetings of the board to be settled by the chairman in consultation with the company secretary.

▶ The company secretary should be responsible to the chairman for the proper administration of meetings of the company, the board and any committees thereof.

▶ The minutes of meetings should record the decisions taken and provide sufficient background to those decisions.

▶ All papers presented at meetings should be identified and retained for reference.

▶ Minutes of committees' meetings should be circulated to the board.

▶ Where the articles of association allow the board to delegate any of its powers to a committee, the board should approve:

  ▷ the membership and quorum of any such committee;

  ▷ its terms of reference; and

  ▷ the extent of any powers delegated to it.

▶ Any director or the company secretary must be able to raise at any board meeting any matter, whether or not it is on the agenda for the meeting.

More information

Chapter 13

Bonus issue (capitalisation issue)

A bonus or capitalisation issue is the means by which the company allots shares that are partly or fully paid, by capitalising reserves. No further payment from the shareholder is normally required. However, if the bonus shares are partly paid, the unpaid portion may be called from the shareholder at some future date.

The company's capacity to issue partly or fully paid shares is included in the model articles for private and public companies, but also requires approval of the shareholders by ordinary resolution. Although a bonus issue is an issue of new shares, no new capital is raised; it is effected by capitalising some or all of the company's distributable reserves.

sch. I reg. 36, sch. 3 reg. 78, SI 2008/3229

Companies may wish to issue shares in this manner for a number of reasons. These include:

▶ to increase the company's issued share capital in order to meet the minimum capital requirement when re-registering as a public company without requiring the shareholders to inject further funds (see page 231);

▶ to declare a bonus issue in conjunction with a rights issue to reduce the potential dilution of the holdings of those shareholders who do not take up any shares under the offer; and

▶ to create a more substantial balance sheet by capitalising reserves into issued share capital.

Checklist

▶ Check the articles of association to ensure the issue of bonus shares is permitted and if any procedures have been stipulated.

▶ Check the articles to ensure that if the company has an authorised share capital, there are sufficient unissued shares available for issue.

▶ Check the articles of association to ensure the directors have authority in terms of s. 551 to issue shares. If not, a resolution to extend or renew the authority will be required (see page 256)

Procedure

▶ Convene a directors' meeting to recommend appropriate resolution(s) to members and to seek member approval either by circulating written resolution(s) or by convening a general meeting. Ensure valid quorum is present.

▶ Issue notice, signed by director or company secretary, together convening the general meeting on 14 clear days' notice for members to consider resolution. Alternatively, a private company may circulate the resolutions by written resolution.   **ss.281,307**

▶ Enclose with the notice a form of proxy if desired. Listed companies must enclose a three-way form of proxy (see page 186).

▶ Consider whether class meeting(s) also required.

▶ If the meeting is to be convened on short notice, the company secretary should arrange for agreement to short notice to be signed by the appropriate number of the members (see page 26).   **s.307(5)**

▶ Copy of notice to be sent to non-member directors and auditor, if any.

▶ Hold general meeting. Ensure valid quorum is present. Resolution put to vote either by show of hands or by poll and to be passed by appropriate majority (ordinary resolution by 50% majority).   **ss.310,502**

▶ Following meeting, issue new share certificates and update register of members. If there is to be a delay before share certificates are issued, it may be appropriate to issue allotment letters giving details of each member's entitlement to new shares. In any event, new share certificates must be issued within two months.   **s.554** **s.769**

Filing requirement

▶ Copies of approved member resolutions.   **s.30**

▶ Form SH01 within one month.   **s.555**

▶ Statement of capital.   **s.555**

Notes

▶ As bonus shares are issued *pro rata*, it should not be necessary to waive any rights of pre-emption, unless the members have the option to renounce their entitlement.

▶ On completion of the bonus issue, the company's accountants, both internal and external, must be informed, so that the appropriate entries to the company's accounts can be made.

▶ If it is necessary to increase or renew s. 551 authority to issue shares (see page 256), it will be necessary to file a copy of the ordinary resolution within 15 days.

More information

 Chapter 12    Chapter 2

Borrowing powers

All companies are deemed to have full capacity unless the articles place specific restrictions on the company.

The articles of listed companies will often restrict the directors' ability to exercise the full borrowing powers of the company. The limitation is often expressed as a multiple of the company's net assets and so will vary over time.

Directors of companies incorporated under previous Companies Acts require specific authority under their articles of association, unless this authority contained in the 'old' Table A has been amended in the articles or by subsequent resolution.

If the directors' capacity to exercise the company's borrowing power is not sufficient for their purposes, the articles of association will need to be amended by special resolution.

Checklist

▶ Check the articles of association for any restriction of either the company's capacity to borrow or the directors' authority to exercise that borrowing capacity.

Filing requirement

None.

More information

Business names

A business name is a name or title by which a company may trade other than its corporate or registered name.

There is no longer a register of business names.

The business stationery of a company using a business name must show the company's registered name in full as well as the business name, in addition to the other statutory requirements (see page 125).

reg. 24, SI 2015/17

Companies using business names must ensure they do not infringe registered names or trademarks, or pass themselves off as other registered companies, partnerships or sole traders.

Checklist

▶ Is the company's registered name shown on all headed paper, email, website, invoices, cheques, etc?

reg. 24, SI 2015/17

▶ Is the company's registered name displayed at all business premises?

regs 21 and 22, SI 2015/17

Filing requirement

None.

Notes

A company that has always been dormant from the date of its incorporation need not have its name on display at its registered office.

reg. 21(2), SI 2015/17

More information

Chapter 4

Chapter 1

Guidance
Incorporation and names

Calls

Where, for any reason, shares have been issued as partly or nil paid, the amounts unpaid can be called by the directors at any time, either in full or in part.

The liability for the unpaid amounts rests with the registered holder.

The company should not accept registration of a transfer of shares on which there remains an unpaid call unless the transferee is willing to pay the unpaid call.

The model articles for private companies do not permit partly or nil paid shares to be issued and accordingly if such shares are to be issued, the articles will require amendment. Table A to the Companies Act 1985 did provide for partly paid shares and contained provisions for the making of calls by directors. The model articles for public companies do contain provisions for the making of calls on partly paid shares.

**art. 21 sch. 1,
SI 2008/3229**

**arts 54–61 sch. 3,
SI 2008/3229**

Checklist

▶ Check the articles of association for the procedure to follow where a call is proposed. The procedure below follows the model wording for public companies.

Procedure

▶ Convene a directors' meeting to approve the making of a call.

▶ The company secretary should arrange the preparation and issue of call notices to members. Each call notice should be addressed to the registered holder or joint holders, as the case may be, and should contain details of the registered member(s), the amounts currently outstanding and the amount now being called, together with details of where and when the payment is due, which must be at least 14 days after the date of the call notice.

▶ Each call notice should carry a distinguishing number and this number should be noted on the register of members, together with a note of the amount being called. The company should compile lists of the payments as they are received and cleared by the bank. Once the date on which the call is due has passed, the list of payments should be reconciled with the register of members and a list of unpaid calls should be prepared.

▶ A reminder letter should be sent to all members that have not paid the call, requesting immediate payment and warning of the potential penalties for non-payment, including forfeiture of shares or suspension of voting rights.

▶ Members should return their share certificates together with a copy of the call notice so that the company can endorse the share certificates, giving details of the paid call. The endorsed share certificate should be returned to the shareholder. Alternatively, the share certificates can be cancelled and new, fully paid share certificates issued.

▶ The register of members should be amended to include details of the additional amounts now paid on the shares.

▶ If a call remains unpaid, interest is due at a rate to be set by the directors but not to exceed 5% above the base lending rate in force from time to time. Directors may waive the obligation to pay interest either in part or in full.

Filing requirement

None.

Notes

▶ Where calls remain unpaid, a number of actions can be taken, although the articles of association should be checked to ensure that the directors have the requisite authority.

▶ The directors may institute proceedings for the forfeiture of the shares, under which circumstance the shares are forfeited by the holder and cancelled or reissued. In the instance of reissue, the company should return to the shareholders the amounts paid by them on the shares.

▶ The articles of association may authorise the directors to withhold any dividends from the shareholder and credit these amounts to the share capital account until such time as the call has been paid.

▶ Alternatively, the shareholder may lose the right to vote until such time as the call has been paid.

▶ It will be necessary to inform the company's auditors of the call and the split between the calls that were paid and any unpaid calls. Occasionally, shares will be issued as partly paid with the balance payable on fixed instalment dates. The procedure to be followed in such circumstances is the same as that for making a call.

More information

 Chapter 13    Chapter 2

Certification of shares

When members are transferring only part of their holding, they may be unwilling to forward their share certificate to the purchaser. In such circumstances, the transferor should forward the certificate and stock transfer form to the company or its share registrar for certifying. The company or its share registrar will then stamp the transfer form stating that the certificate representing the shares on the transfer form has been lodged with the company/share registrar and will return a balance certificate to the transferor if appropriate.

s. 775

Certifications are most commonly used by stockbrokers and market-makers in respect of partial sales for quoted shares. These, however, are becoming less used following the introduction of the paperless settlement system, CREST.

Checklist

▶ Check the register of members to confirm that the share certificate has not previously been cancelled and is valid.

▶ Check that the transferor's details on the transfer form match the holder shown on the share certificate, and that the transfer form is signed by the transferor.

Procedure

▶ Cancel the share certificate and insert on the transfer form reference details for the certification.

▶ Update the register of members to record the certification details and the cancellation of the original share certificate.

▶ Return the now-certified transfer form to the person lodging it.

Filing requirement

None.

More Information

H Chapter 18   CSP Chapter 5

Companies House – addresses of offices

England and Wales
Companies House
Crown Way
Maindy
Cardiff CF14 3UZ
DX 33050 Cardiff 1

Contact Centre: +44 (0)303 1234 500
Lines open: Monday to Friday, 8.30am–6.00pm

Website: www.companieshouse.gov.uk
Email: enquiries@companieshouse.gov.uk

London Information Centre
4 Abbey Orchard Street
Westminster
London
SW1P 2HT

Contact Centre: +44 (0)303 1234 500

Scotland
Companies House
4th Floor, Edinburgh Quay 2
139 Fountainbridge
Edinburgh
EH3 9FF

Contact Centre: +44 (0)303 1234 500

Northern Ireland

Companies House

2nd Floor, The Linenhall

32–38 Linenhall Street

Belfast

BT2 8BG

Contact Centre: +44 (0)303 1234 500

Office hours: Monday to Friday, 9.00am–5.00pm

More information

Companies House website for directions and maps:
www.gov.uk/government/organisations/companies-house/about/access-
and-opening

Companies House – charges

The fees charged by Companies House in force as at 1 May 2017 for incorporation and registration services are as follows.

Service	Web filed	Software	Paper
Incorporation fee		£10	£40
Incorporation fee via Companies House	£12	£30	
Same-day incorporation fee	£40		£100
Change-of-name fee	£8	£8	£10
Same-day change-of-name fee	£30	£30	£50
Re-registration fee			£20
Same-day re-registration fee			£50
Same-day simultaneous re-registration and change-of-name fee			£100
Confirmation fee	£13	£13	£40
Overseas company registration fee			£20
Overseas company change-of-name fee			£10
Overseas company filing accounts fee			£20
Registration of a charge	£15	£15	£23
Voluntary dissolution fee			£10
Reduction of capital supported by solvency statement			£10
Same-day reduction of capital supported by solvency statement			£50
Administrative restoration			£100
Application to suppress address information from public search			£55
Application to suppress address information from credit reference			£100

More information

Full price list available from Companies House website
www.gov.uk/government/organisations/companies-house/about-our-services

Companies House – software filing

Software filing is only available using an approved software package. At present there are about 35 suppliers of software offering some or all of the ability to incorporate companies, file accounts, file forms and register mortgages. A full list and contact information for these suppliers can be found on the Companies House website (www.gov.uk/company-filing-software/filing-other).

Checklist

▶ Proprietary software.

▶ Registration with Companies House.

Procedure

▶ Presenters must first register with Companies House. As part of this process, an account will be opened for the payment of any filing fees.

▶ The company must notify Companies House of a password to authenticate documents and of the presenter transmitting the documents. This password will replace the signature of the company secretary or a director currently required to authenticate all forms.

▶ Groups of companies can choose to have the same password. In order to comply with the Companies Act, the password must be delivered to Companies House in writing by the company, and signed by a serving officer of the company.

▶ When a form detailing the appointment of a director or company secretary is delivered, the appointee is required to indicate his or her consent to act as a director or company secretary by providing three pieces of information that other people would not normally be expected to know. This information will not be displayed on the public file, but will be stored so that it can be retrieved should any question arise as to the validity of the appointment. Such personal information includes: place of birth, mother's maiden name, NI number, passport number, etc. Alternatively, a director or company secretary may agree with Companies House a six-digit personal identification code.

More information

 Chapter 10    www.gov.uk/government/organisations/companies-house

Companies House – web filing

Companies House has introduced an electronic web filing service, currently limited to the more popular forms, with further ones becoming available according to demand. Currently the following forms may be filed using the web filing service:

Company forms

AA01	change of accounting reference date
AA02	dormant company accounts
AD01	change of situation or address of registered office
AD02	notification of single alternative inspection location (SAIL)
AD03	change of location of the company records to the single alternative inspection location (SAIL)
AD04	change of location of the company records to the registered office
annual accounts	audit exempt small full accounts (with abbreviated option)
annual accounts	audit exempt abbreviated accounts
annual accounts	micro-entity accounts
AP01	appointment of director
AP02	appointment of corporate director
AP03	appointment of secretary
AP04	appointment of corporate secretary
AR01	annual return (£13 charge)
CH01	change of particulars for director
CH02	change of particulars for corporate director
CH03	change of particulars for secretary
CH04	change of particulars for corporate secretary
CS01	confirmation statement (£13 charge)
DS02	withdrawal of application to strike off
incorporation (IN01)	private company limited by shares adopting their model articles in their entirety

MR01	particulars of a charge
MR02	particulars of a charge subject to which property or undertaking has been acquired
MR04	statement of satisfaction in full or in part of a charge
MR05	statement that part or the whole of the property charged (a) has been released from the charge (b) no longer forms part of the company's property
NM01	notice of change of name by resolution and special resolution (RES15) (£8 charge)
SH01	return of allotment of shares
TM01	terminating appointment as director
TM02	terminating appointment as secretary

It is not possible to web file full audited accounts.

Limited liability partnership forms

LL AA01	change of accounting reference date of an LLP
LL AD01	change of registered office address of an LLP
LL AD02	notification of the single alternative inspection location (SAIL) of an LLP
LL AD03	change of location of the records to the single alternative inspection location (SAIL) of an LLP
LL AD04	change of location of the records to the registered office of an LLP
LL AP01	appointment of member of an LLP
LL AP02	appointment of corporate member of an LLP
LL AR01	annual return of an LLP (£13 charge)
LL CH01	change of details of a member of an LLP
LL CH02	change of details of a corporate member of an LLP
LL CS01	confirmation statement (£13 charge)
LL DS02	withdrawal of application to strike off
LL MR01	particulars of a charge created by an LLP
LL MR02	particulars of a charge subject to which property or undertaking has been acquired by an LLP
LL MR04	statement of satisfaction in full or in part of a charge by an LLP
LL MR05	statement that part or the whole of the property charged (a) has been released from the charge (b) no longer forms part of the LLP's property
LL TM01	termination of appointment of member of an LLP

Checklist

▶ Registration with Companies House.

Procedure

▶ Presenters must first register with Companies House. As part of this process, an account will be opened for the payment of any filing fees.

▶ The company must notify Companies House of a password to authenticate documents and of the presenter transmitting the documents. This password will replace the signature of the secretary or a director currently required to authenticate all forms.

▶ Groups of companies can choose to have the same password. In order to comply with the Companies Act, the password must be delivered to Companies House in writing by each company, and signed by a serving officer of the relevant company.

More information

 Chapter 7  https:www.gov.uk/government/organisations/
companies-house/about-our-services#webfiling

Company secretary – appointment and reporting lines

A public limited company must appoint a suitably qualified individual to the role of company secretary. Private companies need not appoint or retain a company secretary, but may do so if they wish. Nevertheless, all companies must ensure their statutory obligations are met, so it is good practice for all but the simplest organisations to have an appropriately qualified and experienced company secretary.

ss. 271, 273

s. 270

Regardless of the size of the organisation, the company secretary is a key member of the executive team who is appointed by the board as an officer of the company. They have specific responsibility for advising the board through the chair on all governance matters. The company secretary is also responsible for ensuring good information flows within the board and its committees and between senior management and non-executive directors, as well as facilitating induction and assisting with professional development. The UK Corporate Governance Code states that the appointment and removal of the company secretary is a matter for the board as a whole. The company secretary is responsible to the board of directors collectively rather than to any individual director.

The company secretary will need to have knowledge of the legal, regulatory and administrative framework in which the organisation operates. This will vary from a premium listed public limited company with thousands of shareholders, to a private limited company, a charity or a service provider in the public sector. The individual appointed should have the experience and/or ability to understand the additional demands of the role.

Reporting lines

The company secretary should be in a position to give independent, impartial advice and support to all the directors individually and to the board as a whole. The company secretary should not be subject to undue influence from one or more of the directors and appropriate reporting lines should be established. If the board fails to protect the integrity of the company secretary's position, one of the important in-built internal controls available to the company is likely to be undermined. Appropriate reporting lines for the company secretary will also help to ensure the delivery of the best company secretarial service and the most positive impact on the performance of the board and the organisation.

ICSA recommends that the company secretary should report to the chairman on all matters relating to corporate governance and other duties and responsibilities that concern the whole board. If the company secretary has other executive or administrative duties, they should report to the chief executive or other director who has delegated responsibility. ICSA also recommends (particularly where the company secretary reports to the chairman on all matters) that decisions on remuneration and benefits should be taken (or at least noted) by the board as a whole or the relevant board committee to avoid undue influence.

Checklist

▶ The person named as company secretary, if any, on form IN01 delivered on incorporation of a company is deemed to have been appointed as company secretary upon incorporation.

▶ Subsequent appointments of company secretaries are made by the board of directors in accordance with the provisions of the Act or any provisions contained in their articles of association. **s.276**

▶ If a public company fails to appoint a company secretary, the Secretary of State may issue a direction requiring the appointment of a company secretary and specifying the period in which the appointment must be made, being between one and three months of the date of the direction. **s.272**

▶ The company's auditor cannot be appointed as company secretary. **s.1214**

▶ Company secretaries of public companies must be qualified by profession or experience: **s.273**

▷ They have held the position of secretary in a public company for at least three of the five years preceding their appointment.

▷ They are a member of any of the specified bodies. **s.273(3)**

▷ They are a barrister, advocate or solicitor called or admitted in the UK.

▷ They are a person who, through holding or having held another position, or being a member of another body, appears to the directors to be capable of fulfilling the functions of the role.

Procedure

▶ Convene a directors' meeting to approve the appointment of the company secretary. Ensure valid quorum is present.

▶ File form AP03 or AP04 as appropriate. **s.276**

▶ The necessary entry must be made in the Register of Secretaries. **s.275**

▶ The company secretary is frequently a signatory on the company's bank account, and accordingly it may be necessary to amend the company's bank mandate in addition to notifying the bank of the new appointment and supplying specimen signatures to the bank.

▶ The board will normally consider it necessary for the company secretary to have a service contract.

▶ If the company secretary is to carry out executive duties, it may be considered necessary to include the company secretary on any policy of directors' and officers' indemnity insurance.

Filing requirement

▶ Form AP03 or AP04 within 14 days.

Notes

▶ The appointment of a company secretary may be terminated by the directors. There is no need for shareholder approval. The company secretary may be able to bring an action for breach of contract in such circumstances, and accordingly a compromise agreement may be appropriate.

s. 277

▶ The company secretary must provide a service address; this need not be their residential address. Unlike with directors, there is no need to notify the company of the secretary's usual residential address.

More information

 Chapter I  Chapter II  Guidance booklet GP3

Company secretary – role and responsibilities

The role of the company secretary can cover all areas of a company's activities, depending on the size and nature of the company. The duties of the company secretary are not specified in detail in the Companies Act, although as an officer of the company, the company secretary is liable, along with the directors, for any breaches of the regulations imposed by the Act.

s.1262

The company secretary plays a central role in the legal operation of the organisation and, by ensuring high standards of corporate governance, shareholder relations and board effectiveness, the company secretary can contribute to the company's performance. The UK Corporate Governance Code recognises explicitly the secretary's responsibility for corporate governance, particularly as an independent, impartial adviser.

Research published in July 2014 by ICSA and Henley Business School identified that the independence and discretion of the company secretary, bridging the executive team and main board NEDs, played an increasingly important role in promoting a well-functioning board, which in turn helped to build stakeholder trust. ICSA guidance on the duties and reporting lines of the company secretary divides the role and responsibilities into three broad areas – the board, the company and the shareholders – and then sets out the core duties, which are summarised below.

Checklist

The board

▶ Board/committee meetings

 ▷ Organise the board/committee meetings.

 ▷ Agree meeting agendas with the chairman and/or chief executive and ensure optimal decision making by, for example, allowing appropriate time for discussion, organising and distributing high-quality information to promote good decision making.

 ▷ Ensure that the board and committees are properly constituted and advised, that there are clear terms of reference and that the business of the board and committees is coordinated.

▶ Advise the board on compliance matters and ensure correct procedures are followed.

▶ Provide independent and impartial advice to the board on governance matters.

▶ Advise directors on their statutory duties under the Act and ensure compliance with restrictions in the Act. For example, conflicts of interest, service contracts, loans and other transactions.

▶ Facilitate the induction, professional development and evaluation of directors, including skills audits to ensure appropriate composition of the board.

The company

▶ Memorandum and articles of association

▷ Ensure the company complies with its memorandum and articles of association and draft and incorporate amendments in accordance with the ACT, the LPDT rules and any other procedures.

▶ Registers and returns

▷ Maintain statutory registers (members, director and secretary, interest in voting shares, debenture holders). **ss. 114, 877, 892, 162, 265 and 743**

▷ Ensure that the company meets the periodic compliance requirements of the Registrar of Companies and reports certain changes regarding the company. These will include:

– amended articles of association;

– notices of appointment, removal and resignation of directors and the secretary;

– share capital returns;

– notices of removal or resignation of the auditors;

– change of registered office;

– company resolutions;

– confirmation statements; and

– report and accounts.

▶ General compliance

▷ Monitor and ensure compliance with relevant legal requirements, particularly under the Companies Acts, such as the administration of the registered office, communication and display of the company's identity and arrangements for the public inspection of documents.

The shareholders

▶ Listed, AIM and NEX company obligations

▷ Monitor and ensure compliance with the LPDT Rules, AIM or

NEX Rules and the Takeover Code, including supervising the implementation of the Model Code.

▷ Manage relations with the UK Listing Authority (UKLA), Stock Exchange or NEX Market through the company's advisers.

▷ Release 'regulated information' (i.e. information required to be disclosed under LPDT Rules) and ensure the security of unreleased, price-sensitive information.

▶ General meetings

▷ Organise general meetings as required by the Act, the company's articles of association and the LPDT Rules if applicable.

▷ Prepare and issue notices of meetings and proxy forms.

▷ Support the board and prepare briefing notes for directors.

▷ Ensure correct procedures are followed, especially in relation to voting.

▶ Report and accounts

▷ Coordinate the preparation, publication and distribution of the company's annual report and accounts and interim statements in consultation with the company's internal and external advisers.

▷ Assist the directors in preparing the narrative reporting sections of the report, covering corporate governance disclosures and the work of the board and its committees.

▶ Share registration

Some or all of these tasks may be outsourced to the company's registrar, but the company secretary will need to be responsible for managing the relationship.

▷ Maintenance of the company's register of members.

▷ Payment of dividends and interest.

▷ Issue documentation regarding rights issues and capitalisation issues.

▷ Dealing with transfers and other matters affecting shareholdings.

▷ Dealing with queries and requests from shareholders.

▶ Shareholder communications

▷ Communicate with the shareholders formally (e.g. through circulars) and encourage good shareholder relations by providing appropriate information on the company's website.

▷ Relations with institutional shareholders and their investment protection committees.

▶ Shareholder monitoring

▷ Monitor the register of members to identify any apparent 'stake building' in the company's share by potential takeover bidders.

▷ Make enquiries of members as to beneficial ownership of holdings.

▶ Share and capital issues and restructuring

▷ Implement changes in the structure of the company's share and loan capital.

▷ Devise, implement and administer directors' and employees' share participation schemes.

Notes

There are many other areas in which company secretaries can and often do become involved relating to the management of companies. These might include other aspects of company law, regulation and compliance such as risk management, pensions administration, information security and data protection, and health and safety.

More information

Confirmation statement

With effect from 30 June 2016 the confirmation statement, form CS01, replaced the annual return, form AR01. Introduced under SBEE2015 as a deregulating measure, the confirmation statement is intended to offer an easier and more efficient way for companies to check and confirm information held by the Registrar of Companies rather than having to provide information in the form of the annual return, which for many companies remains unchanged from year to year.

All companies must make a confirmation statement up to a date not more than 12 months after the previous confirmation (or 12 months after incorporation), although a company may choose to make it up to an earlier date. The confirmation statement must be filed with the Registrar of Companies within 14 days of the confirmation date, together with a fee (currently £13 if filed online or £40 if filed in hard copy).

s.853A(1)

The statement confirms that all information that the company is required to have delivered to the Registrar of Companies under s. 853B (Relevant Events) has been delivered or is being delivered at the same time as the confirmation statement. In addition to the statement concerning relevant events, companies must provide updated information primarily relating to their share capital, share ownership and beneficial ownership (ss. 853C–I).

s.853A(2)(a)

s 853A(2)(b)

Checklist

▶ Check if the records at Companies House are up to date and either confirm or complete the confirmation statement information together with any additional forms required to update the public record as set out below.

▶ Provide details of any changes in relevant events during the confirmation period

▶ Provide details of any changes in:

> ▷ the company's business activities or SIC code;

> ▷ information about people with significant control or any changes;

> ▷ statement of capital;

   ▷   trading status of shares; and

   ▷   member information.

▶ File the confirmation statement within 14 days of end of the review
period to which it relates, together with the appropriate filing
fee, if any: £40 if being filed in hard copy, and £13 if being filed
electronically or online.

s.853A(5)

ss.853A(4),(6)

Procedure

▶ A company's first review period begins on the date of incorporation
and ends 12 months later. Subsequent review periods are the period
of 12 months beginning on the day after the previous confirmation
statement. Companies may choose to file a confirmation statement
covering a shorter period than 12 months, but the period cannot
exceed 12 months.

s.853(B)

▶ A confirmation statement is required even where there have been no
changes.

▶ For all companies, details of any relevant events must have already
been notified or be being notified at the same time as the confirmation
statement is submitted using the usual statutory forms. The relevant
events are:

s.853C

   ▷   company's registered office;

   ▷   company's directors and any changes to their registered or
registrable information (see page 65);

s.853D

   ▷   company's secretary and any changes to their registered or
registrable information (see page 65); and

   ▷   changes to the location of any of the company's registers.

▶ In addition, if there has been a change to any of details set out
below, updated information must be provided with the confirmation
statement:

s.853E

   ▷   If the company's business activities have changed, the relevant
SIC code(s).

   ▷   If the company has shares, any change to the statement of capital.
The statement of capital was simplified at the same time as the
introduction of the confirmation statement and comprises details
of the total number of shares of the company, of all classes,
aggregate nominal value and aggregate amount unpaid on
those shares, whether of nominal value or share premium. In
addition, for each share class there must be provided details of
the prescribed particulars of the rights attached to the shares, total
number of shares of that class and the aggregate nominal value of
the shares of that class.

   ▷   Any changes in trading status of the shares. The requirement is
to notify if any of the shares were at any time during the period

admitted to trading on a regulated market and if so whether the shares were admitted to that market throughout the period and whether the company was a DTR5 issuer.

▷ Any changes in members' information. A non-traded company that has not elected to keep its register of members on the public register must provide information about any changes to the names of any members, number of shares of each class held by members, and number and date of registration of any shares transferred during the confirmation period.

▷ If the company is a traded company, for every member who held 5% or more of the issued shares at any time during the period covered by the return, their name, address and holding of shares.

s.853G

Filing requirement

▶ Form CS01.

▶ Filing fee: £40 or £13 as appropriate.

Notes

If a company files more than one confirmation statement in any 12-month period, there is no fee payable for filing the second or subsequent statements.

More information

 Chapter 7    Chapter 11    Guidance
Confirmation statement

Corporate governance – principles and key issues

The overarching corporate governance principles are as follows.

- Fairness
    - All shareholders (minority and majority) are treated equally.
    - Fairness in treatment of stakeholders other than shareholders.
- Accountability
    - Decision-makers who act on behalf of the company should be accountable for the decisions they make.
    - Shareholders should be able to assess the action of the board of directors and committees of the board.
    - Shareholders should have the opportunity to query or challenge them.
- Responsibility
    - The board of directors should accept full responsibility for the powers it is given and the authority it exercises.
    - Executive management should be responsible for the exercise of power delegated to it by the board of directors, and should be accountable to the board for their achievements.
- Transparency
    - Willingness by the company to provide clear information to shareholders and other stakeholders about what the company has done and hopes to achieve, without giving away commercially sensitive information.
    - Should not be confused with 'understandability' – transparency is more concerned with content over form.
    - A principle of good governance is that stakeholders should be informed about what a company is doing and plans to do in the future, and about the risks involved in its business strategies.

Key areas where there could be potential conflicts of interest (between individual directors, the board of directors as a whole, and other stakeholders groups) are:

- financial reporting and auditing;

- directors' remuneration;

- company–stakeholder relations;

- risk-taking and the management of risk;

- effective communication between directors and shareholders; and

- ethical conduct and corporate social responsibility.

Good corporate governance should promote the best long-term interests of the company. Composition of the board, its functions and responsibilities and its effectiveness are therefore key issues of corporate governance.

More information

Chapter 17

CREST settlement

'CREST-compliant articles' is the term used to describe companies whose articles permit settlement in CREST, the dematerialised settlement system for shares of listed, AIM and NEX companies operated by Euroclear UK and Ireland Limited.

New applicants to either of the markets will be required to ensure that their articles are CREST-compliant as a condition of entry. For existing companies this could be by way of either a directors' or a shareholders' resolution. For newly incorporated companies, this power would be incorporated in the articles of association adopted for the purposes of admission.

Enabling the shares to be settled in CREST requires the register of members to be split into two parts: a wholly electronic sub-register maintained by CREST and the certificated part of the register maintained by or on behalf of the company.

The company will need to ensure it has the necessary systems to allow for real-time updating and synchronisation between the electronic sub-register and the certificated register; this task is usually outsourced to a specialist share registration company.

Checklist

▶ Do the articles permit dematerialised holdings?

▶ Has appropriate software been acquired or the share register been outsourced to ensure the register of members is capable of interacting with CREST?

Procedure

▶ Convene a directors' meeting to approve appropriate resolution to amend the articles of association. Ensure valid quorum is present. **reg. 16, SI 2001/3755**

▶ Alternatively, the amendments may be made by special resolution of the shareholders (see page 239).

▶ Where changes are made by directors' resolution, notice must be given to shareholders within 60 days of the date of the resolution.

Filing requirement

▶ Copy of directors' resolution or special resolution within 15 days.

Notes

▶ Enabling CREST settlement is one of the few occasions where the directors can resolve to change the company's articles of association.

▶ Prior to commencement of CREST settlement, an application form must be submitted to Euroclear UK and Ireland Ltd, the system operator, to enable CREST settlement. This process will usually be arranged by the company's share registrars.

More information

 Chapter 18    Chapter 5   www.euroclear.com

Debenture stock

The procedures for issuing, transferring, payment of interest on and redemption of debentures are, broadly speaking, the same as for the issuing of ordinary shares.

Debentures, unlike shares, are loans to the company and are secured against the assets of the company.

Unless restricted by the articles of association, companies have an implied power to issue debentures.

Checklist

▶ Do articles restrict the directors' power to create and issue debentures?

▶ Create trust deed containing:

  ▷ details of the stock, terms of issue, payment of interest, conversion into shares and/or redemption;

  ▷ provisions constituting charges over the assets of the company in favour of the trust deed and giving details of the events by which the charge would be enforceable;

  ▷ details of the Trustees' powers to concur with the company in dealings with the charged assets;

  ▷ where the security is by way of floating charge, a prohibition on the company issuing any further security ranking in priority to the debenture stock without previous consent; and

  ▷ details setting out the form of stock certificate, conditions of redemption, conversion rights and regulations in respect of the Register of Holders, transfer and transmission, and regulations for the conducting and holding of meetings of the debenture holders.

▶ Register allotment of debentures as soon as practical in register of debenture holders and in any event within two months of issue. **s. 741**

▶ Ensure register is available for inspection at the registered office or at its SAIL address (see page 270). **s. 743**

▶ If register is not kept at registered office, file form AD02.

Procedure

▶ Convene a directors' meeting to approve the terms of the trust deed and the issue of debentures.

▶ The company secretary should arrange the preparation and issue of debenture stock certificates to each debenture holder.

s. 741

▶ The company secretary should record the details of the debentures issued in the register of debenture holders.

ss. 859A, 859B

▶ As debentures are secured on the assets of the company, the trust deed and form MG07 or MG08 as appropriate must be submitted to Companies House within 21 days of the creation of the trust deed.

Filing requirement

▶ Trust deed.

▶ Form MG07 or MG08 within 21 days.

▶ Form AD02, if required.

▶ Filing fee £23 (paper), £15 (electronic).

More information

 Chapter 12　　 Chapter 9　　 Guidance booklet GP3

Directors – appointment of corporate director

The Small Business, Enterprise and Employment Act 2015 (SBEE2015) contains additional restrictions on the appointment of corporate directors; however, at the time of writing these provisions have not been implemented and there is no guidance on when they are to be brought into effect.

Although the Act introduced a general ban on the appointment of corporate directors, there are to be a number of exemptions to this ban.

Accordingly, once brought into force, the detail of the legislation must be checked to ensure any proposed appointment of a corporate director is permitted.

s. 12 reg. 17 sch. 1 or reg. 20 sch. 3, SI 2008/3229

Checklist

▶ If there is to be a corporate director, there must also be appointed at least one other director that is a natural person.

s. 155

▶ Is the director disqualified from acting by statute or the articles of association?

▶ Obtain written consent from the entity consenting to be appointed as a director. This can be included in the service contract rather than a stand-alone document if preferred.

Procedure

▶ The following details will be required in order to complete form AP02.

 – Corporate name and registered or principal office.

 – For an EAA company details of the registry it is registered in and its registered number.

 – For a non EAA company its legal form and if applicable details of the registry it is registered in and its registered number.

▶ Although not explicitly prohibited, the duties and responsibilities of the UK corporate governance code make it very unlikely that a corporate director can be appointed to a listed company.

▶ If directors' names are shown on the headed paper, this will need to be updated.

▶ Amend bank mandate if necessary.

▶ Convene a directors' meeting to approve the appointment of a new director. Ensure valid quorum is present.

▶ File completed form AP02 at Companies House.

▶ Notify employees, customers and/or bank, if appropriate.

▶ Update the registers of directors and directors' residential addresses as necessary.

Filing requirement

▶ Form AP02 within 14 days.

Notes

▶ The new director should notify the board of any interest in contracts or other companies with which the company has dealings.

▶ The company secretary should inform the new director of the dates on which forthcoming board meetings are to be held, if these are known.

▶ If the articles of association require that the directors hold a share qualification, it is essential that the director acquires the appropriate shares within two months, or the time limit set down by the articles if shorter.

▶ Appointees are no longer required to sign a statement on the form AP02 consenting to act as a director; instead a statement confirming the entity has consented is confirmed on behalf of the company. Accordingly confirmation of consent should be obtained and retained in the event of any disputed appointments (see page 101).

▶ It may be necessary to add the director to the company's directors' indemnity insurance policy, or indeed it may be necessary to effect such a policy.

More information

Chapter 6

Chapter 11

Guidance booklet GP3

Directors – appointment of individual

When a company is incorporated, the people named in the incorporation papers (form IN01) as directors and who have consented to act are deemed to be appointed on the date of incorporation. Following the appointment of these first directors, any further directors to be selected should be appointed in accordance with the regulations laid down by the company's articles of association.

In general, the articles will allow the existing directors to fill any casual vacancy in their number by themselves or by the members by ordinary resolution.

Occasionally, the articles of association will stipulate qualifications to be held for eligibility for appointment as a director. This often used to be a share qualification, although this is no longer a popular practice.

Additional qualifications would more normally be the holding of a particular professional or technical qualification (e.g. chartered surveyor, architect, etc).

s. 12
reg. 17 sch. 1 or
reg. 20 sch. 3,
SI 2008/3229

Checklist

▶ Check the articles of association to establish whether directors or only shareholders may appoint the new director(s).

▶ Check the articles to ensure any maximum number of directors stipulated in the articles has not already been reached.

▶ Is the proposed director at least 16 years old?

s. 157

▶ If there is to be a sole director, is the proposed director a natural person?

s. 155

▶ Is the director disqualified from acting by statute or the articles of association?

▶ Obtain the director's details required to complete form AP01, including their residential address in addition to a service address.

▶ If appointment is as a non-executive to a listed company, ensure appropriate independence tests can be met if appropriate.

▶ Obtain written consent from the individual consenting to be appointed as a director. This can be included in their employment contract rather than a stand-alone document if preferred.

▶ If directors' names are shown on the headed paper, this will need to be updated.

▶ Amend bank mandate if necessary.

Procedure

▶ Convene a directors' meeting to approve the appointment of a new director. Ensure valid quorum is present.

▶ File completed form AP01 at Companies House.   **s.167**

▶ Notify employees, customers and/or bank, if appropriate.

▶ Notify Stock Exchange if company's shares are listed or traded on AIM.   **LR 9.6.11, AR 17**

▶ Notify NEX if company's shares are traded on the NEX market.   **PL71**

▶ Update the registers of directors and directors' residential addresses as necessary.   **ss.163–165**

Filing requirement

▶ Form AP01 within 14 days.

Notes

▶ The new director should notify the board of any interest in contracts or other companies with which the company has dealings.   **ss.177, 182**

▶ The company secretary should inform the new director of the dates on which forthcoming board meetings are to be held, if these are known.

▶ If the articles of association require that the directors hold a share qualification, it is essential that the director acquires the appropriate shares within two months, or the time limit set down by the articles if shorter.

▶ If the new director is to be an executive director, it may be considered necessary for the director to have a formal service contract with the company.

▶ It may be necessary to add the director to the company's directors' indemnity insurance policy or indeed it may be necessary to effect such a policy.

▶ Appointees are no longer required to sign a statement on form AP01 consenting to act as a director; instead a statement confirming the individual has consented is confirmed on behalf of the company. Accordingly, confirmation of consent should be obtained and retained in the event of any disputed appointments (see page 101).

▶ If this is the director's first appointment as director, he or she should be given guidance as to his or her duties and responsibilities in terms of the Companies Act and his or her duties and responsibilities to members.

▶ HM Revenue & Customs should be informed of the director's appointment.

More information

 Chapter 6    Chapter 11    Guidance booklet GP3

Directors – ceasing to hold office

A director may cease to hold office as a result of his or her death, by statute or under the provisions of the articles of association.

A director may be barred from holding or continuing to hold office as director for the following reasons:

- If the articles require that the director hold a share qualification and the director does not acquire the necessary shares within the time limit specified by the articles if shorter.

- If the director becomes bankrupt (unless permitted to continue by the court).

- If the director is disqualified from holding a directorship by a court order.

Additionally, the articles may stipulate certain events that will require the director to vacate office, including:

- If a director resigns: resignation will not normally require consent of the remaining directors, although this may be required by the articles.

- If a director is absent from board meetings for a specific period without the authority of the board.

- If a director has a Receiving Order made against him or her, or if he or she enters into arrangements with his or her creditors.

- If the director is, or may be, suffering from a mental disorder and either the director has been admitted to hospital pursuant to the Mental Health Act or a court order has been made requiring his or her detention under the Act.

- If a director is removed from office by the remaining directors or by the members in some specified manner. This may include by written resolution of the remaining directors, by notice in writing of the company's holding company or in certain circumstances by their appointer. (For example, the holders of a particular class of shares may have the right to appoint a director and this person may be removed by them.)

In addition to the powers contained in the articles of association or by statute, the shareholders of the company have the right at all times to remove a director by ordinary resolution. Care must be taken when using these provisions.

s. 168

Checklist

▶ The company's bankers should be informed and any necessary amendments made to the bank mandate.

▶ The company secretary should amend the company's register of directors and the register of directors' residential addresses.

ss. 162, 165

▶ If the director's name is shown on the company's letter heading, this should be amended.

▶ If the company maintains a directors' indemnity insurance policy, the insurers should be informed.

▶ The auditors should be informed.

▶ HM Revenue & Customs should be notified.

▶ Any outstanding fees should be paid to the director and arrangements made for the return of any company property (car, computer equipment, etc).

▶ If appropriate, the director should be reminded of any restrictions on his or her future employment contained in his or her contract of employment with the company.

Procedure

▶ Convene a directors' meeting to consider the circumstances of the director whose appointment has ceased. Ensure valid quorum is present.

▶ File completed form TM01 at Companies House.

▶ Update register of directors and register of directors' residential addresses as necessary.

ss. 162, 165

▶ Amend headed paper if directors' names are shown.

▶ Notify Stock Exchange if company's shares are listed or traded on AIM.

LR 9.6.11, AR 17

▶ Notify NEX if company's shares are traded on the NEX market.

IR 71

Filing requirement

▶ Form TM01 within 14 days.

Notes

None.

More information

 Chapter 6　　 Chapter 11　　 Guidance booklet GP3

Enterprise Act 2002
Company Directors' Disqualification Act 1986
Insolvency Act 1986
Small Business, Enterprise and Employment Act 2015

Directors – disqualification

▶ The Company Directors' Disqualification Act 1986 (CDDA1986) consolidated a number of enactments relating to the disqualification of persons from being directors of companies and from being otherwise concerned with company management.

▶ CDDA1986 sets out circumstances where a court may or will (depending on the section) make a disqualification order that prohibits that person from being a director, liquidator or administrator of a company, a receiver or manager of a company's property, or being in any way involved in the promotion, formation or management of a company for the specified period.

CDDA1986 ss. 1–6, 10

▶ Under provisions introduced by the Insolvency Act 2000, a director facing prosecution may voluntarily apply to be disqualified as a director. This voluntary procedure speeds up the disqualification process and significantly reduces the costs for all parties.

▶ SBEE2015 introduced new provisions allowing the courts to take into account overseas convictions for the purposes of determining whether or not to disqualify a person from acting as a director in the UK.

form DQ01

Checklist

▶ Ensure the court order or copy bears the seal of the court.

▶ The company's bankers should be informed and any necessary amendments made to the bank mandate.

▶ The secretary should amend the company's register of directors.

▶ If the director's name is shown on the company's letter heading, this should be amended.

▶ If the company maintains a directors' indemnity insurance policy, the insurers should be informed.

▶ The auditors, if any, should be informed.

▶ HM Revenue & Customs should be notified.

▶ Any outstanding fees should be paid to the director and arrangements made for the return of any company property (car, computer equipment, etc).

▶ If appropriate, the director should be reminded of any restrictions on his or her future employment contained in his or her contract of employment with the company.

Procedure

▶ File completed form TM01 at Companies House.   **s.167**

▶ Update register of directors as necessary.

▶ Amend headed paper if directors' names are shown.

▶ Notify Stock Exchange if company's shares are listed or traded on AIM.   **LR 9.6.11, AR 17**

▶ Notify NEX if company's shares are traded on the NEX.   **IR 71**

Filing requirement

▶ Form TM01 within 14 days.   **s.167**

▶ Copy of disqualification order.

More information

 Chapter 6    Chapter 11   Guidance booklet GP3

Directors – duties

A director's prime duty, which he or she holds together with his or her fellow directors, is to manage the company for the benefit of its members. The directors may delegate some or all of their powers to particular directors (perhaps constituting a committee of the board) and/or other senior officers in the company, but they cannot delegate their duties.

The Companies Act 2006 introduced seven duties of directors. These duties codified, with some amendments, existing case law.

The directors must ensure that suitable arrangements are in place to enable the company to meet its statutory duties and are liable to penalties if the company is in default. Directors of many companies will delegate these duties to the company secretary, and as it is the directors who are liable in the event of default, care must be taken to ensure that the company secretary is suitably qualified.

In many small private companies the directors will often rely on their professional advisers to undertake some of their responsibilities, such as filing accounts and preparing annual returns. Directors must act on the advice of their advisers to ensure that the statutory obligations are met. It is the directors and not the professional advisers who are liable, and in the event of default and prosecution it is the directors who will be called to account.

Checklist

The seven statutory duties are:

1. **To act within their powers:** Directors must act in accordance with the company's constitution and only exercise powers for the purposes for which they are conferred. The company's articles of association should be consulted to ascertain the extent of a director's powers and any limitations placed upon them.

s. 171

2. **To promote the success of the company:** A director must act in the way he or she considers, in good faith, would be most likely to promote the success of the company for the benefit of its members as a whole, and in doing so have regard (among other matters) to:

s. 172

▶ the likely consequences of any decision in the long term;

- the interests of the company's employees;

- the need to foster the company's business relationships with suppliers, customers and others;

- the impact of the company's operations on the community and the environment;

- the desirability of the company maintaining a reputation for high standards of business conduct; and

- the need to act fairly as between members of the company.

3. **To exercise independent judgement.**

s. 173

4. **To exercise reasonable care, skill and diligence:** The duties imposed by ss. 173 and 174 require that a director owes a duty to exercise the same standard of care, skill and diligence that would be exercised by a reasonably diligent person with:

s. 174

- the general knowledge, skill and experience that may reasonably be expected of the person carrying out the same functions as a director in relation to that company (an objective test); and

- the general knowledge, skill and experience that the director actually has (a subjective test).

(For example, a finance director would be expected to have a greater knowledge of finance issues than, say, the HR director (the objective test); but if the HR director is also a qualified accountant, then he or she would be expected to have a greater knowledge than would normally be expected of a HR director, although not necessarily the same knowledge as the finance director (the subjective test).)

5. **To avoid conflicts of interest:** Directors must avoid situations in which they have or might have a direct or indirect interest that conflicts or might conflict with the interests of the company. Of particular importance are conflicts relating to property, information or opportunity regardless of whether the company could take advantage of such opportunities.

s. 175

- The duty does not apply to conflicts arising out of transactions or arrangement between the company and the director.

- Where the company is a private company, authorisation may be given by resolution of the directors, provided there is nothing in the company's articles of association that invalidated the authorisation.

s. 175(2)

- Where the company is a public company, authorisation may be given by resolution of the directors, provided there is specific authority in the company's articles of association that permits directors to authorise such transactions.

- Such authorisation, whether for a private or public company, is only valid if the necessary quorum for a meeting of the directors is present, excluding the director with the conflict of interest and without that director voting.

s. 175(6)

6. **Not to accept benefits from third parties:** Directors must not accept a benefit from a third party being given by virtue of their being a director or due to any action or inaction by the director.   **s. 176**

Benefits received by a director from a person by whom his or her services are provided are not to be regarded as paid by a third party.

The duty is not infringed if the acceptance of the benefit cannot reasonably be regarded as likely to give rise to a conflict of interest.   **s. 177**

7. **To declare interests in any proposed transaction or arrangement:** A director must declare the full nature and extent of any direct or indirect interest in any proposed transaction or arrangement before that transaction or arrangement is entered into. The declaration may be given at a meeting of the directors or by general notification on appointment.   **ss. 184, 185**

Where a previous notification or interest becomes inaccurate or incomplete, additional notification(s) must be made.

Notification is not required where the director is not aware of the interest or is not aware of the transaction or arrangement.

Notification is not required where the nature of the interest is such that it cannot reasonably be regarded as likely to give rise to a conflict of interest, to the extent that the other directors are already aware of the interest without requiring specific notification or where the transaction relates to the director's service contract.

More information

 Chapter 6    Chapter 11    Guidance booklet GP3

Directors – meetings – private companies

There are no fixed rules regarding operation of the board of directors. The articles of association will govern the powers of directors. The maximum or minimum number of directors and the quorum necessary for meetings of the directors will be stipulated.

regs 7–16 sch. 1, SI 2008/3229

Meetings of the directors should be held upon 'reasonable' notice, according to the circumstances of the company or the meeting concerned. Where the board of directors all work in the same office, reasonable notice may well be two to three hours. Where the directors normally meet on a quarterly basis only and do not work at the same location, then reasonable notice may be two weeks, or more.

Meetings are usually called by the company secretary on instructions of the chairman, although any director may request that a meeting be convened or convene it themselves.

reg. 9 sch. 1, SI 2008/3229

Votes at a directors' meeting are taken on the basis of one vote per director. All resolutions are passed by a simple majority. The articles of association of the company may give the chairman a casting vote in circumstances where there are an equal number of votes both for and against a particular resolution.

regs 7, 8, 13, SI 2008/3229

In certain circumstances, usually where one director has invested the majority of the company's funding, the articles may provide for enhanced voting rights for certain specified directors.

Directors may be empowered by the articles of association to appoint someone to attend and vote in their place (an alternate director), when circumstances dictate that they are unable to attend the meeting themselves. Such authority is not contained in the CA2006 model articles for private companies, although it is contained in Table A for companies incorporated prior to 1 October 2009.

regs 65–69 Table A, SI 1985/805

In addition to allowing the reaching of decisions at meetings, the model articles permit private company directors to reach decisions by indicating to each other by any means that they share a common view on any particular matter. Although many formal matters may be decided upon by circulating written resolutions, where a contentious matter requires consideration and an exchange of views, it is important to ensure that all directors are able to participate fully in that debate.

reg. 8(2) sch. 1, SI 2008/3229

Although the day-to-day running of the company will be left to the managing director and the other executive directors, the board should meet to decide upon matters of policy and matters requiring signature on behalf of the board.

Checklist

▶ Pre-CA2006 articles may provide for directors not in the UK not to be entitled to receive notice of meetings.

▶ Has notice been given to all directors entitled to notice?

▶ Have all relevant board papers been circulated sufficiently in advance of the meeting?

▶ At the meeting, is a quorum present at the start and throughout the meeting?

reg. 11 sch. 1, SI 2008/3229

▶ Have participating directors declared any conflicts of interest and considered their statutory duties in reaching their decision?

reg. 16 sch. 3, SI 2008/3229

ss. 171–177

▶ Have minutes been taken and, once approved, kept in the minute book?

reg. 15 sch. 1, SI 2006/3229

s 248

Notes

▶ Members have no right to view the minutes of the directors.

More information

 Chapter 9    Chapter 13

Directors – meetings – public companies

There are no fixed rules regarding operation of the board of directors. The articles of association will govern the powers of directors. The maximum or minimum number of directors and the quorum necessary for meetings of the directors will be stipulated.

regs 7–19 sch.3, SI 2008/3229

Meetings of the directors should be held upon 'reasonable' notice, according to the circumstances of the company or the meeting concerned. Where the board of directors all work in the same office, reasonable notice may well be two to three hours. Where the directors normally meet on a quarterly basis only and do not work at the same location, then reasonable notice may be two weeks, or more.

Meetings are usually called by the company secretary on instructions of the chairman, although any director may request that a meeting be convened or convene it themselves.

reg. 8 sch.3, SI 2008/3229

Votes at a directors' meeting are taken on the basis of one vote per director. All resolutions are passed by a simple majority. The articles of association of the company may give the chairman a casting vote in circumstances where there are an equal number of votes both for and against a particular resolution.

regs 13, 14, SI 2008/3229

In certain circumstances, usually where one director has invested the majority of the company's funding, the articles may provide for enhanced voting rights for certain specified directors.

Directors may be empowered by the articles of association to appoint someone to attend and vote in their place (an alternate director), when circumstances dictate that they are unable to attend the meeting themselves. If a director is appointed as an alternate for another director, that director will have two votes and may cast each vote differently.

reg. 15 sch.3, SI 2008/3229

In addition to allowing the reaching of decisions at meetings, the model articles permit public company directors to reach decisions by any other means, provided they can communicate with each other. Accordingly decisions may be reached by conference video or telephone facilities. Written resolutions of directors are permitted by the model articles. As decisions may require an exchange of views, it is important to ensure that all directors are able to participate fully in that debate.

reg. 9(1)(b) sch.3, SI 2008/3229

regs 17, 18 sch.3, SI 2008/3229

Although the day-to-day running of the company will be left to the managing director and the other executive directors, the board should meet to decide upon matters of policy and matters requiring signature.

Checklist

▶ Pre-CA2006 articles may provide for directors not in the UK not to be entitled to receive notice of meetings.

▶ Has notice been given to all directors entitled to notice?

▶ Have participating directors declared any conflicts of interest and considered their statutory duties in reaching their decision?

reg. 16 sch. 3, SI 2008/3229 ss. 171–177

▶ Have all relevant board papers been circulated sufficiently in advance of the meeting?

▶ At the meeting, is a quorum present at the start and throughout the meeting?

reg. 10 sch. 3, SI 2008/3229

▶ Have minutes been taken and, once approved, kept in the minute book?

s. 248

Notes

▶ Members have no right to view the minutes of the directors.

More information

 Chapter 8    Chapter 13

Directors – objection to appointment

The Small Business, Enterprise and Employment Act 2015 introduced a new procedure under which a person can object to their appointment as a director on the grounds that they did not consent to be appointed.

ss. 1095(4A–4D)

If the objection is upheld, the Registrar has power to rectify the company record and remove form AP01 or AP02 from the company's file.

s. 1095(1)

Checklist

▶ Application can only be made by or on behalf of the person claiming to have been appointed without their consent.

Procedure

▶ The applicant or someone on their behalf must complete and file form RP02a setting out details of the incorrect form lodged and confirming that the application complies with the requirements of s. 1095.

s. 1095(4A)(b)

▶ On receipt of the application the Registrar will send a notice to all directors and company secretary, if any, the registered office and the presenter giving notice of the intention to remove the relevant form from the company's file unless an objection is received within 28 days.

s. 1095(4B)

▶ Provided no objection is received, the relevant form will be removed and the register will be annotated accordingly.

▶ If there are any objections these are indicated by filing form RP03, which must be filed within 28 days of the date of notice by the Registrar.

▶ To object, the company need only provide evidence that the person consented to act.

s. 1096

Filing requirement

▶ Form RP02.

▶ Form RP03, if applicable.

Notes

▶ In the case of any objections, the Registrar is not permitted to remove the form and has no authority to decide the merits of any claim. Where the applicant maintains they have been appointed in error, it will be necessary to make an application to the court.

▶ Application for rectification and removal of forms should only be used in cases of fraud or genuine dispute. Where a form contains a factual inaccuracy, rectification is not normally appropriate and a replacement document should be filed.

More information

 Chapter 6    Chapter 11    Guidance booklet GP6

Directors – removal

Irrespective of any provisions contained in the company's articles of association or a director's service contract, the shareholders can, at any time, remove a director by ordinary resolution.

s.168

Checklist

▶ Will the director resign?

▶ Check the articles to see if the director can be removed by a vote of the remaining directors or by notice from, say, the holding company.

▶ Is the director due to retire by rotation at the next annual general meeting (public companies only)?

▶ Special notice (see page 162) of the proposed removal needs to be given to the company by an officer. **s.168(2)**

▶ The director whose removal is proposed must be sent a copy of the special notice. **s.169(1)**

Procedure

▶ Company secretary, director or a shareholder to give special notice to the company of proposal to remove a director. The special notice must be received at least 28 clear days before the meeting. **s.169(1)**

▶ If the removal is proposed by shareholders, it may be appropriate for them to requisition a general meeting as well (see page 123). **s.303**

▶ A copy of the special notice must be sent to the director whose removal has been proposed. **s.169(1)**

▶ Convene a board meeting to consider the special notice and convene a general meeting if appropriate.

▶ Company secretary or a director to issue a notice convening a general meeting on 14 clear days' notice to consider the resolution as an ordinary resolution. The notice should state on it that special notice has been given. The director whose removal is proposed is entitled to have a written representation circulated with the notice. **s.168** **s.169(3)**

▶ If the resolution is approved, file form TM01 with Companies House.

▶ The company secretary should ensure that the register of directors is amended.

▶ Listed, AIM or NEX companies must make an appropriate announcement no later than the day following the removal.

LR 9.6.11, AR 17, IR 71

Filing requirement

▶ Form TM01 within 14 days.

Notes

▶ The director to be removed has the right to be heard at the general meeting even if he or she is not a shareholder.

▶ Although the meeting can be held at short notice without contravening the provisions relating to the giving of special notice, this may be seen as prejudicial to the director's case and care must be taken when convening the meeting on short notice.

▶ Although the shareholders can remove the director from office, this would not prejudice the director's rights under any service contract, nor would it affect his or her right to take action against the company for any breach.

▶ The removal of a director must be put to a meeting of the members and cannot be dealt with by means of a written resolution by a private company.

s. 168(1)

More information

H Chapter 6   CSP Chapter 11

Directors – residential address

Directors, other than corporate directors (and in the case of an overseas company registered in Great Britain, a representative), must give details of a service address on form AP01 and any change in that address on form CH01.

s.167

If the service address of a director is not their usual residential address, the director must notify the company of their usual residential address and the company must maintain a register of directors' residential addresses. Where the service address is a director's usual residential address, the register of directors' residential addresses need only contain an entry to that effect.

s.165

Although details of the residential address are contained in form AP01, those details are not disclosed on the public file unless required by a court order or where the Registrar has cause to believe that the service address is not effective at bringing documents to the notice of the director.

ss.240–246

More information

 Chapter 6    Chapter 11    Guidance booklet GP3

Directors – residential address suppression

Directors' private address information is no longer disclosed on the public record, for new filings, after 1 October 2009 when directors and company secretaries were permitted to provide a service address.

However, previous forms still show the residential address information.

Due to the nature of the business activities of certain companies, overseas companies and LLPs, their directors, company secretaries and members might be at risk of violence or intimidation.

Such individuals can apply for their residential address information to be suppressed.

ss. 243, 790(ZF) & (ZG), 1088

Checklist

Application may only be made by an individual who is or proposes to be:

▶ a director of a company;

▶ a member of an LLP; or

▶ a director or permanent representative of an overseas company.

Procedure

▶ Applications are available on request from Companies House contact centre, 0303 1234 500.

▶ Complete and file appropriate application form. There are a number of different forms depending on which section the application is being made under and whether it relates to an individual, company, charge holder or a subscriber. All the forms have the prefix 'SR'.

  Whichever SR form is used the following information is required:

  – statement of the grounds for making the application;

  – identifying the company whose activities may place the applicant at risk;

  – the applicants details; and

  – application fee of £100.

Filing requirement

▶ SR form as appropriate.

▶ Statement of grounds and evidence.

▶ Application fee.

▶ Details of company whose activities give rise to the risk of violence or intimidation.

ss. 243, 790(ZF), (ZG), 1088

More information

 Chapter 7

 Guidance booklet GP3

Dissolution

The Registrar is authorised by the Companies Act 2006 to remove from the register those companies that are believed to be defunct. This procedure will frequently be used where a company has failed to file accounts or annual returns, and no response is received to letters sent to the company's registered office.

s.1000

In addition, the directors of a company may voluntarily request that a company be struck off.

s.1003

This procedure may not be used if, within three months of the proposed application, the company has changed its name, traded, disposed of property or rights for value, or engaged in any activity other than that required to effect the dissolution, or where application for a scheme of arrangement or petition or order under the Insolvency Act has been made.

s.1004(1)

s.1005

Checklist

▶ Has the company any assets or liabilities, or does it hold title to any property or assets?

▶ During the three months preceding the application, has the company:

  ▷ changed its name;

  ▷ traded;

  ▷ disposed of any property or rights for value; or

  ▷ engaged in any activity other than that required to effect the dissolution?

▶ Check that insolvency or administration procedures have not commenced.

Procedure

▶ Convene a directors' meeting to consider the dissolution of the company.

▶ If part of a group, enter into a transfer of assets agreement with another group company to 'sweep' up any assets not previously disposed of.

▶ File completed form DS01 at Companies House signed by all directors, where there are no more than two, or a majority of directors, if there are three or more.

▶ A copy of the application must be sent within seven days to any person who at any time on or after the date of application but prior to dissolution or withdrawal was: **ss. 1006, 1007**

  ▷ an employee;

  ▷ a member;

  ▷ a creditor;

  ▷ a director; or

  ▷ a manager or trustee of any pension fund established for the employees.

▶ VAT-registered companies must notify their VAT office.

▶ On receipt of the application, the Registrar will publish a notice in the *Gazette* inviting any objections as to why the company should not be struck off.

▶ If no objections are made within two months of publication in the *Gazette*, the Registrar will strike off the company and publish a further notice in the *Gazette* notifying that the company has been dissolved.   **s. 1003(3)**

Filing requirement

▶ Form DS01.

▶ £10 filing fee.

Notes

▶ The directors may halt the dissolution process by submitting form DS02.   **ss. 1009, 1010**

▶ Care must be taken to ensure that there are no assets remaining in the company as these will pass to the Crown on dissolution under the *bona vacantia* (ownerless property) regime. Within groups of companies, leases are frequently left in the name of dormant subsidiaries.

▶ Where the company has only recently ceased to trade, it will be necessary to contact the company's corporation tax office to settle any liability to tax or confirm that no tax is due, otherwise HM Revenue & Customs are likely to object to the dissolution as a matter of course.

More information

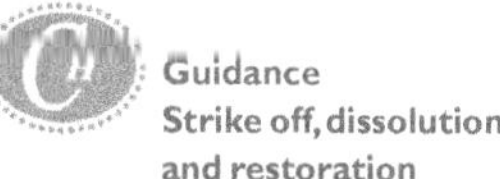

Dividends

Unless shares of any particular class carry a fixed dividend, the declaration and payment of a dividend are at the directors' discretion as set out in its articles.

reg. 30(2) sch. 1,
SI 2008/3229 (Ltd Co)
reg. 70(2) sch. 3,
SI 2008/3229 (PLC Co)

Dividends can be paid only if the company has sufficient distributable profits.

s. 830

The directors may declare a dividend as they see fit in the case of an interim dividend, or subject to the approval of the members by ordinary resolution in the case of the final dividend.

reg. 30 sch 1, reg. 70
sch. 3, SI 2008/3229

The declaration of any dividend should be made by reference to the relevant accounts. These would normally be the most recent annual accounts except where those accounts show that there is insufficient profit available or the dividend is proposed to be paid in the first accounting period. In such cases, interim or initial accounts, as appropriate, will be required. If the annual accounts have a qualified auditors' report, the auditor must issue a statement about whether the qualification is material for determining if a distribution can be made in terms of s. 836.

s. 836(2)

s. 837(4)

For a private company, the interim or initial accounts must enable a reasonable judgement to be made as to the availability of distributable reserves. For a public company, those accounts must be properly prepared in accordance with ss. 395, 396 and 397 of the Companies Act 2006.

ss. 838(1), 839(1)

Where interim accounts are prepared, these must be signed and a copy filed with the Registrar of Companies.

In the case of initial accounts, these must contain a report from the company's auditor and, if the audit report is qualified, a statement from the auditor about whether the qualification is material for determining if a distribution can be made in terms of s. 836. A copy of the signed accounts, audit report and any auditors' statement, if required, must be laid before the members in a general meeting and delivered to the Registrar of Companies.

s. 838(2)–(6)

s. 839(2)–(7)

Checklist

▶ Dividends are usually declared stating both a record date and a later payment date. The record date establishes the date on which the entitlements are to be calculated, and any changes in ownership after that date are ignored.

- On the payment date, dividend cheques and tax vouchers should be completed and issued to members.

- With effect from 31 March 2016, dividend payments no longer have an associated tax credit. Companies are however still required to provide members with a dividend confirmation confirming the amount of tax deducted (currently £nil).

Procedure

- Interim dividend.

  - Convene a directors' meeting to consider the payment of an interim dividend. Ensure sufficient distributable profit is available by reference to relevant accounts.

  - The company secretary arranges the printing of dividend warrants and tax vouchers.

  - Dividend warrants and tax vouchers are despatched to the shareholders.

- Final dividend.

  - Accounts and notice of general meeting are issued to members. If accounts have a qualified audit report, the auditors' statement on their qualification is circulated with the accounts.

  - The general meeting is held.

  - If approval is given to the final dividend, the company secretary arranges payment in the same way as for an interim dividend. Although members can reduce the amount of dividend payable, they cannot approve a payment at a higher rate than that recommended by the directors.

Filing requirement

- Interim or initial accounts if prepared by a public company.

Notes

- The secretary should liaise with their bank or, if relevant, their share registrars concerning the format of the dividend warrant.　　　ss. 838(6), 839(7)

- Schedule of payments and non-cashed cheques must be maintained.

- Often companies maintain a separate dividend account, as once declared and dividend cheques issued, the uncashed funds are no longer a company asset.

More information

Chapter 19　　

Chapter 7

Documents – suggested retention periods

Type of document	Period of retention	
Statutory records		
Certificate of incorporation	Original to be kept permanently	
Certificate to commence business (public company)	Original to be kept permanently	
Articles of association	Original to be kept permanently	
Seal book/register	Original to be kept permanently	
Register of directors and secretaries	Original to be kept permanently	**s. 162**
Register of directors' residential addresses	Original to be kept permanently	**s. 165**
Register of interests in voting shares	Original to be kept permanently	**s. 808**
Register of charges created prior to 6 April 2013	Original to be kept permanently	**s. 876**
Register of members	Current members permanently Former members 10 years	**s. 113** **s. 121**
Register of debenture or loan stockholders	Original to be kept permanently	**s. 743**
Meeting records		
Minutes of general and class meetings, written resolutions	Originals to be kept permanently for meetings held prior to 1 October 2007	**para. 40 sch. 1, SI 2007/2194**
	Ten years after meeting for meetings held after 1 October 2007	**s. 355**
Directors' minutes	Originals to be kept permanently for meetings held prior to 1 October 2007	**para. 19 sch. 1, SI 2007/2194**
	Ten years after meeting for meetings held after 1 October 2007	**s. 248(2)**
Circulars to shareholders including notices of meetings	Master copy to be kept permanently	

Proxy forms/polling cards	One month if no poll demanded One year if poll demanded	

Accounting and financial records

Annual report and accounts	Signed copy to be kept permanently (a stock of spare copies should be maintained for up to five years to meet casual requests)	
Accounting records required by the Companies Acts	Six years for a public company Three years for a private company	**s. 388(4)(b)** **s. 388(4)(a)**
Taxation returns and records	Six years	
Internal financial reports	Six years	
Statements and instructions to banks	Six years	
Tax returns	Permanently	
Expense accounts	Seven years	
Customs and Excise returns	Six years	

Share registration documents	Refer to articles, but typical periods are:	
Forms for application of shares, debentures, etc, forms of acceptance and transfer, renounceable letters of acceptance and allotment, renounceable share certificates, request for designation or redesignation of accounts, letters of request, allotment sheets, letters of indemnity for lost share certificates, stop notices and other court orders	Ten years from date of registration	**reg. 82 sch. 3,** **SI 2008/3229**
Powers of Attorney	Ten years after cessation of membership to which power relates	**s. 121**
Dividend and interest bank mandate forms	Two years after registration	
Cancelled share or stock certificates	One year after cancellation	
Notification of change of address	Two years	
Any contract or memorandum to purchase the company's own shares	Ten years	
Report of an interest in voting shares for investigations requisitioned by members	Six years	
Register of interest in shares when company ceases to be a public company	Six years	

Property records

Deeds of title	Permanently
Leases	Twelve years after lease has terminated
Agreements with architects, builders, etc	Six years after contract completion
Patent and trademark records	Permanently

HR records

Staff personnel records	Seven years after employment ceases
Patent agreements with staff	Twenty years after employment ceases
Applications for jobs	Up to twelve months
Payroll records	Twelve years
Salary registers	Six years
Employment agreements	Permanently
Time cards and piecework records	Two years
Wages records	Six years
Medical records	Twelve years
Industrial training records	Six years
Accident books	Twelve years

Pension records

Trustees and rules (pension schemes)	Permanently
Trustees' minute book	Permanently
Pension fund annual accounts and Inland Revenue approvals	Permanently
Investment records	Permanently
Actuarial valuation records	Permanently
Contribution records	Permanently
Records of ex-pensioners	Six years after cessation of benefit
Pension scheme investment policies	Twelve years after cessation

Insurance records

Group health policies	Twelve years after final cessation of benefit
Group personal accident policies	Twelve years after cessation of benefit
Public liability policies	Permanently
Product liability policies	Permanently

Employers' liability policies	Permanently
Sundry insurance policies	Three years after lapse
Claims correspondence	Three years after settlement
Accident reports and relevant correspondence	Three years after settlement
Insurance schedules	Ten years

Other records

Vehicle registration records, MOT certificates and vehicle maintenance records	Two years after disposal of vehicle
Certificates and other documents of title	Permanently or until investment disposed of
Trust deeds	Originals to be kept permanently
Contracts with customers, suppliers or agents	Six years after expiry
Licensing agreements	Six years after expiry
Rental and hire purchase agreements	Six years after expiry
Indemnities and guarantees	Six years after expiry

Dormant companies

Where a company has not traded during any particular financial period, the company can dispense with the obligation to prepare audited accounts and need only file an abbreviated balance sheet and notes with Companies House. This is a separate dispensation from the audit exemptions considered on page 9.

s.480

Checklist

▶ There must have been no transactions required to be made in the company's accounting records.

s.1169

▶ The company must not:

s.481

▷ be an authorised insurance company, a banking company or e-money issuer, a MiFID investment firm or a UCITS management company; or

▷ carry on insurance market activity.

▶ The company is required to prepare group accounts.

s.480(2)(b)

▶ The company must qualify as a small company (see page 21), or would have but for the fact that it is:

s.480(2)(a)

▷ a public company; or

▷ a member of an ineligible group.

▶ The balance sheet must contain statements immediately above the director's/directors' signature(s) that:

▷ the company is entitled to the exemption;

s.475(2)

▷ the director(s) acknowledge their responsibilities;

s.475(3)(b)

▷ the accounts give a true and fair view;

s.396(2),)

▷ the members have not required the accounts to be audited (this only applies to the set of accounts filed at Companies House).

s.475(3)(a)

Procedure

▶ Non-trading non-audited accounts must be prepared.

▶ Convene a directors' meeting to approve the accounts.

▶ Signed copy to be filed with the Registrar within the same timescales for a trading company (see page 12).

Filing requirement

▶ Copy of the accounts within the appropriate timescale: six months for a public company and nine months for a private company.

Notes

▶ For a company to remain dormant, any costs must be paid by someone other than the company itself and any cash held in a bank must be in a non-interest-bearing account. **s. 1169(3)**

▶ Receipt of payment by the company for the shares taken by the subscribers or any payment made in respect of any change of name, re-registration fees, annual returns or late filing penalties may be disregarded for the purposes of assessing whether a company is dormant.

▶ Although the copy that is filed with the Registrar may be abbreviated and not contain a directors' report, the copy circulated to shareholders must be full accounts, and accordingly a directors' report will be required.

More information

 Chapter 10    Chapter 15    Guidance
Filing accounts

Electronic communications

Subject to any provisions in their articles, and obtaining shareholder consent under schedule 5 to the Companies Act 2006, companies may send written resolutions, notices, annual accounts and related documents to their members in hard copy, in electronic form or by making the documents available for download from a website.

ss. 293(2), 308, 309

When making written resolutions available on a website, these are not valid unless the document(s) is/are available throughout the period commencing with the circulation date and ending on the date the resolution lapses.

s. 299

Notice of a meeting given by publication on a website is not valid unless the notification sent to members states that it concerns a notice of a general meeting, specifies the place, date and time of the meeting and, in the case of a public company, states that the meeting is to be an AGM. The documents must be available throughout the period commencing on the date of notification and ending at the conclusion of the meeting.

s. 309

Notification of the website address may be given in hard copy or by electronic communication, provided the member has provided an address for that purpose.

Quoted companies are required to make their annual report and accounts available on a website as soon as reasonably practical and ending no earlier than the date the following annual report and accounts are made available on the website.

s. 430

Any member receiving documents or information by electronic communication or by publication on a website can request that they receive copies of documents in hard copy and the company must supply those copies within 21 days.

s. 1145

Checklist

▶ To enable shareholders to communicate electronically with the company, ensure notices and forms of proxy contain details of an electronic address to be used by shareholders to send documents or proxies relating to the meeting to the company.

▶ For a company to communicate with its shareholders in electronic form, it must have obtained specific or general consent from shareholders and to an address supplied for that purpose.　**para. 4 sch. 5**

▶ For a company to make information and documents available on a website, it must have specific or general consent from shareholders or where the shareholder is deemed to have consented.　**para. 9 sch. 5**

▶ In addition, listed companies are required to obtain shareholder consent in general meeting to the use of electronic communications.　**DTR 6.1.8**

Notes

None.

More information

Chapter 14

Forfeiture

When shares have been allotted as either nil or partly paid, the balance outstanding on the shares can be called at any time by the directors (see page 57). The amount of this call can be all or part of the balance outstanding.

Any shares on which a call has been made and which remains outstanding may be forfeited provided there is authority contained in the company articles. Companies that have adopted Table A under the former Companies Acts and public companies incorporated after 1 October 2009 and adopting the model articles for a public company will have such provisions in their articles. A private company incorporated after 1 October 2009 and adopting the model articles for a private company will not have such provisions in their articles, as reg. 21 of the model articles for private companies only permits shares to be issued fully paid.

regs 12–22, Table A CA 1985

regs 54–62 sch. 3, SI 2008/3229

The procedures for making a call and subsequent forfeiture must be strictly adhered to. If they are not, the court may overturn any forfeiture. The provisions under which shares may be forfeited are contained in the company's articles of association.

Checklist

▶ Do the articles of association contain forfeiture provisions?

Procedure (taken from the model articles for public companies)

▶ If a call notice has not been paid and forfeiture is to be implemented, the directors must give the member(s) concerned notice.

▶ The company secretary is to issue a notice to the member(s) giving not less than 14 days' notice requiring payment of all outstanding amounts and must state that if the notice is not complied with, the shares are liable to forfeiture.

▶ If the call remains unpaid, the directors must convene a board meeting to consider forfeiture of the shares. This is accomplished by the directors resolving that the shares be forfeited.

▶ Notice of forfeiture is usually sent to the member(s) by the company secretary, but it is not a requirement.

▶ Forfeited shares may be sold or cancelled as the directors see fit.

▶ Details of the forfeiture must be entered in the register of members.

Filing requirement

None.

Notes

▶ If the shareholder cannot or will not pay the call, he or she may wish to surrender the shares. Shares can only be surrendered if they are already liable to be forfeited.

▶ The member whose shares have been forfeited ceases to be a member in respect of such shares as soon as the forfeiture has been entered in the register of members. Such a person does, however, remain liable for any amounts unpaid on the shares.

▶ Forfeited shares may be sold or disposed of on such terms and in such manner as the directors think fit. Forfeited shares that are reissued must be issued at a price not less than the amounts remaining unpaid. When shares are reissued, the original member will no longer be liable for the uncalled amounts once the full amount has been received by the company, from whatever source.   **s.662**

▶ Where the shares are reissued at a price greater than the unpaid amount, then the company shall pay to the original member the additional monies received up to the amount paid by them.

▶ At the end of the financial year, it will be necessary to inform the auditors that certain shares have been forfeited and whether or not they have been reissued.

More information

Chapter 13   
Chapter 2

General meetings

All meetings of members of a private company are general meetings unless there are express provisions in the company's articles that provide for it to hold an annual general meeting or an extraordinary general meeting.

s.301

Any meeting of a public company which is not an annual general meeting is a general meeting. If there is express provision in its articles, an extraordinary general meeting may be held. Where an extraordinary general meeting is held, there is no longer any distinction between that and a general meeting.

s.336

All matters that can be considered at a general meeting of a private company may be undertaken by written resolution, with the exception of considering resolutions for the removal of a director or an auditor.

Procedure

▶ Convene a board meeting to consider the business to be put to shareholders and convene a general meeting if appropriate.

s.302

▶ The company secretary or a director is to issue a notice convening the general meeting on 14 clear days' notice. If appropriate, the notice should state on it that special notice has been given.

s.307

▶ The meeting may be held upon shorter notice if 90% of the members entitled to attend and vote agree in the case of a private company and 95% for a public company general meeting.

s.307(5)

Filing requirement

▶ Copies of relevant resolutions and appropriate forms within 15 days.

s.30

Notes

None.

More information

Chapter 8

Chapter 14

General meetings – requisition

Subject to the company's articles of association, a member or members holding not less than 5% of the paid-up issued share capital and carrying the right to vote may requisition a meeting of the members. **s.303(3)**

If the directors do not convene a meeting within 21 days of receiving the requisition, those who have requisitioned it may convene the meeting themselves for a date not more than three months thereafter. **s.303(3)**

The directors are deemed not to have duly convened the meeting if it is convened for a date more than 28 days after the date of the notice convening the meeting. **s.305**

Checklist
s.304

▶ Does the requisitionist(s) hold the necessary number of shares?

▶ Has notice of the requisition been served on the company either in hard copy or electronic form, and has it been authenticated by the requisitionist(s)?

▶ The request must state the general nature of the business to be considered and may include the text of a resolution that may be properly moved at the meeting. **s.303(6)**

▶ A resolution may be properly moved unless it would be ineffective due to inconsistency with any legislation or the company's constitution, or it is defamatory or is frivolous or vexatious. **s.303(4)**

Procedure
s.303(5)

▶ A letter or electronic communication of requisition and the text of the desired resolution(s) or general nature of the business must be delivered to the company.

▶ Convene a board meeting to consider the request and convene a general meeting if appropriate. If a meeting has been requested, it is not sufficient for the directors of a private company to circulate the proposed resolution as a written resolution.

▶ The directors must convene the meeting within 21 days of receipt. **s. 304**
If approved, the company secretary or a director is to issue a notice
convening a general meeting to be held within 28 days on appropriate
notice to consider the resolution(s).

Filing requirement

▶ There are no requirements specific to the meeting having been
requested, but it will be necessary to file copies of any special
resolutions or relevant ordinary resolutions meeting the criteria
set out in s. 29 within 15 days.

More information

 Chapter 8    Chapter 14

Headed paper

The full name of the company as registered must be shown on all letters, notices and other official publications, e-mails, its website, bills of exchange, promissory notes, cheques and orders for money or goods signed by or on behalf of the company, invoices, receipts and letters of credit. If this provision is not complied with, the signatory of the document in question may be personally liable in the event of default by the company.

s.82

regs 24, 25, SI 2015/17

Where the company operates under a trading name other than its registered name, the registered name will usually be shown at the foot of the page.

Checklist

▶ The company name as registered must be shown.

▶ The place of registration must be shown, e.g. registered in England and Wales, Cardiff, Wales, Scotland or Edinburgh.

▶ The company's registration number must be shown.

▶ The address of the company's registered office must be shown. Where the company's business address and registered office are the same, the fact that the address shown on the headed paper is the registered office must be stated unless the address of the registered office is shown separately.

▶ Where the company is an investment company, as defined in s. 833, this fact must be stated on the headed paper.

▶ In the case of a charity where the company's name does not include the word 'Charity' or 'Charitable', the fact that it is a charity must be stated on the headed paper. If this provision is not complied with, the signatory to any documents may be personally liable in the event of any default by the company.

▶ Where directors' names are shown on headed paper, all the directors' names must be shown and not just some of them. This is particularly important to remember where the directors have personalised stationery. It is not necessary to show the nationality of directors.

▶ If the company has been permitted not to include the word 'limited' in its registered name, the headed paper must disclose that the company is a limited company.

Filing requirement

None.

Notes

▶ When a company changes its registered office, the company's headed paper must be changed to show the new address within 14 days of the date of change. The date of change is the date of registration of form AD01 by the Registrar of Companies.

s.87(3)

▶ Although not necessary, if there is a reference to the company's share capital on the headed paper, this must be to the paid-up share capital.

**reg. 4,
SI 2015/17**

More information

 Chapter 4    Chapter 1

HM Revenue & Customs – Stamp Duty Office

Except in cases where the transactions is exempt from stamp duty, all stock transfer forms with a transfer value of £1,000 or more must be stamped by HM Revenue & Customs.

Companies must not register transfers that are liable to duty if not stamped, as registering such a transfer does not give good title to the underlying shares.

For all enquiries, please contact the HMRC dedicated Enquiry Line.

Enquiry Line Number: 0300 200 3510

Written enquires should be addressed to the Customer Service office:

Customer Service Manager
HMRC Birmingham Stamp Office
9th Floor
City Centre House
30 Union Street
Birmingham
B2 4AR

DX 15001
Birmingham 1

More information

Chapter 18

Chapter 5

Inland Revenue
www.gov.uk/topic/business-tax/stamp-taxes

Incorporation

The majority of companies are formed directly with Companies House, although many are still incorporated on behalf of the ultimate owners by registration agents. It is open to anyone, however, to incorporate a company using the procedure set out below.

Checklist

▶ Check the index of company names maintained by the Registrar of Companies to ensure that the proposed name is not the same as, or too similar to, the name of an existing company. The register can be checked either at Companies House or by accessing the Companies House website at www.gov.uk/government/organisations/companies-house   **s.66**

▶ Additionally, certain words ('sensitive' words) may require justification or approval by some third party (see page 248).   **s.66(4)**

▶ All companies must have at least one subscriber.

▶ Private companies must have at least one director and may have a company secretary; public companies must have at least two directors and a company secretary (who can also be a director).   **s.7**   **s.154**

Procedure

▶ The following documents must be submitted to the Registrar of Companies.   **s.7**

  ▷ The memorandum of association. This must be signed by the subscriber(s) in the presence of at least one witness.

  ▷ Articles of association, which again must be signed by the subscriber(s) and the signature(s) witnessed. Alternatively if the model articles are to be adopted without amendment, there is no requirement to file a copy, as the model articles are adopted by default.   **ss.9(5),20,55**

▷ An application to register a company (form IN01) containing details of the proposed company name, the country of the situation of its registered office, whether the members' liability is limited and if so whether by shares or guarantee and whether the company is to be a private or public company, the names and addresses of the first director(s), company secretary if there is to be one and the situation of the registered office. This form must be signed by the first director(s) and company secretary (if one is being appointed), agreeing to act in that capacity, and must also be signed by the subscriber(s) or their agent(s). **ss. 9–12**

▷ A statement of compliance made by a solicitor or by one of the first directors or company secretary confirming that the necessary documents have been properly prepared. **s. 13**

▷ Where appropriate, formal justification of a 'sensitive' name must be submitted with the incorporation papers. **s. 66**

▷ Where appropriate, a statement on form NE01 to exempt the company from using the word 'limited' as part of its name. **s. 60**

▷ The registration fee payable (£40 if filed in hard copy, £10 if using a software package and £12 if made via Companies House).

Filing requirement

▶ Form IN01. **s. 15**

▶ Memorandum and articles of association.

▶ Filing fee (£30, or £100 for same-day incorporation).

▶ Form NE01 if required.

▶ Justification for name if required.

▶ Statement of compliance.

Notes

▶ By using an appropriate software package, companies can now be incorporated electronically.

▶ Upon incorporation, the Registrar of Companies issues a certificate of incorporation which shows the date of incorporation, the status of the company (i.e. private or public) and the company's registered number.

▶ A private company is entitled to commence business immediately and there is no requirement for the company to obtain a certificate to commence business.

▶ The incorporation process for a public company is essentially the same as that for a private company, with the exception that the form of memorandum and articles of association is different and that the company must have a minimum of two directors and a company secretary.

▶ Before a public company may commence business or exercise its borrowing powers, it must apply for a trading certificate using form SH50. This certificate will only be issued once the company has a nominal issued capital of at least £50,000 (or euro equivalent) with the nominal value of each share at least 25% paid up plus the whole of any premium, if any.

s. 761

s. 584

More information

 Chapter 2    Chapter 1    Guidance booklet GP1

Incorporation – completion formalities

Once a company has been incorporated, there are a number of matters that should be formally noted or approved by the directors.

The first director(s), company secretary, if any, and situation of the registered office will have been determined and shown on application for registration (form IN01), filed with the Registrar of Companies. Particularly where companies are incorporated by registration agents, the first director and any company secretary may well be the agent themselves and accordingly will resign and the registered office will be changed immediately following incorporation.

Some or all of the following matters will require attention.

Checklist

▶ Appoint director(s) and company secretary, if any, to replace incorporation agents.

▶ Appoint a managing director or chairman of the board.

▶ Appoint bankers, including approval of the relevant bank mandate.

▶ Appoint solicitors to act on behalf of the company.

▶ Appoint accountants and auditors.

▶ Change the company's default accounting reference date.

▶ Approve the transfer of the subscriber share(s), if appropriate.

▶ Allot shares in the capital of the company and approve the issue of share certificates.

▶ Dispense with the need for distinguishing numbers on fully paid shares.

▶ Notify the Registrar, if appropriate, of the place where directors' service contracts and the statutory books are situated, if elsewhere than at the registered office.

▶ Some or all of the directors may require service contracts.

▶ The directors may decide to effect directors' indemnity insurance.

▶ Consider arrangements regarding PAYE, VAT, insurance and the possible need to register trademarks in the company's name.

▶ If the company is to have employees, then employers' liability insurance is compulsory.

▶ Appropriate company headed stationery should be obtained. See page 125.

Procedure

▶ Convene a directors' meeting for directors to consider and approve any changes required. Ensure valid quorum is present.

▶ Write up the statutory books to record changes in director(s) and company secretary, transfers or allotment of shares and directors interests.

Filing requirement

▶ As required, forms AP01, AP02, AP03, AP04, AD01, SH01 and AA01 within 15 days.

▶ Form SH50 prior to commencing to trade (public companies only).

Notes

▶ Form AA01, notifying the Registrar of the company's accounting reference date, should be submitted to the Registrar. If this form is not received by the Registrar, the company's first financial year will end on the last day of the month of the anniversary of its incorporation. **s.390**

▶ If a company subsequently decides to have a different accounting reference date, it will be necessary to amend this default accounting reference date on form AA01. **s.45**

▶ If the company is to adopt a company seal, this should be formally approved by the directors. It is no longer necessary for a company to have a seal, as the company may rely on s. 46 of the Companies Act 2006. If the company does rely on this section, documents executed by the directors must be expressed as having been executed on behalf of the company, i.e. 'Executed as a deed this . . . day of . . . 20 . . . on behalf of . . . Limited in the presence of . . . .'.

More information

 Chapter 2    Chapter 1    Guidance booklet GP1

Insolvency – administration

Insolvency legislation is complex and outside the scope of this book. However, it is appropriate for company secretaries to be aware of the procedures applicable to the appointment of an administrator, and these are detailed below.

A company becomes insolvent when it is unable to pay its debts as they fall due. In circumstances where the directors realise the company will become insolvent, but has not reached that point, they might wish to appoint an administrator to manage the company until it is able to continue, be sold or, if these are not possible, to wind up the company.

Part II EA2002

s. 123 IA1986

Checklist

A company is deemed unable to pay its debts if:

▶ it is unable to pay a debt of £750 or more within 21 days of a formal demand in the prescribed form;

▶ execution issued on a judgement remains unsatisfied in whole or in part (England and Wales);

▶ the court is satisfied that the company is unable to meet its debts as they fall due;

▶ the court is satisfied that the value of the company's assets is less than the amount of its liabilities;

▶ a charge for payment on an extract decree, extract registered bond or extract registered process has expired without payment (Scotland); or

▶ a certificate of unenforceability has been granted in respect of judgement (Northern Ireland).

Procedure

▶ There are a number of methods for appointing an administrator, including:

  ▷ on application to the court by the company, a majority of its directors, a qualifying floating charge holder or one or more creditor;

  ▷ an out-of-court appointment by a qualifying floating charge holder;

> ▷ the company or a majority of its directors;

> ▷ the liquidator of the company; and

> ▷ the supervisor of a CVA.

▶ Once a company is in administration, all business documents issued by it must state the name of the administrator and that the business and affairs of the company are being managed by the administrator.

▶ As soon as practical after appointment, the administrator must publicise their appointment, file notice at Companies House and forward a copy to the company and all known creditors

▶ While an administration order is in force, the company cannot be wound up and an administrative receiver cannot be appointed or, if previously appointed, they must vacate office. There are restrictions on enforcing any security over the company's property, selling any goods and starting any legal proceedings.

Filing requirement

▶ Form AM01.

Notes

None.

More information

 Chapter 20    Chapter 18    Guidance
Liquidation and insolvency,
booklets GP08n and GP08s

The Insolvency Service
www.gov.uk/guidance/guidance-on-personal-debt-relief-options-company-liquidation-investigation-and-enforcement

Insolvency – receivership

Insolvency legislation is complex and outside the scope of this book. However, it is appropriate for company secretaries to be aware of the procedures applicable to the appointed of a receiver, and these are detailed below.

An administrative receiver is a receiver or manager of the whole or substantially the whole of a company's property and business, appointed by or on behalf of the holders of debentures of the company secured by a floating charge. An appointee under a fixed charge will normally have no power to manage the business and is, as such, known merely as 'a receiver'.

Receivers are appointed either by the courts or by debenture holders.

Checklist

▶ Check the deed of appointment and a copy of the debenture (or Trust Deed) in order to consider the validity of the debenture and the receiver's appointment.

Procedure

Appointment by the court

▶ A court may appoint a receiver on the application of a mortgagee or a debenture holder in the following circumstances:

▷ where repayment of principal and/or interest is in arrears;

▷ when the security has become crystallised into a specific charge by the making of a Winding-up Order or passing of a resolution to wind up;

▷ where the security of the mortgagee or the debenture holder is in jeopardy;

▷ a receiver may also be appointed by the court on the application either of a contributory (i.e. a person liable to contribute to the assets of the company in the event of its being wound up) or of the company. The court will sometimes appoint a receiver and a manager on a short-term basis if the directors are not fulfilling their functions of management – for instance, because of a dispute between them, and pending a general meeting where there has been no governing body. A court will not, however, appoint a receiver if winding up would be more appropriate.

Appointment by debenture holders

▶ The appointment is made under a deed executed by the debenture holder and is, together with the debenture, evidence of his or her capacity. The appointment of a receiver usually arises in the following circumstances:

  ▷ failure to pay the principal and/or interest in accordance with the terms of the debenture;

  ▷ where a borrowing limit has been exceeded and has not been reduced within a specified period; or

  ▷ a breach of some other provisions in the debenture or trust deed.

Filing requirement

▶ Form RM01.

Notes

▶ The appointment as receiver or manager must be accepted before the end of the next business day following receipt of the instrument of appointment, and shall be deemed to be effective from the time and date the instrument of appointment was received.

More information

		Guidance
H Chapter 22	CSP Chapter 18	Liquidation and insolvency, booklets GP08n and GP08s

The Insolvency Service
www.gov.uk/guidance/guidance-on-personal-debt-relief-options-company-liquidation-investigation-and-enforcement

Insolvency – winding up (liquidation)

Insolvency legislation is complex and outside the scope of this book. However, it is appropriate for company secretaries to be aware of the procedures applicable to the appointment of a liquidator, and these are detailed below.

A company becomes insolvent when it is unable to pay its debts as they fall due. Once this stage has been reached, in order to protect the interests of creditors, employees and shareholders, the directors must take steps for the company's affairs to be wound up. Winding up involves the realisation of the company's assets. The process is administered by a licensed insolvency practitioner who is appointed as liquidator of the company. Winding up is frequently known as liquidation.

Checklist

There are several methods of winding up.

▶ Members' voluntary winding up, only available where the company is solvent, requiring the directors to give a declaration that the company can meet its debts in full, with interest, during the period of 12 months commencing on the date of commencement of winding up.   **ss. 89, 90 IA 1986**

▶ Creditors' voluntary winding up, applicable where a declaration of solvency cannot be given.   **s. 98 IA 1986**

▶ Winding up by the courts.

▶ Winding up by special resolution of the members.

▶ On petition of a judgement creditor where a debt of not less than £750 has not been paid within 21 days of a demand in the prescribed form.   **s. 123 IA 1986**

▶ It is just and equitable that the company be wound up.

▶ The company fails to meet specific statutory requirements such as minimum number of shareholders.   **ss. 122, 124 IA 1986**

Procedure

Members voluntary

▶ The company's board of directors resolves to make a declaration of solvency, which must embody a statement of assets and liabilities, and be made within five weeks immediately before the passing of the resolution to wind up. The declaration has to be filed with the Registrar of Companies within 15 days of the passing of the resolution to wind up.

▶ The board of directors will also authorise the calling of a general meeting at which a special resolution to wind up will be considered. An ordinary resolution will suffice if the period of life of the company has expired or the occurrence of an event on the happening of which the articles provide that the company should be wound up.

▶ If the resolution is passed, it will be necessary to appoint a liquidator. This may be done by an ordinary resolution of the company.

▶ The resolution to wind up, signed by the chairman of the meeting, should be published in the *London Gazette* or the *Edinburgh Gazette*, as appropriate, within 14 days of being passed. The resolution and all documents for publication in each *Gazette* must be authenticated by a solicitor or a member of an established body of accountants or secretaries. The resolution to wind up must also be filed within 15 days with the Registrar of Companies.

▶ The liquidator must, within 14 days of his or her appointment, advertise his or her appointment in each *Gazette* and give notice to the Registrar of Companies.

Creditors voluntary

▶ A meeting of the board of directors will authorise the calling of a general meeting to consider an ordinary resolution that the company, by reason of its liabilities, cannot continue and that it is advisable to wind up.

▶ A meeting of the creditors should be called by the company to be held within 14 days of the members' meeting to consider the resolution to wind up. At least seven days' notice of the meeting must be given to the creditors. Notice of the creditors' meeting should be advertised in the appropriate *Gazette* and two local newspapers.

▶ The notice must state either:

  ▷ the name and address of the insolvency practitioner who will give such information to the creditors before the meeting takes place as they may reasonably require; or

  ▷ a place in the principal area of business of the company where a list of names and addresses of the company's creditors will be available for inspection without charge.

▶ The creditors' meeting will be presided over by one of the directors, who should prepare a statement of affairs in the prescribed form, verified by affidavit, to be laid before the creditors' meeting.

▶ At the general meeting an ordinary resolution is passed to wind up and an ordinary resolution is passed to nominate the liquidator.

▶ At the creditors' meeting, which must be attended by the proposed liquidator, the directors may answer questions put to them by the creditors concerning the administration of the company, although there is no legal requirement for them to do so.

▶ The liquidator shall be the person nominated by the creditors or, where no other person has been so nominated, the person (if any) nominated by the company. Where a different person is nominated by the creditors, any member or creditor of the company may apply to the court within seven days for an order that the members' nomination shall remain liquidator instead of, or jointly with, the creditors' nomination, or that some other person be appointed.

By the court

▶ When the court makes a Winding-up Order, the official receiver becomes the liquidator.

▶ The official receiver may require officers of the company or other persons as specified to prepare, swear and submit a statement of affairs within 21 days.

▶ Separate meetings of creditors and contributories may be summoned by the official receiver at his or her discretion for the appointment of some other person to be liquidator of the company. Contributions are defined by the IA s. 79, but are usually synonymous with the term 'members'. The official receiver remains liquidator if another person is not appointed. The official receiver must summon a meeting for the appointment of another liquidator if 25% of the creditors requisition him or her to do so.

▶ The court may make any appointment or order to give effect to the wishes of the meetings or make any other order that it may think fit.

▶ The creditors and contributories may nominate as liquidator any person who is qualified to act as an insolvency practitioner, and in the absence of a nomination by the creditors, the contributories' nominee (if any) will be the liquidator.

▶ At any time the official receiver may apply to the Secretary of State for the appointment of a liquidator in his or her place. Any such liquidator must send notice of his or her appointment as the court may direct.

Filing requirement

▶ There are a variety of forms that are required depending upon which of the three methods of winding up is used. The liquidator or proposed liquidator will normally arrange filing of the relevant forms and this will not fall to the company secretary.

Notes

▶ On the appointment of a liquidator, all the powers of the directors cease.

▶ The creditors have the power to appoint a liquidation committee, which may sanction the continuation of some of the directors' powers.

▶ The remuneration of the liquidator is fixed by the liquidation committee or, if there is no committee, by the creditors.

More information

 Chapter 22    Chapter 18    Guidance
Liquidation and insolvency,
booklets GP08n and GP08s

The Insolvency Service
www.gov.uk/guidance/guidance-on-personal-debt-relief-options-company-liquidation-
investigation-and-enforcement

Inspection of registers and other documents

The Act requires that every company keep various registers, and stipulates where they must be held and provisions regarding their inspection, other than the register of directors' residential addresses. Inspection of all the registers is free to members and, in the case of the historic register of charges, free to creditors. Anyone else may be required to pay a fee.

Requests to inspect the register of members must be accompanied by a statement identifying the person requesting the information and the purpose for which they require the information. If the company does not believe that the request is being made for a proper purpose, application may be made to the court for a direction either to supply the information or to order the company not to comply with the request. Any application to the court must be made within five days of the request being made.

s.116

s.117

Where a private company has elected to hold some or all of its registers on the central record, entries on those registers after the date of election are automatically available for public inspection, although application to the company will still be required for any earlier entries.

s.128D

Checklist

▶ The general position is that all the registers must be kept at and be available for inspection either at the registered office, the single alternative inspection location (see page 270) or Companies House where an election to keep a register on the central record has been made.

s.1136

▶ The following registers and documents must be available for inspection:

▷ s. 114 (register of members);

▷ s. 128D (historic register of members);

▷ s. 162 (register of directors);

▷ s. 228 (directors' service contracts);

▷ s. 237 (directors' indemnities);

▷ s. 275 (register of secretaries);

▷ s. 358 (records of resolutions, etc);

▷ s. 702 (contracts relating to purchase of own shares);

▷ s. 720 (documents relating to redemption or purchase of own shares out of capital by private company);

▷ s. 743 (register of debenture holders);

▷ s. 790N (register of people with significant control);

▷ s. 790Z (historic PSC register);

▷ s. 805 (report to members of outcome of investigation by public company into interests in its shares);

▷ s. 809 (register of interests in shares disclosed to public company); and

▷ s. 859Q (instruments creating charges).

Filing requirement

▶ Forms AD02, AD03 and AD04 as required.

Notes

▶ The registers and other documents of a public company must be available for inspection for at least two hours between 9.00am and 5.00pm on business days.   **reg. 5, SI 2008/3006**

▶ The registers and other documents of a private company must be available for inspection for at least two hours between 9.00am and 3.00pm on business days, and the company must be given two days' notice of inspection where such request is made during the notice period of a meeting or during the circulation period of a written resolution, and ten days' notice at all other times.   **reg. 4, SI 2008/3009**   **reg 2 SI 2008/3007**

▶ Fees payable:

▷ The company is obliged to provide copies of certain registers and documents upon payment of a fee.   **reg 3 SI 2007/2612**

▷ Fees in respect of inspection of registers by non-members.   **reg 3 SI 2007/3535**

▷ The fee for the inspection of the register of members, register of interests in shares and register of debenture holders.

▷ £3.50 per hour or part thereof during which the register(s) is/are inspected.

▷ Fees for provision of copies of entries in registers and copies of reports.   **reg. 6 SI 2016/339**

▷ The fees for copies of the registers of debentures, register of interests in voting shares and registers of debenture holders or members are:

▷ £1.00 for the first five entries;

> ▷ £30.00 for the next 95 entries or part thereof;

> ▷ £30.00 for the next 900 entries or part thereof;

> ▷ £30.00 for the next 99,000 entries or part thereof; and

> ▷ £30.00 for the remainder of the entries in the register.

▶ The fee for provision of copies of trust deeds, service contracts and minutes is 10 pence per 500 words or part thereof.

▶ The fee for providing a copy of all or part of a PSC register is £12 per request.

More information

 Chapter 7    Chapter 5

Joint shareholders

Occasionally, shares will be issued or transferred jointly to two or more persons. The articles of association of the company may place a limit on the number of holders. Under Stock Exchange and NEX Market rules, listed, AIM and NEX public companies must allow for a minimum of four joint holders.

Suggested solutions are given below to particular problems or queries that can arise in relation to joint holdings.

Joint holders may request that the shares registered in their names be split into two or more accounts, with the holders' names being shown in a different order. Such requests are commonly dealt with without the need for a stock transfer form, provided the request is in writing and signed by all the joint holders. Additionally, it will be necessary for the share certificate to be returned for cancellation and new certificates issued. For ease of administration, however, companies may prefer to deal with such requests by designation of accounts rather than by rearranging the order of the names.

Occasionally, the joint holders will request that the order of the names on the joint account be changed and again most companies will process this without the need for a formal stock transfer form, provided the request is in writing, is signed by all the joint holders and includes confirmation that no sale or disposition has taken place. Again, the share certificate should be returned for cancellation. All communications for the shareholders will be sent to the first-named of the joint holders.

The joint holders may request that communications be sent to someone other than the first-named; however, for administrative reasons this may be impractical. Additionally, the articles of association may prohibit such a request.

Notes

None.

More information

Chapters 2 and 18

Chapters 5, 6, 7 and 14

Joint shareholders – death of one shareholder

When a joint shareholder dies, the surviving holder or holders in whose name or names the shares are registered become the beneficiaries of the share. There is no need for a stock transfer form to be completed. The company will require sight of the death certificate or an authenticated copy of it. The register of members should be amended to note the death of one holder.

The company may require a new dividend mandate to be given.

The share certificate may be either endorsed or cancelled and a new certificate issued.

It is important to establish the correct address for the surviving joint shareholder(s), as if it is the first-named holder that has died, the address details for the next first-named holder may be several years old.

Checklist

- Amend register of members.
- Endorse or issue a replacement share certificate. (Replacement is often more appropriate as otherwise the surviving joint holders will be reminded of the deceased joint holder whenever the records are reviewed.)

Procedure

- Note death details on register of members.
- Confirm correspondence address for surviving joint holder(s).

Filing requirement

None.

Notes

None.

More information

 Chapter 18    Chapters 5 and 6

Loan stock

The procedure for the issue of loan stock, and thereafter the payment of any interest and the holding of meetings, are, subject to a trust deed creating the loan stock, similar to the procedures for the issue, declaration of dividend and requirements for meetings of ordinary shares.

The most important difference is that the loan stock will be created by a trust deed setting out the rights attaching to the stock.

Checklist

▶ Check the articles to ensure directors have authority to create loan stock.

▶ The trust deed should cover:

  ▷ details of the stock, aggregate amount of stock, the units in which it may be issued or transferred and details of repayment and interest;

  ▷ provisions creating a charge over the company's assets and stipulating under what circumstances the security is enforceable;

  ▷ the powers of the trustee. In particular the trustee is usually instructed to concur with the company in all dealings relating to the charged assets;

  ▷ provisions stipulating that no additional charges can be created ranking ahead of the stock without written consent of the loan stockholders; and

  ▷ schedules detailing the repayment conditions, transfer conditions, regulations for meetings and the form of stock certificate.

Procedure

▶ Convene a directors' meeting to approve the creation of the loan stock deed and issue of loan stock. Ensure valid quorum is present.

▶ Enter details in register of loan stock (if kept).

▶ Issue appropriate loan stock certificates.

Filing requirement

▶ None unless secured, in which case the charge needs to be registered (see page 206).

Notes

▶ The company is not required by statute to keep a register of loan stockholders. However, for practical reasons this is usually done and, in such circumstances, the register of loan stockholders should be in the same form as the register of members.

▶ Stock is issued by resolution of the directors as with the share capital, although there is no requirement to file a return with the Registrar of Companies.

More information

 Chapter 12    Chapters 2 and 9

Loan stock – convertible

It is common for the terms of issue of loan stock (more usually *unsecured loan stock*) to include provisions for the loan stock to be converted into share capital. Usually the loan stock will be convertible into equity shares, although the stock may be convertible into another class of shares.

Checklist

▶ Ensure there is no restriction on the number of shares that may be allotted without seeking the consent of members (see page 256).

▶ Ensure directors have authority to grant rights to convert securities into shares.

s.549(1)(b)

Procedure

▶ Convene a directors' meeting to consider the conversion of the stock, whether in full or in part. Ensure valid quorum is present. The precise procedures to be followed will be stipulated in the loan stock deed.

▶ The company secretary should prepare a circular letter to the holders giving details of the conversion procedure, including a form of nomination and acceptance for their use. A form of nomination is necessary in the event that any particular stockholder requires the shares to be registered in another person's name.

▶ As the completed notices of conversion and forms of nomination and acceptance are received, these should be checked against the register of stockholders to ensure that the details are correct. The loan stock certificates should be returned for cancellation. Once the period for conversion has elapsed, a list of shares to be issued should be compiled and the directors should formally allot the shares. A return of allotments should be submitted to the Registrar of Companies within 15 days.

▶ Share certificates evidencing the shares issued should be prepared and issued to the shareholders within two months of the date of allotment.

▶ The register of members should be amended to record the shares now issued, and the register of loan stock should be amended to show the loan stock that has been cancelled.

▶ Where the conversion of the loan stock is only for part of the stock, a balancing loan stock certificate should be issued.

Filing requirement

▶ Form SH01 within 15 days.

Notes

None.

More information

 Chapter 12    Chapters 2 and 9

Loan stock – unsecured

Unsecured loan stock carries a greater risk for investors than secured loan stock and as a result will usually attract a higher rate of interest. Additionally, as an added incentive, the holders may be given options to acquire equity capital in the future, usually by conversion of the unsecured loan stock into equity shares rather than by repayment of the loan. As with secured loan stock, the issue of unsecured loan stock and the rights and privileges attaching to the stock are governed by a trust deed.

Checklist

▶ Check the articles to ensure directors have authority to create loan stock.

▶ The trust deed should cover:

  ▷ details of the terms of issue, amounts payable on the stock and, where these are payable by more than one instalment, dates and terms of the instalments, details of the repayment or redemption of the stock and interest payments, and any rights of conversion or options on shares in the capital of the company;

  ▷ restrictions on further issues of unsecured loan stock without the approval of the existing loan stockholders;

  ▷ restriction on the borrowing powers of the company without prior approval;

  ▷ restrictions on the disposal by the company of certain assets or other sale agreements without prior approval;

  ▷ guarantees by the company that it will maintain sufficient unissued share capital to satisfy any conversion or option rights given to the loan stockholders;

  ▷ the actions open to the stockholders in the event of non-payment of interest or non-redemption of the stock on the due date;

  ▷ details of the trustees to the issue and of any remuneration payable; and

$\triangleright$ schedules containing the form of stock certificates, option certificates, notices of redemption and detailed conditions concerning the redemption, whether in whole or in part, and any conversion rights or options given to the holders.

Procedure

▶ Convene a directors' meeting to approve the creation of the loan stock deed and issue of loan stock. Ensure valid quorum is present.

▶ Enter details in register of loan stock (if kept).

▶ Issue appropriate loan stock certificates.

Filing requirement

None.

Notes

▶ The procedures to be followed for the issue or repayment of unsecured loan stock are the same as for loan stock (see page 146).

▶ The conversion procedure, where relevant, is the same as for convertible loan stock (see page 148).

More information

 Chapter 12    Chapters 2 and 9

Loans to directors

Except under specified circumstances, companies are not permitted to make loans or quasi-loans, nor enter into credit arrangements with their directors, directors of their holding company or persons connected to them unless the transaction has been approved by ordinary resolution of the members. Where the director concerned is a director of the holding company, the transaction must be approved by members of the holding company.

ss. 197–203

Approval is not required where funds are being made available to meet expenditure made or to be made for the purposes of the company or to enable the director to perform his or her duties as a director of the company.

s. 204

Checklist

The following transactions do not require approval from members:

s. 207

▶ quasi-loan of up to £10,000 where repayment required within two months;

s. 207

▶ loan to director of company or holding company not exceeding £10,000;

s. 209

▶ loan to director by relevant company in ordinary course of business on an arm's length, commercial basis. Where a loan is proposed for the purchase of a home, this must be for the director's only or main residence or for the improvement of such a residence; and

s. 204

▶ loan to cover out-of-pocket expenses to be incurred in performance of duties not exceeding £50,000.

Procedure

▶ Check if proposed loan falls within one of the permitted exceptions.

▶ Convene a directors' meeting to consider the making of a loan or credit arrangement to a director. Ensure valid quorum is present.

▶ Ensure director notifies interest in proceedings (see page 96).

- Convene general meeting to approve ordinary resolution or, if a private company, circulate a written resolution.

Filing requirement

None.

Notes

None.

More information

 Chapter 6    Chapters 11 and 16

Memorandum of association

From 1 October 2009, the content of the memorandum of association changed and now only contains details of the subscribers.

s.8

To form a company, one or more persons must subscribe to a memorandum of association.

For an existing company, any other provisions set out in their memorandum are deemed to form part of their articles of association.

Filing requirement

▶ On incorporation, a copy of the memorandum of association is required to be filed with the other incorporation documents.

s.9

Notes

None.

More information

 Chapter 3    Chapter I

Memorandum of association – deletion

For companies incorporated prior to 1 October 2009, the provisions of their memorandum will be treated as provisions in the articles of association. The only exception to this is the details of the subscribers.

s.28
s.8

Accordingly the clauses stating the company name, the liability of the company, the objects of the company, the country of registered office and details of the share capital can now be altered, updated or deleted by amending the articles.

Procedure

▶ Convene a directors' meeting to recommend resolutions to members and to convene a general meeting or, in the case of a private company, circulate a written resolution if appropriate.

▶ Issue notice, signed by director or company secretary, convening general meeting on 14 clear days' notice, or circulate written resolution for members to consider special resolution to amend the articles.

s.21

▶ As a special resolution, the resolution must contain the full text of the proposed changes.

▶ Consider whether a class meeting is also required.

▶ If the meeting is to be convened on short notice, the company secretary should arrange for agreement to short notice to be signed by each of the shareholders.

s.283

▶ Hold general meeting. Ensure valid quorum is present. Resolutions put to vote either by show of hands or by poll and to be passed by appropriate majority (special resolution by 75% majority).

▶ If the resolution is circulated by means of a written resolution, the resolution must receive approval of the holders of at least 75% of the members entitled to vote within 28 days of the circulation date of the resolution.

Filing requirement

▶ Signed copy of special resolution within 15 days.   ss.29(1)(a),30(1)

▶ Amended copy of the articles of association with copy of the resolution.   s.26

    s.31

▶ If the resolution adds, removes or alters the statement of the company's objects, form CC04 must be filed within 15 days.

Notes

▶ Although it is not necessary to issue new copies of the articles of association to the shareholders, the company should ensure that it has a supply for issue to those shareholders who request a copy. In addition, a copy will normally be sent to the company's bankers and to their auditors.   s.27   s.27(4)

▶ If a company files a copy of a resolution amending its articles but does not file a copy of the amended articles, Companies House may issue a notice requiring an amended copy of the articles be filed within a specified time. Failure to file the amended copy within the specified time will mean the company is liable to a £200 fine.

More information

 Chapter 3    Chapter 1    Guidance booklet GP3

Minutes

Directors are required to ensure that minutes are kept of all directors', shareholders' and class meetings, and members' resolutions approved otherwise than at a general or class meeting, and that these are kept in appropriate minute books.

ss. 248, 355

Checklist

▶ Minutes should state the name of the company, the place, date and time of the meeting.

▶ If a list of attendees is not included or attached to the minutes, the minutes should state that a quorum was present.

▶ The minutes should record decisions reached by the meeting together with sufficient detail of the discussions to enable the sense of the meeting to be established.

s. 249

▶ Any specific disagreement by a director with a particular resolution or course of action should be recorded.

▶ Companies that have external regulators will often have particular requirements for their directors' minutes to include more detail of discussions leading up to decisions. For instance, the impact of a business decision or declaration of dividends on the regulated capital of an FCA-regulated company.

Procedure

▶ It is normally the company secretary who takes the minutes of proceedings and who prepares the first draft.

▶ The draft minutes are circulated to those attending for comments.

▶ Although not a requirement, it is useful for the chairman to sign the agreed minutes.

▶ Signed minutes are evidence of the discussions and agreement reached.

Filing requirement

None.

Notes

▶ When draft minutes are circulated for comments, care must be taken to ensure that any suggested amendments do not reflect what a speaker meant to say rather than what was actually said.

▶ Directors are entitled to have access to directors' minutes.

▶ Shareholders may inspect the minutes of shareholder meetings or, on payment of a prescribed fee, request that copies of shareholder minutes be sent to them, within seven days. Shareholders have no right to view minutes of the directors' meetings.   **s.358**

▶ Minutes of directors' and shareholders' meetings must be kept for at least 10 years from the date of the meeting.   **ss.248(2), 355(2)**

More information

 Chapters 8 and 9    Chapters 10, 13 and 14

Name change

A company may change its name by special resolution of the members or by other means provided for in its articles of association.

s.77(1)

Certain words are deemed to be 'sensitive' and require justification or due authority before the Registrar of Companies will allow their use (see page 248).

ss.55–57,1193–1198

Checklist

▶ Check that the proposed name is available by checking the register of company names (www.gov.uk/government/organisations/companies-house).

s.66
ss.1080,1085

▶ The name of a private company must end with either 'limited' or 'ltd', or the Welsh equivalents 'cyfyngedig' or 'cyf'. Certain guarantee or non-profit-making companies and charitable companies are exempt from this provision if they meet qualifying criteria or are a community interest company.

ss.60–62

s.33 C(AICE)A 2004

▶ The name of a public company must end with either 'public limited company' or 'PLC', or the Welsh equivalents 'cwmni cyfngedig cyhoeddus' or 'ccc'. Community interest companies are not subject to this provision.

s.58
s.33 C(AICE)A2004

▶ Does the name contain only permitted characters?

s.57
reg.4 and sch.2, SI 2008

▶ Is the name misleading or does it contain sensitive words or expressions?

ss.54–56,65
SI 2015/17

▶ Although not a legal requirement, it is advisable to check the proposed names against the trademark registry and registered internet domain names so as to limit the possibility of objections being raised with the company names adjudicator by third parties with goodwill in the name.

s.69

Procedure

▶ Convene a directors' meeting to recommend the appropriate special resolution to members and to convene a general meeting or circulate a written resolution as appropriate. Alternatively use any other relevant procedure contained in the company's articles of association. Ensure valid quorum is present.

▶ Where a general meeting is to be held, issue notice, signed by director or company secretary, on 14 clear days' notice for members to consider resolution.

▶ Enclose with the notice a form of proxy if desired. Listed companies must enclose a three-way form of proxy (see page 186).

▶ If the meeting is to be convened on short notice, the company secretary should arrange for agreement to short notice to be signed by each of the members.

▶ Hold general meeting. Ensure valid quorum is present. Resolution put to vote either by show of hands or by poll and to be passed by appropriate majority (special resolution by 75% majority).

▶ Amend articles of association if these contain a company name clause.

▶ Alternatively the directors may be directed by the Secretary of State to change the name of the company, in which case a resolution of shareholders is not required. **ss.64, 1033**

▶ If authorised by the articles of association, the directors of a company can resolve to change the name of the company without requiring any additional consent from the members. **s.79**

Filing requirement

▶ Copy of change of resolution within 15 days. **ss.78(1), 79(1)**

▶ Form RES15.

▶ Notice of change of name on form NM01, NM02, NM04 or NM05 as appropriate.

▶ Filing fee £10 (same-day fee £50). Filing fee £8 if filed online (£30 for same-day change filed online).

▶ Justification for sensitive word(s) if required. **s.26**

▶ Amended copy of articles of association, if required.

Notes

▶ The change of name only takes effect when the Registrar issues a revised certificate of incorporation. **s.80**

▶ Once the Registrar has issued the revised certificate of incorporation, it will be necessary to obtain new headed stationery, amend email and website disclosures, and obtain a new company seal where the company has a seal. **s.82**

▶ Arrange for the name of the company's bank accounts to be changed and arrange for the company's articles of association to be amended and reprinted.

▶ Notify the company's suppliers and customers of the change of name, the VAT authorities, HM Revenue & Customs for both corporation tax and PAYE, pension scheme, title deeds, trademark registrations, data protection registration, insurers, etc. Signs at the company's premises or on the company's cars, vans and lorries will also require amendment.

▶ Listed, AIM and NEX companies must make appropriate market disclosures.

More information

 Chapter 4　　 Chapter 1　　 Guidance booklet GP3

Notice – special

Certain resolutions require that 28 days' special notice of the intention to put that resolution be given to the company. Other than where resolutions are proposed by shareholders, this special notice would be given by a director or the company secretary.

s.312

Checklist

The following resolutions require special notice to be given to the company:

▶ removal of a director (see page 103);

s.168

▶ removal of auditors or appointment as auditors of persons other than the retiring auditors (see page 45); and

s.511

▶ appointment of auditors to fill casual vacancies or reappointment of auditors following appointment by directors to fill casual vacancies (see pages 39 and 47).

s.515

Procedure

▶ Letter to the company stating the intention to propose appropriate resolution and stating that special notice is being given must be lodged at the company's registered office at least 28 days prior to the meeting.

s.312

▶ The company must, where practical, give its members notice of any such resolution in the same manner and at the same time as it gives notice of the meeting. If that is not possible, it must give at least 14 days' notice by newspaper advertisement or such other method provided in its articles.

s.312(2)

s.312(3)

▶ If the resolution relates to the proposed removal of a director, a copy of the special notice must be sent as soon as possible to the director concerned.

Filing requirement

None.

Notes

▶ If after special notice has been given the meeting is convened for
a date sooner than in 28 days, notice is deemed properly given,
although not within the time required.

s.312(4)

More information

 Chapter 8    Chapter 14

Notices – content

Checklist

▶ Notices should contain:

   ▷ company name;

   ▷ date and time of meeting;   **s.311(1)(a)**

   ▷ place of meeting; and   **s.311(1)(b)**

   ▷ general nature of business to be transacted.   **s.311(2)**

▶ Notice of a public company or traded private company AGM must state that the meeting is to be an AGM.   **s.337(1)**

▶ Where a special resolution is to be proposed, the notice must state that the resolution is to be proposed as a special resolution and contain the text of the resolution.   **s.283(6)**

▶ For listed, AIM and NEX companies, resolutions on substantially different matters should be separate resolutions and not bundled.

▶ Public companies must consider the appointment or reappointment of directors as separate resolutions unless a resolution permitting multiple appointments by single resolution has previously been approved.   **s.160**

▶ A statement that members may appoint proxies who need not themselves be members.   **s.325**

▶ Companies whose shares are settled in CREST will usually state a date not more than 48 hours before the meeting as the cut-off for registrations to determine entitlement to attend and vote. In practice, due to the difficulty in establishing the entitlement to attend part-way through a trading day, the cut-off is usually stated as being the holdings at the close of business on the pre-penultimate day before the day of the meeting.   **s.41 USR1985**

Procedure

▶ Convene a directors' meeting to recommend appropriate resolution(s) to members and to convene a general meeting. Ensure valid quorum is present.

▶ Issue notice either in hard copy, in electronic form or by means of a website.   **s.308**

▶ Issue with the notice a form of proxy if desired. Listed companies must enclose a three-way form of proxy (see page 186).

▶ Consider whether class meeting(s) also required.

▶ If the meeting is to be convened on short notice, the company secretary should arrange for agreement to short notice to be signed by each of the shareholders.

Filing requirement

None.

Notes

None.

More information

 Chapter 8    Chapter 14

Notices – periods

Although directors' meetings may be held on 'reasonable' notice, there are strict rules governing the minimum notice periods for shareholders' meetings.

Checklist

▶ Annual general meeting of a public company	21 days	**s.307(2)(a)**
▶ General meeting of a public company	14 days	**s.307(2)(b)**
▶ General meeting of a private company	14 days	**s.307(1)**
▶ Notice to company of intention to put resolution	28 days	**s.312**
▶ General meeting of a traded company that is not an AGM, where electronic proxy voting is available and a resolution permitting notice of not less than 14 days has been passed at either the previous AGM or a subsequent general meeting	14 days	**s.307A**

Procedure

▶ Convene a directors' meeting to recommend appropriate resolution(s) to members and to convene a general meeting. Ensure valid quorum is present.   **s.308**

▶ Issue notice either in hard copy, in electronic form or by means of a website.

▶ Issue with the notice a form of proxy if desired. Listed companies must enclose a three-way form of proxy (see page 186).

▶ Consider whether class meeting(s) also required.

▶ If the meeting is to be convened on short notice, the company secretary should arrange for agreement to short notice to be signed by each of the shareholders.

Filing requirement

None.

Notes

▶ Period of notice is stated in 'clear' days. The articles should be consulted to ascertain what constitutes 'clear' days for the particular company. For example, the company's articles may state that the day of receipt must be classed as 48 hours and not 24 hours after posting.

▶ Under the UK Corporate Governance Code, listed companies should give 20 working days' notice of their AGM and 14 for a GM.

▶ Companies formed prior to 1 October 2009 must take great care to check their articles, as these are very likely to contain the notice periods under the former Companies Act which are longer in certain circumstances.

More information

 Chapter 8    Chapter 14

Overseas company

The provisions relating to overseas companies are contained in ss. 1044–1059 and the Overseas Companies Regulations 2009 SI 2009/1801 ('OCR').

Any overseas company that opens a UK establishment must register certain particulars with the Registrar of Companies. A UK establishment is either a branch within the meaning of the eleventh Company Law Directive or a place of business that is not a branch. **OCR reg. 3**

The previous distinction and different filing regime for branches and places of business have been replaced by one registration regime.

If an overseas company has already registered details for another UK establishment, details applicable to both registrations need not be repeated but may be referred to. **OCR reg. 5(2)**

Checklist

▶ If the parent company's incorporation documents are not in English, a certified translation will be required.

▶ If another UK establishment has been registered, details of that registration will be required. **OCR regs. 5 and 6**

Procedure

▶ Complete form OS IN01, containing:

  ▷ the company's registered name;

  ▷ its legal form (public, private, etc);

  ▷ if registered in its country of incorporation, its registered number and the identity of the register;

  ▷ details of directors and secretary, or their equivalents;

  ▷ the authority of the directors to represent the company and their capacity to bind the company in dealings with third parties together with a statement of whether this authority may be exercised solely or jointly with other directors; and

  ▷ whether the company is a credit or financial institution.

- If the overseas company is not incorporated in a member state of the European Union, the following additional information must be provided:

  OCR reg. 5(2)

  ▷ the legislation under which the company was incorporated;

  ▷ the address of the principal place of business, the country of incorporation, the objects of the company and the amount of its issued share capital; and

  ▷ the accounting reference date and time allowed for filing of accounts available for public inspection (required if the company wishes to take advantage of the right to file in the UK accounts prepared and disclosed in its country of incorporation).

- In respect of the UK establishment, the following information should be registered:

  OCR reg. 6(2)

  ▷ the address of the establishment;

  ▷ the date on which it was opened;

  ▷ the business carried on;

  ▷ the establishment's trading name if different from the company's registered name;

  ▷ the name and service address of all persons resident in the UK authorised to accept service on behalf of the company in respect of that establishment;

  ▷ the name and address of all persons authorised to represent the company as permanent representatives for the business of that establishment; and

  ▷ the authority of the permanent representatives to contract on behalf of the establishment and whether they may exercise such authority solely or, if jointly, the name of the person(s).

- A statement of how the company intends to meet its obligations relating to accounts and whether those will be met by the establishment being registered or by another UK establishment.

  OCR reg. 7

Filing requirement

- Form OS IN01.

- A certified copy of the company's constitutional documents.

- A copy of the latest set of audited accounts required to be published by parent law.

- If these documents have been previously filed by another UK establishment, they may be referred to rather than filed again.

- Registration fee of £20, same-day registration £100.

Notes

▶ The constitutional document need only be submitted once and must be referred to for other branch registrations.

▶ Any alterations to the constitutional documents must be notified on the appropriate form.

OCR reg. 14

▶ Each overseas company with a UK establishment that is required by its parent law to prepare, have audited and disclose accounts or is incorporated in an EAA state and is required by its parent law to prepare and disclose accounts but is not required to have those accounts audited to deliver them must register its annual report and accounts.

OCR regs. 68–74

OCR regs. 31 and 32

OCR regs. 36 and 37

▶ Each overseas company to which the above criteria do not apply must prepare accounts and deliver a copy to companies as if it were a company incorporated in the UK.

OCR regs 58–65

▶ A UK establishment owning property over which charges have been given is required to register details with the Registrar.

▶ Every UK establishment of an overseas company shall state the registered branch number and the place of registration of the branch on its headed paper, invoices, etc. If the overseas company is not from an EU member state, the following additional information must be stated:

▷ the identity of the register and its country of incorporation;

▷ its registered number, if any;

▷ the legal form of the company;

▷ if the liability of its members is limited, that fact;

▷ the location of its registered office or principal place of business; and

▷ whether it is in liquidation or other form of insolvency.

▶ Where an overseas company that has UK establishment(s) is being wound up it must, within 14 days of the commencement of the winding up, give details of its name, particulars of the winding up and the date upon which the winding up is or will be effective. Within 14 days of appointment, the liquidator must notify his or her name and address, the date of his or her appointment and a description of his or her powers. Following the termination of the winding up for whatever reason, the liquidator must file details of the termination within 14 days. Details must be given for each UK establishment, although one return may be made, provided the registered numbers of each UK establishment are stated on the return.

More information

 Chapter 24    Chapters 1, 5, 6, 10 and 16   Guidance booklet GPO1

Polls

The rules governing the demanding of a poll will be laid down in the company's articles or in the appropriate model articles if the company has not adopted its own articles. The provisions of ss. 321 and 322 must be considered, however, when drafting a company's articles covering voting on a poll, since by those sections certain provisions are rendered void.

The checklists and procedure set out below are based upon the relevant model articles set out in SI 2009/3229.

Private companies – sch. 1, SI 2009/3229

Checklist

▶ Check articles to see if model articles provisions adopted.

▶ Has the demand for a poll been validly made:　　　　　　　　　　**reg. 44(1)**

　▷ in advance of the general meeting; or

　▷ at the meeting on or before the declaration of the result on a show of hands?

▶ Where model article provisions have been adopted, a poll may be　**reg. 44(2)**
demanded by:

　▷ the chairman;

　▷ the directors;

　▷ at least two persons having the right to vote at the meeting; or

　▷ one or more persons representing not less than one-tenth of the total voting rights of all the members having the right to vote at the meeting.

▶ Demand for a poll may only be withdrawn if the poll has not taken　**reg. 44(3)**
place and the chairman agrees.

▶ The poll must be taken immediately in such manner as the chairman　**reg. 44(4)**
directs.

Public companies – *sch. 3, SI 2009/3229*

Checklist

▶ Check articles to see if model articles provisions adopted.

▶ Has the demand for a poll been validly made: **reg. 36(1)**

  ▷ in advance of the general meeting; or

  ▷ at the meeting on or before the declaration of the result on a show
    of hands?

▶ Where model article provisions have been adopted, a poll may be   **reg. 36(2)**
  demanded by:

  ▷ the chairman;

  ▷ the directors;

  ▷ at least two persons having the right to vote at the meeting; or

  ▷ one or more persons representing not less than one-tenth of the
    total voting rights of all the members having the right to vote at the
    meeting.

▶ Demand for a poll may only be withdrawn if the poll has not taken   **reg. 36(3)**
  place and the chairman agrees.

▶ The poll may be taken in such manner as the chairman directs, but   **reg. 37(5)**
  must be taken within 30 days.

▶ The chairman may appoint scrutineers, who need not be members,   **reg. 37(2)**
  and may decide how, where and when the results will be declared.

▶ Polls on the election of a chairman or adjournment of the meeting   **reg. 37(4)**
  must be taken immediately.

▶ No notice need be given if the time and place are announced at the   **reg. 37(7), (8)**
  meeting, otherwise seven days' notice is required.

Quoted companies

Checklist

There are additional provisions which quoted companies must adhere to.

▶ A quoted company must publish on a website the results of any poll
  votes including date of the meeting, text of the resolution and the   **s. 341**
  number of votes cast in favour of and against the resolution.

▶ Members representing at least 5% of the total voting rights or 100
  members or more may request an independent report on a poll taken
  or to be taken at a general meeting. The request may be in hard copy   **s. 342**
  or in electronic form, must identify the poll(s) to which it relates, must
  be authenticated by all those members requesting it and must be
  received by the company not later than one week after the date the
  poll is taken.

▶ Where an independent assessor has been appointed, the company
must publish on a website details of the appointment, the identity
of the assessor, the text of the resolution(s) and a copy of the
independent assessor's report.

s.351

Procedure

▶ An announcement should be drafted for the chairman, which can be
read out if a poll is demanded, to inform members of the procedure
to be followed, or, if the poll is to take place at a later date, of the date
and time for the taking of the poll and the procedure to be followed.

▶ It may be appropriate for the chairman to suggest that since proxies
already lodged are overwhelmingly in favour of the resolution, the
person or persons requesting the poll may decide to withdraw their
demand.

▶ If the demand for a poll is not withdrawn, the validity of the demand
should be checked by confirming that those who have demanded it
are, in fact, members or proxies or, for example, if only one member is
demanding it, that he or she holds not less than one-tenth of the total
voting rights. It is usually the scrutineers' responsibility to check the
validity of the demand for the poll.

▶ If the scrutineers advise that the poll has not been properly
demanded, the chairman will make a statement to this effect and
the meeting will usually proceed to its next business after having
put the matter on which the poll was requested to the vote by a
show of hands (if this had not already been done at the time the poll
was demanded). Polls on procedural resolutions should take place
immediately.

▶ If the demand for the poll is valid and is not withdrawn, the chairman
will advise the meeting to this effect. If the chairman did not advise the
meeting as to the proxy position when the poll was first demanded,
this could now be done. Assuming the poll is still not withdrawn, the
chairman will read the statement announcing the time for holding of
the poll (e.g. either immediately, at the conclusion of the meeting or
at a later date). It is usual practice for the poll to be held at the end of
the meeting and for it to be kept open for one hour. The meeting then
proceeds to its next business until the conclusion of the business of
the meeting.

▶ At the end of the meeting, the chairman declares the meeting closed
and informs the members as to the procedure for the conduct of the
poll. He or she explains that those who have appointed a proxy need
not complete a ballot paper unless they wished to alter their vote.

▶ Stewards then distribute ballot papers to those present. These are
collected by staff after completion by the members and proxy holders,
and handed to the scrutineers.

▶ The scrutineers, especially if they are the company's auditors, have their own instructions with regard to the checking of the ballot papers, verification of the holdings, and preparation of a report and final certificate of the result of the poll. This is handed to the chairman, who then declares the results of the poll. In the case of a listed company, or a company whose shares are traded on AIM or NEX, the result of the poll is notified to the Stock Exchange or NEX as appropriate.

Filing requirement

None.

Notes

▶ As procedures can vary from company to company, it is essential that the articles of association are checked to ensure the correct procedure is followed.

▶ In order for a demand for a poll to be valid, it must be called for before or immediately on the declaration by the chairman of the result of the vote on a show of hands.

More information

H Chapter 8   **CSP** Chapter 14

Powers of Attorney – corporate

A corporate Power of Attorney is an appointment by a company of a person or persons to act on its behalf as set out in the document creating the Power of Attorney. Attorneys are usually appointed by companies to act on their behalf overseas, although an attorney may be appointed within the UK.

Although the Powers of Attorney Act 1971 sets out a short-form Power of Attorney used to confer wide powers on the attorney, this is unlikely to be used by a company, as a corporate Power of Attorney is more likely to be for a specific purpose and would therefore be in a longer form, setting out the precise details of the Powers of Attorney. A long-form Power of Attorney would need to be used by a Scottish or Northern Ireland company, as the Powers of Attorney Act 1971 does not apply in those countries.

The Power of Attorney need not be given under seal, provided it is stated as being executed as a deed on behalf of the company.

The directors' authority to delegate their authority to an attorney is contained in the articles of association.

reg. 5(b) schs 1 and 3, SI 2009/3229

Checklist

▶ Check the articles of association to ensure directors may delegate their authority to an attorney.

Procedure

▶ Convene a directors' meeting to approve the terms of the attorney's appointment. Ensure valid quorum is present.

▶ The document creating the Power of Attorney is to be executed in accordance with the articles of association, usually any two directors, one director and the company secretary or by a sole director duly witnessed.

▶ Any changes required to be made to an existing Power of Attorney will require a variation to the original agreement.

Filing requirement

None.

Notes

None.

More information

 Chapter 6

Powers of Attorney – member

Individuals may give either a general or specific power of attorney under the provisions of the Powers of Attorney Act 1971 or a lasting power of attorney (LPA) under the Mental Capacity Act 2005. The LPA has replaced the enduring power of attorney given under the Powers of Attorney Act 1971, although an enduring power of attorney created prior to 1 October 2007 remains valid provided, in the case of a donor who has become mentally incapable, the enduring power of attorney has been registered under MCA2005 with the public guardian.

Checklist

▶ The document received for registration must be the original document, bearing a stamp duty impression if granted prior to 26 March 1985, or an authenticated copy of it.

▶ Care must be taken to ensure that the person granting the power of attorney is indeed a member of the company and holds the appropriate number of shares. It may be that the power of attorney is being granted by a member who has only recently acquired shares either by allotment, by renunciation of bonus or rights issue, or by transfer.

Procedure

Where a power of attorney is received for registration, the following procedure should be maintained:

▶ The company should retain a copy of the power of attorney for its records.

▶ The terms of the power of attorney must be checked to see whether one attorney is being appointed or more than one. In the case of more than one attorney, it will be necessary to check whether one attorney acting on his or her own has power to effect transfers, or whether all attorneys must act together.

▶ The power of attorney may change the registered address for the shareholder and the matter of to whom any future dividends must be made.

- ▶ If the power of attorney is in order, the company's registration stamp should be affixed to the original document and returned to the person giving the power of attorney.

- ▶ On every occasion that documents are executed by the attorney, this should be cross-referenced with the copy of the power of attorney retained by the company to ensure that the terms of the power of attorney have been complied with.

- ▶ Neither the name in the register of members nor the original share certificate requires amendment, since the beneficial owner is not changing and, indeed, as the register of members is a public document, the appointment of a power of attorney should not be noted on it.

- ▶ A power of attorney can be revoked or changed by the person giving the power of attorney at any time or, alternatively, the power of attorney may be given for a specific occasion or for a specific length of time.

Filing requirement

None.

Notes

None.

More information

 Chapter 18    Chapter 6

Pre-emption rights – allotment

Any new equity securities (ordinary shares or rights to convert securities into or subscribe for ordinary shares) to be issued by a company must first be offered to existing members in proportion to the number of shares they already hold. An ordinary share is defined as a share without restriction on their entitlement to participate in dividends or return of capital. This provision safeguards members, as their holding of shares can only be diluted if they do not take up shares. **s.561** **s.560**

However, private companies may forgo these provisions in their articles of association and either substitute 'tailor-made' pre-emption provisions or delete pre-emption provisions entirely or may exclude the provisions by special resolution. **s.567**

Public companies may only relax these provisions by special resolution. Many private companies are incorporated with articles of association that remove the statutory pre-emption rights and substitute alternative provisions. Commonly the first allotment following incorporation is exempt from any pre-emption provisions. **s.569**

Where directors have been given authority to issue shares under s. 551 either generally or by special resolution, they may be given power either in the articles or by special resolution to allot shares as if s. 561 did not apply. **ss.570,571**

Listed companies and those whose shares are traded on AIM or NEX will usually seek an annual renewal of a limited waiver of pre-emption rights to enable ad hoc share issues during the year. **ss.573,724**

These pre-emption provisions also apply to the sale of any treasury shares held by a limited company.

Checklist

▶ Do the articles exclude or vary the statutory pre-emption provisions of s. 567 (private companies only)?

▶ Is any previous waiver still valid or has that authority been used by previous share issues or time expired?

▶ If the company has only a small number of shareholders, it may be more practical to arrange for the shareholders to waive their pre-emption rights by notice in writing or written resolution, as otherwise a general meeting will be required.

▶ If there is a shareholders' investment or similar agreement, this may contain pre-emption provisions that override the articles of association.

Procedure

▶ Convene a directors' meeting to recommend appropriate special resolution to waive pre-emption provisions to members and to seek members' approval by written resolution (private companies only) or at a general meeting. Ensure valid quorum is present.   **s.307**   **s.297**

▶ Issue notice, signed by director or company secretary, on 14 clear days' notice (21 days if to be put to a public company's AGM) for members to consider resolution.

▶ Enclose with the notice a form of proxy if desired. Listed companies must enclose a three-way form of proxy (see page 186).

▶ If the meeting is to be convened on short notice, the company secretary should arrange for agreement to short notice to be signed by each of the shareholders.

▶ Hold general meeting. Ensure valid quorum is present. Resolution put to vote either by show of hands or by poll and to be passed by appropriate majority (special resolution by 75% majority).

▶ Where circulated as a written resolution by a private company, the requisite majority must be achieved within 28 days of circulation.   **s.29**

▶ Amend articles of association if necessary.   **s.26**

Filing requirement

▶ Copy of resolution within 15 days.

▶ Amended copy of articles of association if appropriate.

Notes

▶ It is not necessary to waive pre-emption rights for a rights, bonus or capitalisation issue as these are *pro rata* issues except where overseas shareholders are excluded. For example, many rights issues of publicly traded companies exclude overseas territories where to participate in the offer would require an offer document prepared under local laws to be registered in that overseas territory.

▶ Where there is more than one class of shares, each class may have different pre-emption rights.

▶ Listed companies will follow the recommendations of the Pre-Emption Group. This was set up in 2005 to produce a Statement of Principles to be taken into account when considering the case for disapplying pre-emption rights. This Statement of Principles was revised in 2015 with further clarification issued in 2016. The group's members represent listed companies, investors and intermediaries (www.pre-emptiongroup.org.uk).

More information

H Chapter 13   CSP Chapter 2

Pre-emption rights – transfer

There are no statutory pre-emption rights on the transfer of shares. However, many private companies and some public companies will have pre-emption rights embodied within their articles of association. Although the provisions usually stipulate a strict procedure to follow when shares are to be transferred, these provisions are frequently waived in circumstances where the transfer is agreed by all the shareholders. The provisions would, however, be used in a contentious transfer. In such circumstances the pre-emption provisions must be followed strictly.

Checklist

▶ Check the articles of association to see whether pre-emption rights apply to the transfer.

▶ If the share transfer is not contentious, it may be appropriate for the existing shareholders to waive their rights of pre-emption by notice in writing.

▶ Alternatively, the transfer may be non-contentious but due to the large number of shareholders, the rights of pre-emption may best be waived by special resolution at a general meeting.

Procedure

▶ Where the transfer is likely to be contentious or it is deemed inappropriate or impractical to request members waive their rights of pre-emption, it will be necessary to follow strictly the pre-emption procedure, as set down in the articles. This procedure will often take a number of weeks to complete and may require the company's auditor or accountant to certify the fair value for the shares.

Filing requirement

None.

Notes

▶ Where a company's articles of association do contain pre-emption rights on transfer, there may be special dispensations for transfers between family members or group companies.

▶ Where shares are to be transferred following the death of a shareholder, the pre-emption provisions may be deemed to have been brought into effect and the shares offered to the existing shareholders even if the appropriate notice has not been given by the executor(s).

More information

H Chapter 18   CSP Chapter 2

Private or public company?

The majority of companies are private companies limited by shares.
However, there are three types of private company, each with qualities
better suited to certain activities than others. Additionally, rather than
incorporating a company, entrepreneurs may prefer an unincorporated
trading entity such as a partnership or sole trader, or a mix of the two in
the form of an LLP.

The following table shows the more common factors to consider when
assessing what form of trading entity to use.

	PLC	Ltd	Unltd	Guar	LLP	Uninc
Is the company to trade for profit?	✓	✓	✓		✓	✓
Is it to be a charitable or non-profit-making body such as an association?				✓		✓
Is the liability of the members to be:						
limited	✓	✓		✓	✓	
or unlimited?			✓			✓
(Some professional associations require their members to trade without limited liability.)						
Is financial information regarding the company to be kept confidential?						
Yes			✓			✓
No	✓	✓		✓	✓	
Are the profits of the business to be assessed for tax on:						
the owners					✓	✓
or the trading vehicle?	✓	✓	✓	✓		
Are shares in the business to be offered for subscription to:						
the public (>50 persons)	✓					
or a defined, restricted membership?		✓	✓	✓	✓	✓

KEY

PLC	Public limited company	Guar	Guarantee
Ltd	Limited	LLP	Limited liability partnership
Unltd	Unlimited	Uninc	Unincorporated

More information

 Chapter 2    Chapter 1

Proxies

Members unable to attend a meeting can appoint one or more proxies to attend and vote in their place. A proxy need not be a member of the company.

s.324

A proxy can vote on a poll or on a show of hands. Proxies are entitled to exercise all of their appointors rights to speak at the meeting, including the right to call or join in a demand for a poll.

ss.282(3)(b), 283(4) (b), 284(2)(b)

Companies need not appoint a proxy, as they may appoint a representative who may attend on their behalf with the same rights as if they were a shareholder in their own right. However, where a corporation wishes to appoint multiple appointees, making such appointments as proxies gives greater flexibility, as where multiple corporate representatives are appointed by the same corporate member, only one of them can exercise the voting rights.

s.323(1)

s.323(3)

Proxies can either be appointed with specific instructions on how to vote or left to use their discretion. If the proxy is instructed how to vote, they must vote in accordance with those instructions.

The notice convening a members' meeting must disclose the members' rights to appoint proxies under s. 324 or any more extensive rights contained in the company's articles of association.

s.325

Checklist

s.326

▶ Where a company issues proxy forms, they must be sent to all members entitled to vote at the meeting.

▶ Normally proxies must be registered with the company not less than 48 hours prior to the meeting and it is unlawful for the company to require that these be lodged more than 48 hours prior to the meeting excluding any day that is not a business day.

s.327(2)

Filing requirement

None.

Notes

▶ Public companies listed on the Stock Exchange or AIM must issue three-way proxies. **LR 9.3.6**

▶ Most companies will word the proxy form to appoint the chairman as proxy unless a specific person is chosen.

▶ Members can attend and vote in person even if they have lodged a proxy form and attendance will often automatically revoke the appointment of a proxy. Accordingly a check should be made at the meeting to discard any proxies received from those attending.

More information

 Chapter 8    Chapters I and I4

Purchase of own shares – out of capital

It is possible, under certain circumstances, for a private company to purchase its own shares out of capital provided that the purchase is not restricted or prohibited by the company's articles of association. Additionally, there are restrictions on the company's ability to use its reserves to purchase its own shares and care must be taken to ensure that any profits available are utilised first as purchases out of capital can only be made (whether in whole or in part) if there are no distributable reserves available.

ss. 690, 709

s. 710

Checklist

▶ Is the company a private company?

s. 709(1)

▶ Has the company no distributable reserves or will the purchase use up all available distributable reserves?

s. 710(1)

▶ Check articles to ensure company is not prohibited from purchasing its own shares.

▶ Accounts must be drawn up to a date within three months of the date of the directors' statement made under s. 714 and must be used to calculate the permissible capital payment.

ss. 712(6), (7)

▶ If the company's accounts are not audited, an auditor must be appointed.

▶ Will the directors be able to confirm the company's ability to pay its debts immediately after the payment and for the following 12 months, and will the auditor be able to confirm that such a statement is reasonable?

ss. 714(3), (6)

Procedure

▶ Convene a directors' meeting to approve the making of a statement specifying the permissible capital payment and confirming the company's ability to meet its debts, recommending the purchase to members and either to convene a general meeting or to circulate a written resolution to obtain members' approval. Ensure valid quorum is present.

s. 714

▶ Issue notice, signed by director or company secretary, on 14 clear days' notice or circulate written resolution for members to consider special resolution(s). Included with the notice or written resolution must be an auditors' report and the terms of the purchase. The special resolution must be approved within one week of the date of the directors' statement made under s. 714.

ss.716,718

s.714

▶ Enclose with the notice a form of proxy if desired.

▶ A copy of the agreement, or a written schedule of its terms if the contract is not in writing, must be made available for inspection by the members of the company at the company's registered office for not less than 15 days prior to the meeting and at the meeting itself. The schedule of the terms must include the names of any members holding shares which it is proposed be purchased and, if the written contract does not show these names, a schedule must be attached showing the names and the number of shares to which the contract relates. Where a previously approved contract is being varied, the terms of the variation must be available for inspection by the members.

ss.693,696(2)

▶ This requirement for the documents to be made available for inspection to the members prior to the meeting restricts the ability of the company to hold the meeting at shorter notice than 15 days. Where the resolutions are to be passed by written resolution of the members, a copy of the contract and/or any schedule must be supplied to the members no later than the date upon which they receive a copy of the written resolution for signature.

s.696(2)(b)

▶ Directors to make the statutory declaration specifying the permissible capital payment within one week before the date of the meeting.

s.714

▶ Hold general meeting. Ensure valid quorum is present. Resolution put to vote either by show of hands or by poll and to be passed by appropriate majority (special resolution by 75% majority).

s.716

▶ Within one week of the passing of the special resolution, the company must publish a notice in the *London Gazette* giving details of the proposed payment and notify creditors either individually or by newspaper advertisement published within one week of the passing of the resolution. Creditors may make application to the court to cancel the resolution, provided such application is made within five weeks of the date of approval of the special resolution.

s.719

s.721

▶ If an application is made, the court will decide whether to cancel the resolution, reject the application or make such modification to the proposed purchase as it deems appropriate.

s.721(4)

▶ If no objections are received, the payment may be made at the end of the five-week period and must be made within seven weeks of the date of approval of the special resolution.

s.723(1)

▶ Once the company has purchased the shares, a return on form SH03 must be submitted to the Registrar, stating the number of shares and the class of shares, together with the nominal value of the shares and

s.707

the date on which they were repurchased. The purchase of shares by a company is subject to stamp duty where the amount payable exceeds £1,000, the duty being payable on the consideration and not the nominal value at the rate of 0.5% (rounded up to the nearest £5).

▶ Issue consideration cheques and cancel share certificates relating to shares purchased. Update register of members.

Filing requirement

▶ Copy of special resolution within 15 days.

▶ Amended copy of articles of association, if amended.

    s.30

▶ Directors' and auditors' statement.

    ss.26,714

▶ Notification in *London Gazette* of proposed payment.

    s.719(1)

▶ Advertisement in appropriate newspapers or notice given to all creditors.

    s.719(2)

▶ Stamped form SH03 within 28 days.

    s.707

Notes

▶ The resolution will be invalid if any member of the company holding shares which it is proposed be repurchased exercises the voting rights attaching to those shares, and the resolution would not have been passed if those shares had not been voted.

    s.695

▶ Copies of the contracts must be retained for 10 years.

    s.702(3)

More information

 Chapter 14    Chapter 8

See also reduction of capital on pages 198–200.

Purchase of own shares – out of profit

It is possible under certain circumstances for public and private companies to purchase their own fully paid shares, provided that the purchase is not restricted or prohibited by the company's articles of association. Additionally, there are restrictions on the company's ability to use its reserves to purchase its own shares and care must be taken to ensure that the company has sufficient distributable reserves for the purpose. It may also be possible for the company to issue new shares to fund the redemption.

ss.690,691

s.692(2)

Shares may be purchased as an off-market purchase in pursuance of a purchase contract approved in advance by members or by a market purchase on a recognised investment exchange.

s.693(1)

Checklist

▶ Does the company have sufficient distributable reserves to fund the purchase?

▶ Check articles to ensure company is permitted to purchase its own shares.

Procedure – off-market purchase

▶ Convene a directors' meeting to recommend the purchase to members and to convene a general meeting or circulate a written resolution in the case of a private company. Ensure valid quorum is present.

▶ Issue notice, signed by director or company secretary, on 14 clear days' notice for members to consider resolution(s). Where approval is being sought by written resolution, a copy of the purchase contract or the terms of the purchase must be circulated with the written resolution.

ss.694,696(2(a))

▶ Enclose with the notice a form of proxy if desired. Listed companies must enclose a three-way form of proxy (see page 186).

▶ A copy of the agreement, or a written schedule of its terms if the
contract is not in writing, must be made available for inspection by
the members of the company at the company's registered office for
not less than 15 days prior to the meeting and at the meeting itself.
The schedule of the terms must include the names of any members
holding shares which it is proposed be purchased and, if the written
contract does not show these names, a schedule must be attached
showing the names and the number of shares to which the contract
relates. Where a previously approved contract is being varied,
the terms of the variation must be available for inspection by the
members.

                              s.696(2)(b)

▶ This requirement for the documents to be made available for
inspection to the members prior to the meeting restricts the ability of
the company to hold the meeting at shorter notice than 15 days.

▶ Hold general meeting. Ensure valid quorum is present. Resolution
put to vote either by show of hands or by poll and to be passed by
appropriate majority (ordinary resolution by 50% majority).

▶ Once the company has purchased the shares, a return on form SH03
must be submitted to the Registrar, stating the number of shares and
the class of shares, together with the nominal value of the shares and
the date on which they were repurchased. The repurchase of shares
by a company is subject to stamp duty, the duty being payable on the
consideration and not the nominal value at the rate of 0.5% (rounded
up to the nearest £5).

▶ Issue consideration cheques and cancel share certificates relating to
shares purchased. Update register of members.

Procedure – market purchase

▶ A company may only make a market purchase of its own shares if the
purchase has been approved in advance by ordinary resolution.
   s.701(1)

▶ The resolution may be a general authorisation or limited to the
purchase of shares of a particular class or description and may also be
an unconditional authority or conditional.
   s.701(2)

▶ The authority must specify the maximum number of shares that may
be purchased, the maximum and minimum process that may be paid,
and the date not more than 18 months from the date of the resolution
when the authority lapses.
   s.701(3),(5)

Filing requirement

▶ Copy of special resolution within 15 days.   **s.30**

▶ Amended copy of articles of association, if amended.   **s.26**

▶ Stamped form SH03 within 28 days.   **s.707**

Notes

▶ In the case of a public company, the resolution must state the date upon which the authority is to lapse, being not more than 18 months from the date of the resolution.　**s.694(5)**

▶ The resolution will be invalid if any member of the company holding shares which it is proposed be repurchased exercises the voting rights attaching to those shares, and the resolution would not have been passed if those shares had not been voted.　**s.695**

▶ Where a contract for an off-market purchase of shares has been approved, a copy of the contract or, if not in writing, a written memorandum of its terms must be kept at the registered office or another specified place for at least 10 years commencing on the date the purchase of shares was completed or the contract otherwise determines.　**s.702**

More information

 Chapter 14　 Chapter 8

Quorum – directors' meetings

The quorum for a meeting is the minimum number of directors that must be present and entitled to vote in order to constitute a valid meeting. The articles will normally stipulate the quorum. Unless modified, the default quorum established by the model articles for both private and public companies and by Table A for pre-CA2006 incorporated companies is two directors. They also provide for the directors to change the quorum as they see fit; however, any resolution to raise or lower the quorum must be taken at a directors' meeting at which a quorum is present.

reg. 11 sch. 1, reg. 10 sch. 3, SI 2008/3229 reg. 89 Table A

If the articles are silent on the question of a quorum and specifically preclude the provisions of the model articles, then the quorum will default to a majority of the directors in office from time to time.

The quorum must be maintained during the course of a meeting. If the number of directors present falls below the quorum, the meeting must stand adjourned until a quorum (not necessarily the same directors) is present. This can be difficult where directors are interested in the business before the meeting and excluded from voting and from being counted in the quorum.

Checklist

▶ Is a quorum present?

▶ Is a quorum maintained and present for each item of business, especially in circumstances where one or more directors may have a conflict of interests?

▶ If a director is also an alternate for another director, he or she will not count as 'two' people for the purposes of determining whether a quorum is present unless there is specific power in the articles.

▶ Directors 'present' by telephone/video conferencing etc will be included in the quorum.

Filing requirement

None.

Notes

None.

More information

 Chapter 8    Chapter 2

Quorum – shareholders' meetings

The quorum for a meeting is the minimum number of members that must be present and entitled to vote in order to constitute a valid meeting. In the absence of any provisions in the articles of association, the default quorum is two members or, where the company has only one member, the quorum is reduced to one.

s.318

None of the model articles specifies a quorum.

The model articles for both private and public companies waive the quorum requirement on any resolution to appoint a chairman for the meeting.

reg. 38 sch. 1, reg. 30 sch. 3, SI 2008/3229

The model articles require the quorum to be present within half an hour of the time at which the meeting was due to start and if not, the chairman must adjourn the meeting. When adjourning a meeting, the chairman must stipulate either the time and place to which it is adjourned or state that the meeting will continue at a time and place fixed by the directors.

reg. 41 sch. 1, reg. 33 sch. 3, SI 2008/3229

Occasionally the articles will stipulate that at the adjourned meeting those members attending, if any, shall constitute a valid quorum.

Checklist

▶ Check articles to establish quorum.

▶ Is a quorum present at the time the meeting has been convened to be held?

▶ If not present, is a quorum present within half an hour?

▶ Is a quorum maintained throughout the meeting?

Filing requirement

None.

Notes

None.

More information

 Chapter 8    Chapter 14

Reduction of capital – by court order

The Act provides for public and private companies to reduce their share capital by special resolution of the members and subject to confirmation by the court. No specific authority is required in the articles of association. A private company will only use this process in circumstances where the directors are unable to provide a solvency statement.

Application to the court comprises three key dates:

- application made to the court;
- the directions hearing; and
- court hearing.

It is common practice to agree the application date in advance so that the application and accompanying documents can be filed immediately following the conclusion of the general meeting.

The claim form sets out details of the capital structure following the reduction, relevant details from the articles and financial position, as well as details of the resolution approved by the shareholders.

Details of the proposed reduction can be notified direct to creditors as well as by national advertisement.

Reduction of capital proceedings are rarely opposed and confirmation will be given unless:

- the court is not satisfied that creditors are safeguarded;
- the court is not satisfied that the reduction is fair and equitable to shareholders;
- the necessary formalities have not been completed adequately; or
- the reduction is intended solely for the avoidance of tax.

Checklist

- Check articles to ensure no restriction on reduction of capital.
- Where the reduction is part of a scheme of arrangement, it is possible to reduce the share capital to zero followed by an immediate issue of shares.

s.641(2)

▶ If the company is a PLC, will the reduction result in the issued capital falling below the minimum share capital requirement?

▶ Check articles to ensure no restriction on reduction of capital.

▶ There must remain at least one issued share following completion of the reduction of capital.

▶ Will all directors sign the declaration of solvency?

Procedure

▶ Convene a directors' meeting to recommend the reduction of capital to members and either to convene a general meeting or to circulate a written resolution (private companies only) to obtain members' approval. Ensure valid quorum is present.

▶ Issue notice, signed by director or company secretary, on 14 clear days' notice or circulate written resolution for members to consider special resolution(s).

▶ Enclose with the notice a form of proxy if desired.

▶ Hold general meeting or circulate written resolution. Ensure valid quorum is present. Resolution put to vote either by show of hands or by poll and to be passed by appropriate majority (special resolution by 75% majority).

▶ Within 15 days of the passing of the resolution, file a copy of the special resolution with Companies House.

▶ Application must be made to the court to approve the special resolution.

▶ Provided the court is satisfied that the proposed reduction meets all the jurisdictional and procedural requirements, it will make an order confirming the reduction.

▶ A copy of the court order and a statement of capital on form SH19 and the filing fee (£10) must be filed at Companies House.

▶ The reduction becomes effective upon registration of the documents by the Registrar of Companies. The Registrar must certify the registration of the court order.

▶ Issue consideration cheques if appropriate and cancel share certificates relating to shares reduced. Update register of members. Issue balancing share certificates if appropriate.

Filing requirement

▶ Copy of special resolution.

▶ Court order.

▶ Form SH19.

▶ Filing fee £10.

Notes

None.

More information

 Chapter 14    Chapter 6

Reduction of capital – simplified process

Private companies proposing to make small value purchases of shares may take advantage of a simplified process.

Checklist

▶ Check articles to ensure no restriction on reduction of capital.

▶ The aggregate purchase consideration in any financial year must not exceed the lower of £15,000 or 5% of fully paid share capital, at the beginning of the financial year.

s..692(1ZA)

▶ The articles of association must contain authority for the company to purchase its own shares.

▶ The purchase must be made out of capital.

s.694(2)

▶ There must remain at least one issued share following completion of the reduction of capital.

s.696

Procedure

▶ Convene a directors' meeting to recommend the reduction of capital to members and either to convene a general meeting or to circulate a written resolution to obtain members' approval to the terms of the proposed purchase contract. Ensure valid quorum is present.

s.698

▶ Ensure a copy of the proposed contract of purchase (or a written memorandum of its terms if it is not in writing) is made available for inspection by members of the company at the company's registered office for not less than 15 days prior to the meeting and is available for inspection at the meeting.

▶ Issue notice, signed by director or company secretary, on 14 clear days' notice or circulate written resolution for members to consider special resolution(s).

▶ Enclose with the notice a form of proxy if desired.

▶ Hold general meeting or circulate written resolution. Ensure valid quorum is present. Resolution put to vote either by show of hands or by poll and to be passed by appropriate majority (ordinary resolution by 50% majority).

- The votes of any member whose shares are being repurchased should be disregarded for the purposes of establishing whether there is the necessary majority in favour of the resolution.

- The reduction becomes effective upon registration of the documents by the Registrar of Companies.

- Issue consideration cheques if appropriate and cancel share certificates relating to shares reduced. Update register of members. Issue balancing share certificates if appropriate.

Filing requirement

- Copy of ordinary resolution.

- Form SH19.

- Filing fee £10.

Notes

- The purchase may also be made under a contingent purchase whereby a company becomes entitled or obliged to purchase its own shares, provided this has been authorised by ordinary resolution. Authorities may be varied, revoked or renewed by an ordinary resolution. If the articles do not contain authority for the company to purchase its own shares, the articles should be amended by special resolution of the members.

- The memorandum of terms made available for inspection must include the names of the members holding the shares to which the contract relates. If it is the contract itself that is available for inspection, it must have annexed to it a written memorandum specifying the names if they do not appear in the contract itself. Similar arrangements must be made in the case of the variation of an existing contract, which also has to be approved by an ordinary resolution.

- A private company may authorise the purchase of its own shares by written resolution under s. 288. To be valid, a copy of the proposed contract or a memorandum of its terms must be made available to each member no later than the date on which the written resolution is forwarded to them for approval and signature. In practice, it is normal to circulate a copy of the contract or the memorandum of its terms, together with the written resolution for signature and return.

More information

 Chapter 14    Chapter 6

Reduction of capital – supported by solvency statement

The Act provides for private companies to reduce their share capital by special resolution of the members, provided the resolution is supported by a solvency statement. No specific authority is required in the articles of association.

s.642

The solvency statement must be declared by the directors not more than 15 days prior to the date of the resolution and this must be registered at Companies House within 15 days, together with a statement of revised capital on form SH19, confirmation of the date of the solvency statement and the special resolution of the members.

s.644

The solvency statement requires each director to confirm that, in his or her opinion, there are no grounds at the date of the statement that the company could not meets its debts and that during the period of 12 months following the statement, the company will be able to pay its debts as they fall due.

Checklist

▶ Check articles to ensure no restriction on reduction of capital.

▶ There must remain at least one issued share following completion of the reduction of capital.

▶ Will all directors sign the declaration of solvency?

Procedure

▶ Convene a directors' meeting to approve giving of the solvency statement, recommending the reduction of capital to members and either to convene a general meeting or to circulate a written resolution to obtain members' approval. Ensure valid quorum is present.

▶ Issue notice, signed by director or company secretary, on 14 clear days' notice or circulate written resolution for members to consider special resolution(s). Included with the notice or written resolution must be a copy of the solvency statement. The special resolution must be approved within 15 days of the date of the directors' solvency statement made under s. 642.

▶ Enclose with the notice a form of proxy if desired.

▶ Hold general meeting or circulate written resolution. Ensure valid quorum is present. Resolution put to vote either by show of hands or by poll and to be passed by appropriate majority (special resolution by 75% majority).

▶ Within 15 days of the passing of the resolution, file a copy of the special resolution, solvency statement, statement confirming the solvency statement made within 15 days prior to the resolution and circulated to members and form SH19 with Companies House, together with filing fee of £10.

▶ The reduction becomes effective upon registration of the documents by the Registrar of Companies.

▶ Issue consideration cheques if appropriate and cancel share certificates relating to shares reduced. Update register of members. Issue balancing share certificates if appropriate.

Filing requirement

▶ Copy of special resolution.

▶ Solvency statement.

▶ Statement by directors that solvency statement made within 15 days prior to general meeting.

▶ Form SH19.

▶ Filing fee £10.

Notes

▶ The purchase may also be made under a contingent purchase whereby a company becomes entitled or obliged to purchase its own shares, provided this has been authorised by ordinary resolution. Authorities may be varied, revoked or renewed by an ordinary resolution. If the articles do not contain authority for the company to purchase its own shares, they should be amended by special resolution of the members.

▶ The memorandum of terms made available for inspection must include the names of the members holding the shares to which the contract relates. If it is the contract itself that is available for inspection, it must have annexed to it a written memorandum specifying the names if they do not appear in the contract itself. Similar arrangements must be made in the case of the variation of an existing contract, which also has to be approved by a special resolution.

▶ A private company may authorise the purchase of its own shares by written resolution under s. 288. To be valid, a copy of the proposed contract or a memorandum of its terms must be made available to each member no later than the date on which the written resolution is forwarded to them for approval and signature. In practice, it is normal to circulate a copy of the contract or the memorandum of its terms, together with the written resolution for signature and return.

More information

Register of charges

Companies are no longer required to keep a register of charges for charges created on or after 6 April 2013. In place of this requirement, copies of charges (and any amendments to them) and instruments creating a charge (if applicable) must be made available for inspection at either the company's registered office or SAIL address.

ss. 859(P)
and (Q)

In practice, companies will still need to maintain a record in order to monitor outstanding charges, and it is likely that some sort of register will be maintained. Such a register or record is not required to be made available for public inspection.

The requirement to keep and maintain a register of charges remains in place for charges created before 6 April 2013.

Checklist

▶ Does the change relate to a charge created before 6 April 2013?

   ▷ If yes, note satisfaction, in full or part in register of charges.

   ▷ If no, then no entries need be made in the register of charges.

Filing requirement

Pre-6 April 2013 charge
▶ Form MR05 or MR06 as appropriate.

Post-6 April 2013 charges
▶ Form MR01, MR02, MR03, MR06, MR08, MR09 or MR10 to register a new, modified or satisfied charge as appropriate.

▶ Filing fee for new charges £15 electronic, £23 paper.

Notes

▶ Registration of new charges must be completed with 21 days of the creation of the charge.

▶ Copies of charges and any instruments creating a charge must be kept available for inspection at the registered office or SAIL address.

More information

 Chapters 7 and 20

 Chapter 10

 Guidance booklet GP3

Register of directors

All companies are required to maintain a register of directors and this must be available for inspection at the registered office or SAIL address. `s. 162`

Private companies may elect to keep their register of directors on the central register. When an election is in place there is no requirement for access to be provided to the register of directors previously maintained by the company. `s. 167A`

It is important to note that when such an election is in place, a director's full date of birth will be freely accessible to anyone searching the company's record at Companies House. `s. 1136`

Checklist

▶ Is an election under s. 167A in force?

Procedure

▶ Where the company maintains its register of directors, the following information must be recorded: `s. 163`

  ▷ For a director who is a natural person, his or her current and any former name(s) (within the previous 20 years), service address, nationality, business occupation and date of birth. `s. 164`

  ▷ For a corporate director, corporate name, registered or principal office, in the case of an EAA registered company, details of the state and register in which the company is registered and its registered number, for a non-EAA company, details of the legal form of the company and law by which it is governed and, if applicable, details of the register in which the company is registered and its registered number.

Filing requirement

▶ Form AD03 or AD04 as appropriate.

▶ Form EH01 if an election under s. 167A is made.

Notes

▶ If the company maintains its register of directors, this must be kept at either its registered office or its SAIL address.   **s.162(3)**

▶ Unless the register of directors has always been kept at the company's registered office, details of its location must be notified to Companies House.   **s.162(4)**

More information

 Chapters 6 and 7

 Chapters 10 and 11

 Guidance Company registers

Register of directors' usual residential addresses

All companies are required to maintain a register of directors' usual residential addresses in respect of all its directors that are natural persons. This register should not be made available for inspection.

s. 165

s. 1136

Private companies may elect to keep their register of directors' usual residential addresses on the central register. It is important to note that when such an election is in place, a director's residential address information will be freely accessible to anyone searching the company's record at Companies House.

s. 167A

Checklist

▶ Is an election under s. 167A in force?

Procedure

▶ Where the company maintains its register of directors' usual residential addresses, the following information must be recorded:

▷ Each director's usual residential address unless this is the same address as recorded in the register of directors as his or her service address, in which case the register need only contain an entry to that effect.

s. 165

Filing requirement

▶ Form EH02 if an election under s. 167A is made.

Notes

None.

More information

Register of members

All companies are required to maintain a register of members and this must be available for inspection at the registered office or SAIL address.

ss. 112, 114
s. 1136

Private companies may elect to keep their register of members on the central register. It is important to note that when such an election is in place, a member's address information will be freely accessible to anyone searching the company's record at Companies House.

s. 128A

Checklist

▶ Is an election under s. 128A in force?

Procedure

▶ Where the company maintains its register of members, the following information must be recorded:

▷ Name and address of each member and names of all joint holders.

▷ The date on which each member was registered as a member.

▷ The date each member ceased to be a member.

▶ Companies that have a share capital must also record:

▷ the number of shares held by each member including any distinguishing numbers, if any, and the class of share where there is more than one; and

▷ the amount paid or agreed to be paid on the shares.

Filing requirement

▶ Form EH05 if an election under s. 128A is made.

Notes

▶ If the company maintains its register of members, this must be kept at either its registered office or its SAIL address.

▶ Unless the register of members has always been kept at the company's registered office, details of its location must be notified to Companies House.

▶ Records relating to former members may be deleted 10 years after they ceased to be a member.

More information

Chapters 7 and 18

Chapters 5 and 10

Guidance Company records

Register of members – rectification

The Act does not contain specific authority for a company to rectify the register of members. The courts may order rectification of the register of members by the removal or addition of a person from or to the register. Original Orders will bear the seal of the court or, alternatively, a duly authenticated office copy of the Order may be registered.

s.125

In practice, however, minor clerical errors are informally corrected on the register under the authority of a responsible officer following receipt by the company or its registrar of a duly completed form of request for rectification of transferee details following the registration of a transfer of shares.

Where there is a substantial difference between the registered details and the rectification request (e.g. a completely different name and address), great care must be taken and unless there has been a patent error, a court order should be obtained.

Checklist

▶ The Order should be checked to ensure that the holding referred to corresponds with a registered shareholding in the company. Identification will be facilitated by returning the relevant share certificate.

Procedure

▶ The amendments authorised in the Order should be made to the register of members, and the date of the Order and its registration should be entered as the authority for the amendment.

▶ The existing share certificate may be endorsed as appropriate, although it is preferable that a new share certificate be prepared.

▶ The company's registration stamp should be affixed to the Order, which should be returned to the sender together with the endorsed or replacement share certificate.

▶ If a dividend mandate is currently in force, it may be appropriate for this to be amended, cancelled or renewed.

Filing requirement

None.

Notes

None.

More information

 Chapter 18    Chapter 6

Register of people with significant control

The register of people with significant control (the PSC Register) was introduced under SBEE2015 to provide greater transparency of ownership of UK companies. Up until its introduction, the majority of UK companies needed to disclose details only of the registered holder of their shares and not of beneficial ownership. The new sections in the Act are supported by the Register of People with Significant Control Regulations 2016 (SI 2016/339) (the PSC Regs).

ss. 790A-790ZG

From 6 April 2016 all companies other than those qualifying for exemption are required to keep a PSC Register. From 26 June 2017 the exemptions are being narrowed and rather than applying to all companies subject to DTR5, exemption will only be available to listed companies.

s. 790B

As noted above, the purpose of the PSC Register is to increase transparency in ownership and accordingly the register is of natural persons. As a result, where the immediate ownership is through another corporate entity or a trust, companies are required to move up to the next layer of ownership until the ultimate owner(s) are identified.

Procedure

▶ If the company does not have a PSC or has been unable to obtain confirmed details of their PSCs, one of a number of permitted statements must be entered into the PSC Register and updated as required.

s. 790E

▶ It may be perfectly obvious who the beneficial owner(s) is and no further steps are needed to identify them. For instance, for a private company with a sole shareholder and director, no investigation will be required. However, where the share structure is more complex or where there are trust or corporate members, it may be necessary for enquiries to be made of those members to establish beneficial ownership.

s. 790D

▶ The PSC Register can never be blank and in circumstances where beneficial ownership has not yet been established, there are a number of permitted statements to describe the position and which will require updating as the enquiries continue.

s. 790M

▶ These permitted statements are as follows:

Part 4 PSC Regs 2016

▷ The company knows or has reasonable cause to believe that there is no registrable person or registrable relevant legal entity in relation to the company.

▷ The company knows or has reasonable cause to believe that there is a registrable person in relation to the company but it has not identified the registrable person.

▷ The company has identified a registrable person in relation to the company, but all of the required particulars of that person have not been confirmed.

▷ The company has not yet completed taking reasonable steps to find out if there is anyone who is a registrable person or a registrable relevant legal entity in relation to the company.

▷ The company has given a notice under section 790D of the Act which has not been complied with.

▷ The addressee has failed to comply with a notice given by the company under section 790E of the Act.

▷ The company has issued a restrictions notice under paragraph 1 of Schedule 1B to the Act.

▶ Although in general, it is details of individual ownership that must be recorded in the PSC Register, there are two other types of entity that are permitted. Accordingly there are three types of ownership structure whose details must be entered into a company's PSC Register. The categories are individual, registrable relevant legal entity (RLE) and other registrable person.

▶ The information to be registered about each category of ownership is as follows:

▷ For an individual person:

– the date the individual became a registrable person;

s.790K(1)

– name;

– country/state of residence;

– nationality;

– service address;

– usual residential address (this is not shown on the public record);

– date of birth (only the month and year are shown on the public record); and

– the nature of their control over the company.

▷ For a registrable relevant legal entity (RLE) (such as a company):

– the date that they became a registrable RLE;

- corporate name;
- address;
- legal form of the corporate body;
- governing law under which the RLE was registered;
- place of registration (if applicable);
- registration number (if applicable); and
- the nature of their control over the company.

▷ For another registrable person (such as a corporation sole or local authority):

- the date on which they became a registrable person in relation to the company in question;
- name;
- principal office;
- the legal form of the person;
- law by which they are governed; and
- the nature of their control over the company.

Checklist

▶ A PSC is anyone in the company who meets at least one of the four conditions set out in the Register of People with Significant Control Regulations 2016 (SI 339/2016). Some companies will have no PSCs while others may have several. The majority of companies will have one PSC, reflecting that the majority of companies have a sole shareholder.

▶ A PSC is a person who:　　　　　　　　　　　　　　　　　　**Sch 2 PSC Regs**

▷ holds, directly or indirectly, more than 25% of the shares;

▷ holds, directly or indirectly, more than 25% of the voting rights;

▷ holds the right, directly or indirectly, to appoint or remove a majority of directors;

▷ otherwise has the right to exercise, or actually exercises, significant influence or control over the company; and

▷ has the right to exercise, or actually exercises, significant influence or control over the activities of a trust or firm that is not a legal person, the trustees or members of which would satisfy any of the four conditions above.

▶ There are prescribed statements to be used to describe the nature of control in respect of each of the five conditions, and these are set out in Schedule 2 of the Register of People with Significant Control Regulations 2016.

▷ Once a PSC, RLE or other registrable person has been identified, in addition to updating their PSC Register, notice must be filed at Companies House.

Filing requirement

▷ Form EH04 if an election under s. 790X is made.   **s. 790G**

▷ Form PSC01, PSC02 or PSC03 to disclose identity of PSC, RLE or other registrable person, as relevant.   **s. 790H**

Notes

▷ Where a company issues a request to a member requesting details of beneficial ownership, the member has a duty to supply the requested information and to update the company in the event of any changes to that information.

More information

 Chapter 7    Chapter 10    Guidance Company records, PSC requirements for companies and limited liability partnerships

Register of secretaries

All companies are required to maintain a register of secretaries and this must be available for inspection at the registered office or SAIL address.

s.275(1)

Private companies may elect to keep their register of directors on the central register. When an election is in place, there is no requirement for access to be provided to the register of secretaries previously maintained by the company.

s.279A

s.1136

Checklist

▶ Is an election under s. 279A in force?

Procedure

▶ Where the company maintains its register of secretaries, the following information must be recorded:

▷ For a company secretary that is a natural person: his or her current and any former name(s) (within the previous 20 years) and service address.

s.163

▷ For a corporate company secretary: corporate name, registered or principal office, in the case of an EAA registered company, details of the state and register in which the company is registered and its registered number, for a non-EAA company, details of the legal form of the company and law by which it is governed and, if applicable, details of the register in which the company is registered and its registered number.

s.164

Filing requirement

▶ Form AD03 or AD04 as appropriate

▶ Form EH03 if an election under s. 279A is made.

s.275(3)

s.275(4)

Notes

▶ If the company maintains its register of secretaries, this must be kept at either its registered office or its SAIL address.

▶ Unless the register of secretaries has always been kept at the company's registered office, details of its location must be notified to Companies House.

More information

 Chapters 1 and 7

 Chapters 10 and 11

 Guidance Company registers

Registered office

All companies must have an address at which legal documents can be served. This is known as the registered office. On incorporation, the first registered office will be the address detailed on form IN01. Any change in registered office must be notified to Companies House on form AD01 to be effective. The registered office must be situated in the country of registration.

The registered office address must be shown on the company's business stationery, emails and its website(s) (see page 125).

s.86

s.87

s.82
reg. 24 SI 2015/17

Checklist

▶ Is the proposed registered office address in the country of incorporation?

s.9(2)(b)

▶ Is the proposed address a physical building? (PO Box addresses are not permitted.)

▶ Headed stationery must show the (new) registered office address within 14 days of any change.

s.87(2)

▶ The company's name must be displayed at the registered office.

reg. 21 SI 2015/17

▶ Are the statutory registers kept at the registered office? If the registered office is changed, have the statutory registers been moved to the new location?

▶ If the registers are not/no longer kept at the registered office, notify Companies House (forms AD02, AD03).

Procedure

▶ Convene a directors' meeting to approve change in registered office address. Ensure valid quorum is present.

▶ File form AD01.

s.87

Filing requirement

▶ Form AD01 within 14 days.

Notes

- Notify bankers, auditors, solicitors, HM Revenue & Customs (corporation tax, PAYE, share schemes, VAT) and other interested persons.

- The change does not become effective until the form is received and accepted as valid by the Registrar of Companies. **s.87(2)**

- Documents delivered to the old address within 14 days of the date of change are validly served on the company. **s.87(3)**

- The company's headed stationery must show the new registered office address not later than 14 days after the date that the notice was submitted to the Registrar of Companies. **s.87(3)**

More information

 Chapter 7    Chapter I    Guidance Booklet GP3

Registered office – objection to use of address

The Small Business, Enterprise and Employment Act 2015 introduced a new procedure under which an objection may be made to the use by a company of an address as its registered office without consent. This situation can often occur where a company uses the address of one of its professional advisers or a service agent but does not then change the address when the company no longer uses that firm's services.

s.1097A

If the objection is upheld, the Registrar has power to change the company's registered address to the Companies House office in the jurisdication of the company.

s.1097A(2)(h)

Checklist

▶ Application will normally be made by or on behalf of the person whose address is being misused but may be made by any person.

Procedure

▶ The applicant or someone on their behalf must complete and file form RP07 setting out their name and address, identity of the company concerned, the address being used as the registered office and the grounds for the application.

▶ On receipt of the application the Registrar will consider the merits of the application. If there is little or no chance of success the application will be dismissed. Alternatively, the Registrar may decide, or have already started the process, to strike off the company, in which case the application is superfluous and will be dismissed.

▶ If the Registrar accepts the application they will send a notice to all directors and company secretary, if any, at their service and residential addresses and to the company at its registered office giving notice of the objection and that the registered office address will be changed unless, within 28 days, the company voluntarily changes it, an objection is received or the applicant withdraws the application.

▶ Provided no objection is received the Registrar will change the registered office to the default address and notify the company and the applicant.

▶ To object, the company need only provide evidence of proprietary rights in the address, written agreement entitling the company to use the address or a utility bill addressed to the company at that address within the previous six months.

Filing requirement

▶ Form RP07.

Notes

▶ If the default address is imposed on the company, documents may be validly served on the company at that address, but there is no obligation on the Registrar to open any mail received by them.

▶ Officers of the company may make application to the Registrar to collect any mail received.

More information

 Chapter 1    Guidance
Registrar's rules and powers

Registration of charges

Particulars of every charge to which the Companies Act 2006 applies, created by a company registered in England and Wales, Scotland or Northern Ireland, should, within 21 days of its creation, be delivered for registration to Companies House together with a certified copy of any instrument creating or evidencing the charge.

s.859A

It is the duty of the company that creates a charge, or acquires property that is subject to a charge, to deliver to the Registrar the prescribed particulars of the charge within 21 days of the charge's creation, or the acquisition, as the case may be, using form MR01. A filing fee (currently £15 (online) or £23 (paper)) is payable. Although the obligation of registration is placed on the company, any interested party may effect this and it is, in practice, usual for the chargee, debenture holder or trustees to deal with the registration to ensure that their position is fully protected.

s.859A(4)

On receipt, the Registrar of Companies will enter details of the charge in the register kept for each company for the purpose and will also issue a certificate of registration, which states the amount thereby secured and is conclusive evidence that the registration requirements have been complied with. A copy of the certificate of registration must be endorsed by the company on every debenture or certificate of debenture stock secured by the registered charge.

s.859I

Checklist

▶ Charge must be registered within 21 days of creation by the company or the person to whom the charge is entrusted.

s.859A(4)

▶ Check articles of association to ensure the company's capacity to create a charge on its assets is not restricted in any way. Many listed companies will have the borrowing powers restricted to a multiple of their balance sheet value.

Procedure

▶ Convene a directors' meeting to approve the creation of a charge over some or all of the company's assets. Ensure valid quorum is present.

▶ Certified copies of the security document must be delivered to Companies House for registration within 21 days of the date of creation of the security. The security document must be accompanied by 'the prescribed particulars of the charge', set out on form MR01 for most forms of charge, form MR03 for a series of debentures and form MR02 where property is acquired subject to an existing mortgage or charge.

▶ If the security relates to real property, the security document or particulars of the security should also be sent to the Land Registry or the appropriate charge registered at the Land Charges Registry.

s.859P

▶ A copy of every instrument creating a charge requiring registration must be kept at the registered office or a specified place of inspection.

Filing requirement

ss.859P and Q

▶ Certified copy security document within 21 days.

▶ Form MR01, MR02, MR03, MR06, MR07, MR08, MR09 or MR10 as appropriate within 21 days.

s.859H

▶ Filing fee £15 (online) or £23 (paper).

Notes

s.859F

▶ If a charge is not properly registered with the Registrar of Companies, any security on the company's property or undertaking conferred by the charge is void against the liquidator or administrator and any creditor of the company, but not the company itself.

▶ The court has power under the Companies Act 2006, on the application of a company or any interested person, to extend the time for registration of the charge or to rectify an omission or misstatement of any particular relating to a charge.

More information

Chapter 20

Chapter 1

Guidance booklet GP3

Related party transactions

Where a director or a person 'connected' with a director acquires a substantial non-cash asset from the company, or disposes of such an asset to the company, in most instances, shareholder approval must be sought.

s.190(1)

A substantial transaction is one with a value of more than £5,000 and that exceeds the lower limit of £100,000, or 10% of the company's net assets.

s.191(2)

If the director or the connected person is also a director of the company's holding company, then approval of the members of the holding company must also be sought.

s.190(2)

Procedure

▶ Convene a directors' meeting to recommend an appropriate special resolution to members and to convene a general meeting or seek approval by written resolution in the case of a private company. Ensure valid quorum is present.

▶ Issue notice signed by director or company secretary, on 14 clear days' notice for members to consider resolution.

s.307

▶ Enclose with the notice a form of proxy if desired.

▶ If the meeting is to be convened on short notice, the company secretary should arrange for agreement to short notice to be signed by each of the shareholders.

s.307(5)

▶ Hold general meeting. Ensure valid quorum is present. Resolution put to vote either by show of hands or by poll and to be passed by appropriate majority (ordinary resolution by 50% majority).

s.282

Filing requirement

None.

Notes

▶ Transactions between companies of a wholly owned group do not require approval. **s.192**

▶ Where a transaction has not received approval of the members, the transaction will usually be voidable by the company. **s.195**

▶ Where a transaction was not approved in advance, it may be affirmed by members within a reasonable period. **s.196**

▶ Transactions undertaken on behalf of the director or connected person on a recognised Stock Exchange by an 'independent' broker do not require approval.

▶ Where a director acquires a non-cash asset by virtue of being a member of the company, approval is not required. **s.192**

▶ Any arrangements entered into which have not received prior or retrospective approval between a director, connected person or holding company and the company make that director or connected person liable to the company for any gain arising out of the transaction or any losses suffered by the company. **s.195**

More information

 Chapter 6    Chapters 11 and 16

Re-registration – limited company as unlimited

Provided that all members consent, a private limited company may be re-registered as an unlimited company.

s.102

In practice this is seldom done; however, companies may choose to do so to keep their financial affairs secret, as unlimited companies do not need to file their accounts. Additionally, prior to dissolution, conversion to unlimited status can facilitate the return of funds to shareholders that may not be possible as a limited company, due to the constraints on distribution of profit and return of capital.

Checklist

▶ If the company has previously re-registered from unlimited to limited, this cannot be reversed.

s.102(2)

▶ Will all members consent to the change?

s.102(1)(a)

▶ Change company's stationery to reflect new status (see page 125).

Procedure

▶ Convene a directors' meeting to recommend appropriate resolutions to members and to convene a general meeting or circulate a written resolution. Additionally, resolutions to make certain amendments to the articles will be required to reflect the company's new status. Ensure valid quorum is present.

s.302

▶ Where a general meeting is to be held, issue notice, signed by director or company secretary, on 14 clear days' notice for members to consider resolutions.

s.307(1)

▶ Enclose with the notice a form of proxy if desired.

▶ If the meeting is to be convened on short notice, the company secretary should arrange for agreement to short notice to be signed by each of the members.

s.307(5)

▶ Hold general meeting. Ensure valid quorum is present. Resolution put to vote either by show of hands or by poll and to be passed by unanimous consent of all members.

s.102(1)(a)

▶ Application is then made to the Registrar of Companies on form RR05 within 15 days, together with a copy of the resolution detailing the alterations to the articles of association appropriate for an unlimited company and an amended copy of the articles, together with a fee (currently £20, or £50 same-day). **ss. 26, 103**

▶ Each member of the company must confirm in writing on form RR05 that they wish the company to be re-registered as an unlimited company, together with a statement of compliance by the directors that every member has agreed to the re-registration, either personally or by their duly authorised agent. **s. 103(4)**

▶ If the application is accepted, the Registrar issues a new certificate of incorporation stating the company's unlimited status, whereupon the alterations to the articles of association set out in the application take effect. There is no need for the members to pass a special resolution approving these amendments. **s. 104**

Filing requirement

▶ Form RR05.

▶ Filing fee £20 (same-day fee £50).

▶ Copy of resolution. **s. 103**

▶ Amended copy of memorandum and articles of association. **s. 26**

Notes

▶ Unlimited companies do not normally need to file a copy of their accounts with the Registrar of Companies.

▶ Once the Registrar has issued the certificate of re-registration, it will be necessary to obtain new headed stationery, and a new company seal where the company has a seal.

▶ Arrange for the name of the company's bank accounts to be changed.

▶ Notify the company's suppliers and customers of the change of name, HM Revenue & Customs for corporation tax, PAYE and VAT, pension scheme, title deeds, trademark registrations, data protection registration, insurers, etc. Signs at the company's premises and/or on the company's cars, vans and lorries will also require amendment.

More information

 Chapter 2    Chapter 1    Guidance booklet GP3

Re-registration – private company as public

Provided that a private limited company can satisfy five conditions it can, by special resolution of the members, re-register as a public limited company.

ss. 90, 97

Shares recently issued for a non-cash consideration may need to have the consideration valued.

s. 93

Checklist

▶ Does the company have share capital?

s. 90(2)(a)

▶ The issued share capital of the company must have a nominal value of at least £50,000 or the prescribed euro equivalent, and each share must be paid up to at least 25% of its nominal value together with all of any premium.

ss. 90(2)(b), 91, 763, reg. 2, SI 2008/729

▶ The application for re-registration must be received by the Registrar of Companies within seven months of its year-end and a copy of an audited balance sheet must be filed on or before the date of application for re-registration. Normally the balance sheet is taken from the latest audited accounts; however, a balance sheet may be submitted made up to an appropriate date not more than seven months prior to the application.

ss. 90(2)(c), 92

▶ The company's auditors must give a statement to the effect that the net assets of the company are not less than its called-up share capital and undistributable reserves and, where the audit report to the audited accounts is qualified, that the subject of their qualification is not material for determining that the assets are greater than the called-up share capital and undistributable reserves.

s. 92

▶ If shares have been issued otherwise than for cash during the period between the balance sheet date and the date of application for re-registration, the provisions of s. 593 must be complied with. These require an independent valuer to value the consideration received by the company. These provisions do not apply to a share exchange or proposed merger with another company.

s. 90(2)(d)

s. 593

s. 93(7)(b)

▶ The company must not previously have been re-registered as an unlimited company.   **s.90(2)(e)**

▶ If the company does not have one, a company secretary must be appointed.   **s.271**

Procedure

▶ Convene a directors' meeting to recommend an appropriate special resolution to members and to convene a general meeting or circulate a written resolution. Additionally, resolutions to make certain amendments to the articles will be required to reflect the company's new status. Ensure valid quorum is present.   **s.302**

▶ Issue notice, signed by director or company secretary, on 21 clear days' notice for members to consider resolution.   **s.307(1)**

▶ Enclose with the notice a form of proxy if desired.

▶ If the meeting is to be convened on short notice, the company secretary should arrange for agreement to short notice to be signed by each of the shareholders.   **s.307(5)**

▶ Hold general meeting. Ensure valid quorum is present. Resolution put to vote either by show of hands or by poll and to be passed by appropriate majority (special resolution by 75% majority).

▶ File all necessary documents, as set out below, with Companies House within 15 days of passing the resolutions.   **s.30**

▶ If the application is accepted, the Registrar issues a new certificate of incorporation stating the company's PLC status, whereupon the alterations to the memorandum and articles of association set out in the application take effect. There is no need for the members to pass a special resolution approving these amendments.   **s.96**

Filing requirement

▶ Form RR01.

▶ A copy of the relevant balance sheet.

▶ A copy of the audit report.

▶ A copy of the auditors' statement.

▶ A copy of the amended articles of association.

▶ A copy of the special resolutions.

▶ Re-registration fee (currently £20; same-day fee £50).

Notes

▶ A company that has been re-registered as unlimited cannot subsequently be re-registered as a public company.   **s.90(2)(e)**

▶ If the company has insufficient share capital, additional shares must be issued. This is often achieved by a bonus issue, as a company seeking re-registration will normally have adequate reserves. **s. 763**

▶ There is no obligation for a public company's shares to be quoted. Many private companies re-register for the marketing advantages of being a PLC.

▶ The regulations governing PLCs, the actions of their directors and the preparation of accounts are more onerous than for private companies.

▶ Once the Registrar has issued the certificate of re-registration, it will be necessary to obtain new headed stationery, and a new company seal where the company has a seal.

▶ Arrange for the name of the company's bank accounts to be changed.

▶ Notify the company's suppliers and customers of the change of name: HM Revenue & Customs for corporation tax, PAYE and VAT, pension scheme, title deeds, trademark registrations, data protection registration, insurers, etc. Signs at the company's premises and/or on the company's cars, vans and lorries will also require amendment.

More information

 Chapter 2    Chapter 1    Guidance booklet GP3

Re-registration – public company as private

This procedure is becoming more common as more stringent and restrictive provisions for public companies, in particular accounting provisions, continue to increase their scope and effect.

There are no particular qualifying criteria and all public companies, subject to any other regulatory requirements such as FCA, UKLA, etc, could be re-registered as private companies.

s.97

A public company can be registered as a private company limited by shares or guarantee, or as a private unlimited company.

s.89(b),(e)

Procedure – change to private limited

▶ Convene a directors' meeting to recommend appropriate special resolution to members and to convene a general meeting. Additionally, resolutions to make certain amendments to the articles will be required to reflect the company's new status. Ensure valid quorum is present.

ss.97,302

▶ Issue notice, signed by director or company secretary, on 14 clear days' notice for members to consider resolution, or 21 days' notice if the resolution(s) are to be put at an annual general meeting.

s.307(1)

▶ Enclose with the notice a form of proxy if desired.

▶ If the meeting is to be convened on short notice, the company secretary should arrange for agreement to short notice to be signed by each of the shareholders.

s.307(5

▶ Hold general meeting. Ensure valid quorum is present. Resolution put to vote either by show of hands or by poll and to be passed by appropriate majority (special resolution by 75% majority).

▶ File all necessary documents with Companies House within 15 days of passing the resolutions.

s.30

▶ Within 28 days of the passing of the resolution, an application may be made to the court for the cancellation of the resolution. This application may be made only by a holder or holders of at least 5% of the issued share capital of the company (or of any class of shares)

s.98

or by not fewer than 50 of the company's members. If such an application is made, the court may confirm or cancel the resolution, or impose certain conditions on its approval. The company must file a copy of any order made by the court with the Registrar within 15 days of the making of the order or within such period as may be determined by the court.

▶ If no application is made to the court within 28 days of the passing of the resolution, an application for re-registration as a private company should be submitted to the Registrar on form RR02, signed by a director or secretary, together with a copy of the amended articles of association. If all shareholders voted in favour of the resolution, form RR02 may be filed immediately.   **s. 97(1)(c), (2)**

▶ If accepted, the Registrar issues a new certificate of incorporation stating the company's limited status, whereupon the alterations to the memorandum and articles of association set out in the application take effect. There is no need for the members to pass a special resolution approving these amendments.   **s. 101**

Procedure – change to private unlimited

The procedure for a re-registration as a private unlimited company are the same as for re-registering as a private limited company, except as follows:

▶ The resolution to re-register requires consent of all members entitled to vote.   **s. 109(1)(a)**

▶ The company must not previously have been re-registered as a private limited or unlimited company.   **s. 109(2)**

▶ The application form is form RR07.   **s. 110**

Filing requirement

▶ Copy of special resolution.

▶ Form RR02 or RR07.

▶ Copy of amended articles of association.

▶ Statement of compliance.

▶ Copy of the court order, if appropriate.

▶ Re-registration fee (currently £20; same-day fee £50).

Notes

▶ Once the Registrar has issued the certificate of re-registration, it will be necessary to obtain new headed stationery and a new company seal, where the company has a seal.

▶ Arrange for the name of the company's bank accounts to be changed.

▶ Notify the company's suppliers and customers of the change of name: HM Revenue & Customs for corporation tax, PAYE and VAT, pension scheme, title deeds, trademark registrations, data protection registration, insurers, etc. Signs at the company's premises and/or on the company's cars, vans and lorries will also require amendment.

▶ In addition to the voluntary re-registration as a private company, a public company may be *required* to re-register by the court where its issued share capital is below the authorised minimum. This would normally only occur on a reduction of capital or redemption of redeemable shares. In such an event, the court may authorise the re-registration to be effective without a special resolution being passed and may specify in the order the amendments to be made to the memorandum and articles of association.

s.650

More information

 Chapter 2    Chapter 1    Guidance booklet GP3

Resolutions – filing requirements

A copy of the following resolutions must be filed with the Registrar of Companies within 15 days of approval.

s.30

Checklist

▶ Special resolutions:

▷ Resolutions or agreements that have been agreed to by all the members of a company, but that, if not so agreed to, would not have been effective for their purpose unless (as the case may be) they had been passed as special resolutions. Resolutions or agreements that have been agreed to by all the members of some class of shareholders but that, if not so agreed to, would not have been effective for their purpose unless they had been passed by some particular majority or otherwise in some particular manner, and all resolutions or agreements that effectively bind all the members of any class of shareholders, though not agreed to by all those members.

s.29

▷ A resolution passed by the directors of a company in compliance with a direction to change name by Secretary of State.

s.67

▷ A resolution of a company to give, vary, revoke or renew an authority to the directors for allotment of relevant securities.

ss.550,551

▷ A resolution conferring, varying, revoking or renewing authority for market purchase of company's own shares.

s.701

▷ A resolution for voluntary winding up.

s.84 IA 1986

▷ A directors' resolution to amend the Articles of Association of the company to allow title to securities to be transferred through CREST.

▷ Forms IC01 or IC02: notification of intention to carry on business or cease to carry on business as an investment company.

Procedure

None.

Notes

None.

More information

 Chapter 7  Chapter 14  Guidance booklet GP3

Resolutions – majority

The majorities required to pass resolutions are as follows:

Checklist

▶ Ordinary resolutions: simple majority. **s. 282**

▶ Special resolutions: 75% majority. **s. 282**

Procedure

None.

Filing requirement

None.

Notes

▶ The majority for type of resolution is of those members entitled to attend and vote *and* who are present and voting at a general meeting in person or by proxy.

▶ At a meeting on a show of hands, each member or their proxy has one vote. **ss. 282(3), 283(4)**

▶ On a poll vote, each member or their proxy has one vote per share. **ss. 282(4), 283(5)**

▶ For written resolution of a private company, the majority is calculated by reference to each member's total voting rights. **ss. 282(2), 283(2)**

More information

 Chapter 7    Chapter 14

Resolutions – written: private companies

A private company may, by written resolution of members, pass resolutions that would otherwise require a general meeting to be held.

ss. 282, 283, 288

Checklist

▶ Is the company a private company?

▶ Are sufficient members available to sign the written resolution?

Procedure

▶ Written resolutions must be approved with members representing sufficient voting rights to meet the simple or 75% majority required for ordinary and special resolutions, respectively.

ss. 282(2), 283(2)

▶ The signatures need not all appear on the same document, provided that all the signed documents are in the same form; the resolution is effective and dated when signed by or on behalf of the last member to sign.

▶ If the appropriate majority has not been reached within 28 days of the date of circulation, the resolution lapses.

s. 297

▶ The original signed copies of a written resolution should be inserted in the company's minute book in the normal manner.

▶ As the majority of resolutions for a private company may now be passed by written resolution, certain changes have been necessitated to the circulation of documentation to shareholders. Accordingly, documents that are required to be circulated to shareholders with a notice of a general meeting or that are to be made available at the company's registered office for inspection prior to the meeting must, where a written resolution is to be used, be circulated to each member before or at the same time as the resolution is supplied for signature. Such documents include:

  ▷ a written statement to be given by directors pursuant to a special resolution, waiving the rights of pre-emption on the allotment of shares;

s. 571(6)

▷ a copy of the purchase contract, or written memorandum of its terms relating to the off-market purchase or contingent purchase by a company of its own shares; **s.701**

▷ a declaration of compliance and the auditors' report relating to the purchase by a company of its own shares out of capital; **s.718**

▷ a solvency statement by directors in support of a non-court reduction of capital; **s.641**

▷ a written memorandum setting out the terms of a proposed director's service contract for a term of more than two years; and

▷ disclosure of matters relating to the approval of a director's expenditure to enable him or her to perform their duties properly.

Filing requirement

▶ Copy of resolution signed by all shareholders within 15 days. **s.30**

Notes

▶ There are two resolutions that cannot be passed by a written resolution under any circumstances:

▷ the removal of a director pursuant to before the expiration of his or her period of office; and

▷ the removal of an auditor before the expiration of his or her period of office.

▶ Where any particular member is interested in the matter to be approved by written resolution and would not be eligible to vote at a general meeting, he or she is similarly barred from voting by written resolution on the same matter.

More information

 Chapter 7  Chapter 14

Restoration – administrative

Where a company has been struck off the Register and dissolved using the procedures set out in ss. 1000 or 1001, the former directors or former members may apply to the Registrar to have the company restored to the Register. Such application must be made within six years of the date of dissolution of the company.

s. 1024(1),(2)

s. 1024(4)

It should be noted that where a company has been wound up and dissolved, any application for restoration must made to the court (see page 244).

s. 1029

Prior to restoration, it will be necessary to bring the company's statutory records up to date. This will normally involve the completion of all outstanding annual returns and the preparation of accounts as well as any changes in shareholdings, officers or other statutory details of the company to be filed and obtaining the consent of the relevant Crown Representative if any property has vested *bona vacantia*.

s. 1025

Checklist

▶ If dissolved under ss. 1000 or 1001, restoration application must be within six years.

s. 1024(1)

▶ The company must have been carrying on business or have been in operation at the time of dissolution.

s. 1025(2)

▶ The Crown Representative, usually the Treasury Solicitor, must consent in writing to the restoration where any property has vested *bona vacantia*.

s. 1025(3)

▶ All documents required to bring the company's record at Companies House up to date must be delivered to the Registrar together with payment of any filing penalties outstanding at the date of dissolution.

s. 1025(5)

Procedure

▶ Ensure conditions of s. 1025 have been met and all appropriate documents lodged with the Registrar.

s. 1026(1)

▶ File form RT01 together with a statement of compliance that the requirements for administrative restoration are met.

s. 1026(2)

▶ If the Registrar decides that the application is successful, written confirmation is issued to the applicant and the company's name is restored to the Register of companies together with publication of that fact in the *Gazette*.

s.1027

Filing requirement

▶ All necessary forms, annual returns and accounts to bring the company's records up to date.

▶ Late filing penalties as appropriate.

▶ Restoration fee, currently £100.

Notes

▶ In addition to the restoration fee payable to the Registrar of Companies, the company will also be required to pay the costs of the Crown Representative, if any, and the penalties for late submission of accounts, as appropriate. Where late filing penalties were levied in respect of accounts required to be filed prior to dissolution, these are at the minimum statutory penalty rate.

▶ In practice, restoration is often required where a company has been dissolved by the Registrar (for failure to file returns and/or accounts) or at the request of the directors/shareholders and it is subsequently found that the company has valuable assets. In these circumstances, it is necessary for the company to be restored to the Register for the assets to be reclaimed, as the assets of a dissolved company automatically attach to the Crown. It is becoming increasingly common for a company with assets to be dissolved as a result of oversight on the part of directors: either neglect in filing statutory documents, or requesting the Registrar to strike off the company without properly checking that the company has no assets. For example, particular care should be taken when requesting the dissolution of a subsidiary that the legal ownership of property has passed to its holding company or fellow subsidiary. It is not uncommon for the appropriate book entries to be made, for example, transferring the lease of a property to another group company without ensuring that the legal transfer of title is also effected.

More information

Chapter 22

Chapter 19

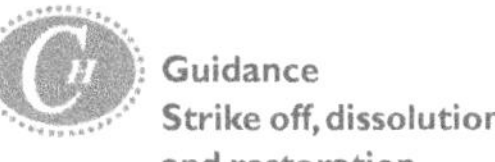
Guidance
Strike off, dissolution and restoration

Restoration – by court order

Application to the court may be made to restore a company dissolved:

- under the Insolvency Acts;   s.1029(1)

- at the conclusion of an administration; or

- either by the registrar under ss. 1000 or 1001, or under the voluntary dissolution procedures under s. 1003.   s.1024(4)

Application is made to the High Court, usually the Registrar of Companies Court in London. Cases can also be heard in District Registries or County Courts that have authority to wind up a company. For companies incorporated in Scotland, application is made to the Court of Session or, where the issued capital does not exceed £120,000, to the Sheriff Court in the Sheriffdom where the registered office was located. Companies incorporated in Northern Ireland should apply to the Royal Court of Justice in Belfast.

Application may be made by any person having an interest in the company including the Secretary of State, former directors or members, any creditor, former liquidator, persons with contractual arrangements with the company, managers or trustees of pension funds, etc.   s.1029(2)

Prior to restoration, it will be necessary to bring the company's statutory records up to date. This will normally involve the completion of all outstanding annual returns and the preparation of audited accounts as well as any changes in shareholdings, officers or other statutory details of the company to be filed.

Checklist

- Restoration to pursue personal injury claims may be made at any time.   s.1030(1)

- Except as noted below, in all other cases application must be made within six years of the date of dissolution of the company.   s.1030(4)

- The exception is where a company was dissolved under ss. 1000 or 1001 and an application for administrative restoration under s. 1024 has been rejected. In such circumstances, an application to court must be made within 28 days of the notice of the decision by the Registrar to reject the application under s. 1024.   s.1030(5)

Procedure

▶ The restoration process requires an application to the court and accordingly the services of a solicitor are required. In the circumstances, the procedure is not detailed here.

Filing requirement

▶ All necessary forms, annual returns and accounts to bring the company's records up to date.

▶ Late filing penalties as appropriate.

Notes

▶ In addition to the restoration fee payable to the Registrar of Companies (currently £100), the company will also be required to pay the legal costs of the Registrar (currently between £250 and £300) and the penalties for late submission of accounts, as appropriate. Where late filing penalties are levied in respect of accounts required to be filed prior to restoration, these are at the minimum statutory penalty rate.

▶ In practice, restoration is often required where a company has been dissolved by the Registrar (for failure to file returns and/or accounts) or at the request of the directors/shareholders and it is subsequently found that the company has valuable assets. In these circumstances, it is necessary for the company to be restored to the Register for the assets to be reclaimed, as the assets of a dissolved company automatically attach to the Crown. It is becoming increasingly common for a company with assets to be dissolved as a result of oversight on the part of directors: either neglect in filing statutory documents, or requesting the Registrar to strike off the company without properly checking that the company has no assets. For example, particular care should be taken when requesting the dissolution of a subsidiary that the legal ownership of property has passed to its holding company or fellow subsidiary. It is not uncommon for the appropriate book entries to be made, for example, transferring the lease of a property to another group company without ensuring that the legal transfer of title is also effected.

▶ Occasionally, a company that has been dissolved will be found to have a large outstanding creditor. In such circumstances, the creditor may apply to the court to have the company restored to the Register at the company's cost, to enable him or her to pursue the claim.

More information

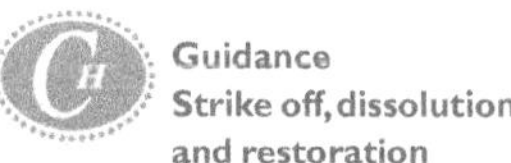

Rights issue

A rights issue is an issue of shares to the existing shareholders *pro rata* to their existing holdings.

Rights issues are used by companies to obtain additional funding from the company's shareholders rather than obtaining working capital by borrowing from banks or other financial institutions.

Checklist

▶ Check the articles to ensure there is no restriction on the maximum number of shares that may be issued. If not, it will be necessary to increase or remove that restriction (see page 37).

▶ Check the articles of association to ensure the directors have authority in terms of ss. 550 or 551 to issue shares. If not, a resolution to renew the authority will be required (see page 37).

▶ If the company has overseas shareholders, it may be necessary to exclude them from the rights issue due to securities legislation in their country, in which case the company must have sufficient waiver of pre-emption rights in terms of ss. 567–571.

▶ If the rights issue is to be made by way of renounceable letters of allotment, the articles of association must be checked to ensure that no pre-emption rights on allotment are infringed.

Procedure

▶ Convene a directors' meeting to approve resolutions declaring the rights issue and resolve to issue the provisional allotment letters to the company's shareholders. Ensure valid quorum is present.

▶ If it is intended that the existing members may renounce their entitlement to third parties, these letters include letters of renunciation.

▶ Once the closing date for the acceptance of the allotment letters has been reached, the directors will meet to allot those shares taken up.

▶ The company secretary should ensure that appropriate share certificates are prepared and issued to the shareholders and that form SH01 is filed with the Registrar of Companies within 15 days. **s.555**

▶ The company secretary should ensure that the register of members is written up to reflect the issue of shares.

Filing requirement

▶ Form SH01.

▶ Copies of any ordinary and special resolutions, as necessary. **s.30**

More information

Sensitive words

Certain words and phrases ('sensitive' words) require the consent of the Secretary of State for the Department for Business, Energy and Industrial Strategy before their use is allowed in a company name. Alternatively, the Secretary of State may require that appropriate authority be obtained from a relevant body. The schedule of sensitive words was reviewed and substantially reduced, with the new regime coming into effect from 31 January 2015.

ss. 54, 55

SI 2014/3140

The sensitive words that require the consent of the Secretary of State for Business, Innovation and Skills are:

▶ words that imply pre-eminence or a particular status or function;

▶ words that imply a connection with the UK Government, a devolved administration, local authority or specified public authorities;

▶ words that represent regulated activities; and

▶ words whose use could be an offence.

For a company to use one or more of these sensitive words in its name, the use must be justified.

The Registrar of Companies has issued guidelines giving details of the criteria to be used, and these are set out below. It should be noted, however, that these are not definitive criteria and in every case the decision on whether or not to allow a particular name to be used will rest with the Secretary of State for the Department for Business, Energy and Industrial Strategy.

Guidance GP1

Checklist

▶ **Words and expressions specified for the purposes of sections 55(1) and 1194(1) of the 2006 Act:** Accredit, Accreditation, Accredited, Accrediting, Adjudicator, Association, Assurance, Assurer, Audit office, Auditor General, *Banc, Bank, Banking, Benevolent, *Breatainn, *Breatannach, *Brenhiniaeth, *Brenhinol, *Brenin, Britain, British, Chamber of commerce, Charitable, Charity, Charter, Chartered, Child maintenance, Child support, *Coimisean, *Comhairle, *Comisiwn, Commission, Co-operative, Council, *Cyngor, Dental, Dentistry, *Diùc, *Dug, Duke, Ei Fawrhydi, England, English, Federation, Foundation, Friendly Society, Fund, Government,

*Gwasanaeth iechyd, Health centre, Health service, Health visitor,
His Majesty, HPSS, HSC, Inspectorate, Institute, Institution, Insurance,
Insurer, Judicial appointment, King, Licensing, *Llywodraeth, Medical
centre, Midwife, Midwifery, *Mòrachd, Mutual, NHS, Northern Ireland,
Northern Irish, Nurse, Nursing, Oifis sgrùdaidh, *Oilthigh, Ombudsman,
*Ombwdsmon, *Parlamaid, Parliament, Parliamentarian, Parliamentary,
Patent, Patentee, Police, Polytechnic, Post office, *Prifysgol, Prince,
*Prionnsa, *Prydain, *Prydeinig, Queen, Reassurance, Reassurer, Registrar,
Regulator, Reinsurance, Reinsurer, *Riaghaltas, *Rìgh, Rìoghachd Aonaichte,
Rìoghail, Rìoghalachd, Royal, Royalty, Scotland, Scottish, Senedd, Sheffield,
Siambr fasnach, Social service, Society, Special school, Standards, Stock
exchange, Swyddfa archwilio, *Teyrnas Gyfunol, *Teyrnas Unedig, Trade
union, Tribunal, Trust, *Tywysog, Underwrite, Underwriting, University,
Wales, Welsh, Windsor.

▶ **Words and expressions specified for the purposes of section 55(1)
of the 2006 Act:** Alba, Albannach, *Cymraeg, *Cymreig, *Cymru, Na h-Alba.

▶ **List of government departments and other bodies whose views must
be sought**

Part 1: Applications where situation of registered office or principal place
of business is irrelevant

*Word or expression
specified under
regulation 3*

*Specified government department or other body
whose view must be sought*

Accredit	Department for Business, Energy and Industrial Strategy
Accreditation	Department for Business, Energy and Industrial Strategy
Accredited	Department for Business, Energy and Industrial Strategy
Accrediting	Department for Business, Energy and Industrial Strategy
Assurance	Financial Conduct Authority
Assurer	Financial Conduct Authority
Banc	Financial Conduct Authority
Bank	Financial Conduct Authority
Banking	Financial Conduct Authority
Brenhiniaeth	The Welsh Assembly Government
Brenhinol	The Welsh Assembly Government
Brenin	The Welsh Assembly Government
Child maintenance	Department for Work and Pensions
Child support	Department for Work and Pensions
Dental	General Dental Council
Dentistry	General Dental Council
Diùc	The Scottish Government
Dug	The Welsh Assembly Government
Ei Fawrhydi	The Welsh Assembly Government
Friendly Society	Financial Conduct Authority
Fund	Financial Conduct Authority
Gwasanaeth iechyd	The Welsh Assembly Government
Health visitor	Nursing & Midwifery Council
HPSS	Department of Health, Social Services and Public Safety
HSC	Department of Health, Social Services and Public Safety

Word or expression specified under regulation 3	*Specified government department or other body whose view must be sought*
Insurance	Financial Conduct Authority
Insurer	Financial Conduct Authority
Judicial appointment	Ministry of Justice
Llywodraeth	The Welsh Assembly Government
Medical centre	Department of Health, Social Services and Public Safety
Midwife	Nursing & Midwifery Council
Midwifery	Nursing & Midwifery Council
Mòrachd	The Scottish Government
Mutual	Financial Conduct Authority
NHS	Department of Health
Nurse	Nursing & Midwifery Council
Nursing	Nursing & Midwifery Council
Oifis sgrùdaidh	Audit Scotland
Oilthigh	The Scottish Government
Parlamaid	The Scottish Parliamentary Corporate Body
Parliament	The Corporate Officer of the House of Lords and the Corporate Officer of the House of Commons
Parliamentarian	The Corporate Officer of the House of Lords and the Corporate Officer of the House of Commons
Parliamentary	The Corporate Officer of the House of Lords and the Corporate Officer of the House of Commons
Patent	The Patent Office
Patentee	The Patent Office
Polytechnic	Department for Business, Energy and Industrial Strategy
Prifysgol	The Welsh Assembly Government
Prionnsa	The Scottish Government
Reassurance	Financial Conduct Authority
Reassurer	Financial Conduct Authority
Reinsurance	Financial Conduct Authority
Reinsurer	Financial Conduct Authority
Riaghaltas	The Scottish Government
Rìgh	The Scottish Government
Rìoghail	The Scottish Government
Rìoghalachd	The Scottish Government
Senedd	The National Assembly for Wales
Sheffield	The Company of Cutlers in Hallamshire
Swyddfa archwilio	Auditor General for Wales
Tywysog	The Welsh Assembly Government
Underwrite	Financial Conduct Authority
Underwriting	Financial Conduct Authority

▶ **Applications where situation of registered office or principal place of business is relevant**

Word or expression specified under regulation 3	Specified government department or other body whose view must be sought under regulation			
	6(a)	6(b)	6(c)	6(d)
Audit office	Comptroller & Auditor General	Auditor General for Wales	Audit Scotland	Audit Office Northern Ireland
Charitable Charity	The Charity Commission	The Charity Commission	Office of the Scottish Charity Regulator	The Charity Commission
Duke His Majesty King Prince Queen Royal Royalty	Ministry of Justice	The Welsh Assembly Government	The Scottish Government	Ministry of Justice
Health centre Health service	Department of Health	The Welsh Assembly Government	The Scottish Government	Department of Health, Social Services and Public Safety
Police	The Home Office	The Home Office	The Scottish Government	Department of Justice in Northern Ireland
Special school	Department for Education	The Welsh Assembly Government	The Scottish Government	Department for Education
University	Department for Business, Innovation and Skills	The Welsh Assembly Government	The Scottish Government	Department for Employment and Learning

Procedure

▶ Where any word or phrase requires the consent of the Secretary of State or from a relevant body, advice should be sought from Companies House as to the form of the authority required. Companies House guidance 'Incorporation and names' sets out details of the relevant body that must provide approval and an overview of the circumstances in which approval will be given.

Filing requirement

None.

Notes

None.

More information

 Chapter 4, Appendix    Chapter 1    Guidance
Incorporation and names

Share certificate – duplicates

Share certificates are evidence of title and so care must be taken when issuing duplicate certificates.

Checklist

▶ Check that there is no difference between the identity of the registered shareholder and the person requesting the duplicate.

Procedure

In the event of a shareholder losing his or her share certificate, the following procedure should be carried out.

▶ The shareholder should be sent a form of indemnity in respect of the issue of a duplicate certificate. This is to protect the company should the original share certificate fall into the wrong hands and an attempt be made to transfer the shares fraudulently.

▶ The form of indemnity should be signed by the shareholder and, for most quoted public limited companies, it will be necessary for the indemnity to be guaranteed by a bank or insurance company.

▶ On receipt by the company of a completed indemnity form, a duplicate share certificate should be prepared and issued to the shareholder.

▶ If the original share certificate is found, it should be returned to the company and cancelled.

Filing requirement

None.

Notes

None.

More information

H Chapter 18   CSP Chapter 5

Shareholders – probate

Where a shareholder dies, the shares form part of their estate; their executors can give valid instructions in respect of those shares. In circumstances where the deceased shareholder left a will, the executors will apply for a grant of probate which gives them the authority to deal with the deceased's affairs. A company should accept for registration any grant of probate for confirmation, or a properly validated copy, provided that it bears the court seal. If there is no will, the document will be Letters of Administration.

Checklist

▶ A careful check must be made to ensure that the details shown on the grant of probate correspond with the entry in the register of members. If there is any doubt as to whether the deceased is indeed a shareholder of the company, then the company should obtain a declaration of identity from the executors. This will usually be given by the solicitors acting for the estate, although the deceased's bankers can also give a declaration of identity.

s.774

Procedure

▶ The date of death and the date of registration of the probate, together with the name(s) and address(es) of the executor(s), should be noted in the register of members and the register should be amended to show the word 'deceased' after the shareholder's name. The postal address for correspondence should be amended to that of the executor and should be addressed to the 'Executor of [shareholder's name] deceased'.

▶ The share certificates should be endorsed with the fact and date of death, the date of registration of probate and the name(s) and address(es) of the executor(s). The endorsement should be validated with the company's security seal.

▶ The company's security seal should be impressed on the probate, and this probate, together with the amended share certificate, should be returned to the person who lodged them. A new dividend mandate form may also be enclosed, as any existing mandate will have been revoked on the death of the shareholder.

Filing requirement

None.

Notes

▶ The company may request that the executor(s) transfer the shares to themselves, as this simplifies further requests and the need to validate instructions no longer applies. This transfer may, however, invoke the pre-emption provisions contained in the articles of association.

More information

 Chapter 18  Chapter 6

Shares – application and allotment

Checklist

▶ Prior to any allotment of shares, the directors should ensure that they **ss.550,551**
have sufficient authority to allot shares and that the statutory pre-
emption provisions on the allotment of shares or, if different, any **s.561**
provisions contained in the company's articles of association are not
infringed or, to the extent that they are, that the necessary waivers
have been received from the members, either in writing or in general
meeting.

▶ If the company's articles restrict the aggregate number of issued
shares, it will be necessary to convene a general meeting or circulate
a written resolution in the case of a private company to remove the
restriction to increase the directors' authority to allot shares and to
waive any pre-emption rights as necessary (see below).

Procedure

▶ A form of application should be made available for those persons
wishing to subscribe for shares. Private companies must take care **s.112**
when drafting an application letter to ensure that it is not regarded
as an invitation to the public to subscribe for shares. Only public
companies can issue shares to the public. **ss.755,756**

▶ Those persons wishing to subscribe for the shares will complete
the application form and return this to the company together with a
cheque in full or part payment for the shares, as appropriate.

▶ Once the application forms and remittances have been received, the **s.554**
remittance cheques should be banked as soon as possible.

▶ Convene a directors' meeting to approve the applications, issue
of shares, issue of share certificates and updating of the register of
members. Ensure valid quorum is present.

▶ As soon as possible, share certificates should be issued to the **s.769**
applicants, and in any event not more than two months from the date
of allotment.

▶ Companies whose shares are publicly traded may have their shares held in uncertificated form in CREST.

▶ Within one month of the date of allotment, a return of allotments (form SH01) should be filed with the Registrar of Companies.   **s.555**

▶ If the shares are all fully paid, it will not be necessary for them to have distinguishing numbers.

Filing requirement

▶ Form SH01 within one month.

Notes

▶ Under certain circumstances, fully paid and partly paid shares of the same class may be regarded as two different classes of shares.

More information

Chapter 18

Chapter 2

Shares – consolidation

Occasionally, it will be necessary to consolidate the share capital of
the company into shares of a greater nominal value. For instance, a
consolidation of 4,000 25p shares into £1.00 shares will result in the
authorised share capital being 1,000 shares of £1.00 each.

s.618

Occasionally, a quoted public limited company will consolidate its shares
into shares of a higher nominal value where the shares have a very low
market price. The consolidation of the shares will effectively increase the
market price and make it easier to trade in the shares.

Alternatively, consolidation of shares will be used in capital reconstruction
or capital reduction schemes. For instance, a company may decide to
reduce its capital from £1.00 shares to 50p shares and then consolidate
the shares into £1.00 shares, thus achieving a 50% capital reduction while
retaining a nominal value of £1.00 for the shares.

Procedure

▶ Convene a directors' meeting to recommend an appropriate ordinary
resolution to members and to convene a general meeting or circulate
a written resolution in the case of a private company. Ensure valid
quorum is present.

s.302

▶ Issue notice, signed by director or company secretary, on 14 clear
days' notice for members to consider resolution.

s.307

▶ Enclose with the notice a form of proxy if desired.

▶ If the meeting is to be convened on short notice, the company
secretary should arrange for agreement to short notice to be signed
by each of the shareholders.

s.307(5)

▶ Hold general meeting. Ensure valid quorum is present. Resolution
put to vote either by show of hands or by poll and to be passed by
appropriate majority (ordinary resolution by 50% majority).

▶ File copy of resolution and form SH02 at Companies House.

ss.30,619

▶ The register of members will require amendment to show details of
the new number of shares and nominal value of the shares currently
held, and any distinguishing numbers will require reallocation.

▶ If there are any fractions of shares arising on the consolidation, these should be sold for the benefit of the members concerned or, alternatively, occasionally new shares can be issued, credited as fully paid, to round their holding up to the nearest whole number.

▶ All existing share certificates should be recalled, either for amendment or cancellation, and new share certificates should be issued.

Filing requirement

▶ Form SH02 within one month.

Notes

None.

More information

 Chapter 12    Chapter 2

Shares – convertible

As the name implies, these are shares that can be converted from one class to another, either at some specific time in the future, on the occurrence of a specific event or at the option of the company or the shareholder.

ss. 549, 550, 551

Convertible shares will often be issued so that the company can attract additional funds, with the shares being issued with enhanced dividend rights. After a period of time, the shares would be converted to ordinary shares, thus reducing the dividends payable by the company.

The issue of convertible shares is similar to loans to the company, but with repayment of the loan at the end of its term being replaced by conversion to ordinary shares.

Checklist

The following points should be considered when convertible shares are being created:

▶ whether the shares could carry pre-emption rights on allotment or transfer;

▶ the amount, if any, of dividend and whether this should be preferential;

▶ whether the shares should carry voting rights;

▶ whether the shares should carry a preferential right to the return of capital on any winding up or distribution and whether the shares should participate in any surplus;

▶ the terms of conversion, including whether conversion should be at the option of the company, the shareholder or both, or at predetermined dates, and the basis of conversion to ordinary shares;

▶ creation of the shares will require alterations to the articles of association and must be authorised by the shareholders by ordinary and special resolutions at a general meeting or by written resolution in the case of a private company; and

▶ once the shares have been created, any further changes to the articles of association may require approval of the holders of the convertible shares at a separate class meeting, whether or not they are voting shares.

Procedure

▶ The procedure to be followed on conversion of the shares is the same as that to be followed on the conversion of convertible loan stock (see page 148).

Filing requirement

▶ Form SH01 on issue of shares.

Notes

None.

More information

 Chapters 12 and 13    Chapter 2

Shares – cumulative

The dividend payable on such shares is 'cumulative' – that is, any dividend not paid on the shares in one year will be accumulated and paid in succeeding years.

As dividends can be paid only out of distributable profits available for the purpose, the dividend may not be paid in a particular year as the company has insufficient distributable profit. In these circumstances, the unpaid dividend will accumulate until such time as the company has sufficient distributable profit to pay a dividend and any arrears to date.

It would be unusual for cumulative shares not to have a fixed dividend, as the directors would only declare a discretionary dividend in circumstances where the company has profits available for distribution.

Checklist

The following points should be considered when cumulative shares are being created:

▶ whether the shares should carry pre-emption rights on allotment or transfer;

▶ whether the shares will have a preferential right to the return of capital and whether this should be limited to the amounts paid up or credited as paid up on the shares, or whether they should participate in any surplus;

▶ whether the shares should be voting shares;

▶ the amount of the fixed dividend and any preferential payment terms, i.e. before or after any dividend to be declared on any other class of shares;

▶ the creation of the shares will require alterations to the articles of association of the company. If the shares are to be created after the incorporation of the company, the creation of the shares will require the consent of the shareholders by ordinary and special resolutions at a general meeting or by written resolution in the case of a private company;

▶ any subsequent alteration to the articles may also require approval of the holders of any cumulative shares if the alteration changes their class rights. This approval will be required at a separate class meeting and is required even where the particular class of shares are non-voting; and

▶ whether or not the shares should be redeemable or convertible at some future date.

Procedure

None.

Filing requirement

None.

Notes

None.

More information

 Chapter 12    Chapter 7

Shares – redeemable

A limited company having a share capital may, if authorised by its articles of association, issue shares that are redeemable or that are liable to be redeemed at the option of the company or the shareholder. The articles of a public company must include specific authority for the issue of redeemable shares.

s. 684

s. 684(3)

Checklist

▶ At the time of issue of redeemable shares, there must be in issue shares that are not redeemable. This is to ensure that the issued share capital of the company cannot all be redeemed, leaving the company with no shareholders.

s. 684(4)

▶ Redeemable shares can only be redeemed if they are fully paid.

s. 686(1)

▶ The terms of redemption may provide for payment in cash on a date later than redemption, failing which they must be paid for on redemption.

s. 686(2), (3)

▶ Public companies may only redeem shares out of the distributable profits or out of the proceeds of a fresh issue of shares made for that purpose. Under certain circumstances, private companies may redeem shares out of capital.

s. 687

▶ Redeemed shares are treated as cancelled on redemption, the amount of the issued share capital being reduced by the nominal value of the shares.

s. 688

Procedure

▶ The process for the redemption of shares is identical to that for purchase of shares by the company (see pages 188–193).

Filing requirement

▶ Form SH02 within one month.

Notes

None.

More information

 Chapter 14    Chapter 8

Shares – transfer

The transfer of shares in a company are governed by the provisions of the company's articles of association and ss. 770–782 of the Act.

Companies adopting either of the model articles will not have any restrictions on the transferability of shares; however, many private companies will adopt pre-emption provisions on the transfer of shares.

Public companies whose shares are publicly traded are not permitted to restrict the transfer of shares except in a few specified circumstances, such as transfers to more than four joint holders or transfer of shares over which the company has a lien.

Checklist

▶ Is the transferee a shareholder?

▶ Is the stock transfer form completed correctly and signed by the transferor? **s. 770(1)(a)**

▶ Is the form stamped or certified as exempt? **s. 770(1)(b)**

▶ Is the form accompanied by share certificates evidencing title to at least the number of shares being transferred?

Procedure

▶ The transferor should complete a stock transfer form giving details of the shares to be transferred, their own name and address as transferor, and the name and address of the transferee. The form should be signed by the transferor and, where the shares are partly paid, by the transferee.

▶ Prior to registration by the company, it will be necessary for the stock transfer form to be stamped by HM Revenue & Customs (see page 127) unless the transfer is exempt from duty and has been signed and certified on the reverse. Stamp duty is payable by the purchaser of the shares. Duty is due on transfers with a consideration of more than £1,000. The current rate for stamp duty is 0.5%, rounded up to the nearest £5, of the consideration paid or payable (whether or not the consideration is cash).

▶ The stamped stock transfer form, together with the original share certificate, should be forwarded to the company or its registrar (as appropriate) for registration.

▶ Upon receipt of a stock transfer form, the company should check that the details of the transferor are correct and that the share certificate is valid. If the original share certificate has been mislaid, it will be necessary for the transferor to complete an indemnity in respect of this lost certificate.

▶ Many private companies have detailed pre-emption provisions on the transfer of shares and care must be taken to ensure that these are followed. Alternatively, the pre-emption rights may be waived by the remaining shareholders.

▶ The transfer of shares requires approval from the board of directors, who should also authorise the issue of a share certificate to the transferee and of any balancing certificate to the transferor.

▶ Details of the transfer must be entered in the register of members.

▶ Transfers must be processed or rejected within two months of receipt. Where they are rejected, the reasons for refusal must be provided.

s.771(1)

Filing requirement

▶ Share transfers are not notified to Companies House; however, details of the transfers of shares in non-traded companies must be shown on the company's next confirmation statement.

s.856(3)(b)

More information

 Chapter 7    Chapter 10

Shares – transmission

Transmission is the process by which title to shares is transferred by operation of law rather than a sale or transfer by a shareholder. The most common form of transmission of shares is on the death of a shareholder.

Checklist

▶ Is the transferee a shareholder?

▶ Is the stock transfer form completed correctly and signed by the executor or personal representative?   **s.770(1)(a)**

▶ Is the form stamped or certified as exempt?   **s.770(1)(b)**

▶ Is the form accompanied by share certificates evidencing title to at least the number of shares being transferred?

Procedure

▶ A stock transfer form should be completed giving details of the shares to be transferred, the name and address of the registered holder as transferor and the name and address of the transferee. The form should be signed by the person lodging the form together with documentary evidence of their authority, such as a grant of probate.

▶ Prior to registration by the company, it will be necessary for the stock transfer form to be stamped by HM Revenue & Customs (see page 127), unless the transfer is exempt from duty and has been signed and certified on the reverse. Most transmissions of shares are not liable to stamp duty and the form should be certified accordingly.

▶ The stamped stock transfer form, together with the original share certificate, should be forwarded to the company or its registrar (as appropriate) for registration.

▶ Upon receipt of a stock transfer form, the company should check that the details of the transferor are correct and that the share certificate is valid. If the original share certificate has been mislaid, it will be necessary for the transferor to complete an indemnity in respect of this lost certificate.

▶ Many private companies have detailed pre-emption provisions on the transfer of shares and care must be taken to ensure that these are followed. Alternatively, the pre-emption rights may be waived by the remaining shareholders.

▶ The transfer of shares requires approval from the board of directors, who should also authorise the issue of a share certificate to the transferee and of any balancing certificate to the transferor.

▶ Details of the transfer must be entered in the register of members.

▶ Transfers must be processed or rejected within two months of receipt.

▶ Where they are rejected, the reasons for refusal must be provided.

Filing requirement

▶ Share transfers are not notified to Companies House; however, details of the transfer of shares in non-traded companies must be shown on the company's next confirmation statement.

Notes

None.

More information

 Chapter 7    Chapter 10

Single alternative inspection location (SAIL) address

There are particular requirements with regard to the place where various statutory records or records are kept and where they may be inspected. As an alternative to the registered office address, companies can choose to keep and make available for inspection some or all of the records and registers at a single alternative inspection location, also referred to as the SAIL address.

Checklist

▶ Any, or all, of the registers or documents that must be kept available for inspection by members or the public may be kept at the SAIL address (see page 141).

▶ There can only be one alternative inspection address, and this must be in the same part of the United Kingdom in which the company is registered.

▶ Ensure that there are adequate processes in place at the SAIL address to facilitate the upkeep and inspection of the registers.

Procedure

▶ The directors should formally agree the transfer of register(s) to the SAIL address or their return to the registered office.

▶ Notify Companies House using forms AD02, AD03 and AD04 as appropriate.

▶ Transfer relevant records to SAIL address.

Filing requirement

▶ Forms AD02, AD03 and AD04 as appropriate.

Notes

▶ For companies using the services of a share registrar due to the requirement that there can only be one SAIL address and that will be the address where the register of members can be inspected, the remaining registers will need to be located at the registered office.

More information

 Chapter 7    Chapter 10    Guidance booklet GP3

Statutory forms and filing periods

Type	Description	CA2006 section(s)	Form code	Filing period	Web filing available
Accounts					
	Change of accounting reference date	392	AA01	Effective on registration	Yes
	Dormant company accounts (DCA)	441	AA02	9 months	Yes
	Notice of resolution removing auditors from office	512	AA03	14 days	
	Statement of guarantee by a parent undertaking of a subsidiary company	394A, 448A, 479A	AA06	On submission of unaudited subsidiary accounts	
Change of constitution					
	Notice of restriction on the company's articles	23	CC01	Effective on registration	
	Notice of removal of restriction on the company's articles	23	CC02	Effective on registration	
	Statement of compliance where amendment of articles restricted	24	CC03	Effective on registration	
	Statement of company's objects	31	CC04	Effective on registration	
	Change of constitution by enactment	34	CC05	Effective on registration	
	Change of constitution by order of court or other authority	35	CC06	Effective on registration	

Type	Description	CA2006 section(s)		Filing period	Web filing available
Change of name					
	Exemption from requirement as to use of 'limited' or 'cyfyngedig' on change of name	60	NE01	On application	
	Notice of change of name by resolution	78	NM01	On application	Yes
	Notice of change of name by conditional resolution	78	NM02	On application	
	Notice confirming satisfaction of the conditional resolution for change of name	78	NM03	On application	
	Notice of change of name by means provided for in the articles	79	NM04	On application	
	Notice of change of name by resolution of directors	64 or 1033	NM05	On application	
	Request to seek comments of government department or other specified body on change of name	56	NM06	On application	
Change of registered office					
	Change of registered office address	87	AD01	Effective on registration	Yes
	Notice to change the situation of an England and Wales company or a Welsh company	88	AD05	Effective on registration	
Company records					
	Notification of single alternative inspection location (SAIL)	114. 162, 228, 237, 275, 358, 702, 805, 809, 877, 859Q, 892	AD02	Effective on registration	Yes

Type	Description	CA2006 section(s)		Filing period	Web filing available
	Change of location of the company records to the single alternative inspection location (SAIL)	114, 128D, 162, 228, 237, 275, 358, 702, 720, 743, 790N, 790Z, 805, 809, 859Q, 877, 892	AD03	Effective on registration	Yes
	Change of location of the company records to the registered office	114, 128D, 162, 228, 237, 275, 358, 702, 720, 743, 790N, 790Z, 805, 809, 859Q, 877, 892	AD04	Effective on registration	Yes
	Election to keep information from register of directors on the central (public) register	167A	EH01	Effective on registration	Yes
	Election to keep information from register of directors on the central (public) register	167A	EH02	Effective on registration	Yes
	Election to keep information from register of directors on the central (public) register	279A	EH03	Effective on registration	Yes
	Election to keep information from register of people with significant control (PSC) on the central (public) register	790X	EH04	Effective on registration	Yes
	Election to keep information from register of members on the central (public) register	128B	EH05	Effective on registration	Yes
	Update to members' information held on the central (public) register	128E	EH06	As soon as possible once obligation to notify commences	

Type	Description	CA2006 section(s)	Form code	Filing period	Web filing available
	Withdrawal of election to keep information from register of directors on the central (public) register	167E	EW01	Effective on registration	Yes
	Withdrawal of election to keep information from register of directors' usual residential addresses on the central (public) register	167E	EW02	Effective on registration	Yes
	Withdrawal of election to keep information from register of secretaries on the central (public) register	279E	EW03	Effective on registration	Yes
	Withdrawal of election to keep information from register of people with significant control (PSC) on the central (public) register	790ZD	EW04	Effective on registration	Yes
	Withdrawal of election to keep members' information on the central (public) register	128J	EW05	Effective on registration	Yes
Confirmation statement					
	Confirmation statement	853A	CS01	14 days	Yes
Directors and secretaries					
	Appointment of director	167, 167D	AP01	14 days	Yes
	Appointment of corporate director	167, 167D	AP02	14 days	Yes
	Appointment of secretary	276, 279D	AP03	14 days	Yes
	Appointment of corporate secretary	276, 279D	AP04	14 days	Yes
	Change of director's details	167, 167D	CH01	14 days	Yes
	Change of corporate director's details	167, 167D	CH02	14 days	Yes
	Change of secretary's details	276, 279D	CH03	14 days	Yes

Type	Description	CA2006 section(s)	Form code	Filing period	Web filing available
	Change of corporate secretary's details	276	CH04	14 days	Yes
	Termination of appointment of director	167, 167D	TM01	14 days	Yes
	Termination of appointment of secretary	276, 279D	TM02	14 days	Yes
Incorporation					
	Application to register a company	9	IN01	On application	Yes
Investment companies					
	Notice of intention to carry on business as an investment company	833(1)	IC01	Effective on registration	
	Notice that a company no longer wishes to be an investment company	833(4)	IC02	Effective on registration	
Mortgage					
	Particulars of an instrument of alteration to a floating charge created by a company registered in Scotland	ss. 410, 466 CA1985	466 (Scot)	21 days	
	Particulars of a charge	859A, 859J	MR01	21 days	Yes
	Particulars of a charge subject to which property or undertaking has been acquired	859C, 859J	MR02	Effective on registration	Yes
	Particulars for the registration of a charge to secure a series of debentures	859B, 859J	MR03	21 days	
	Statement of satisfaction in full or in part of a charge	859L	MR04	Effective on registration	Yes
	Statement that part or the whole of the property charged (a) has been released from the charge, (b) no longer forms part of the company's property or undertaking	859L	MR05	Effective on registration	

Type	Description	CA2006 section(s)	Form code	Filing period	Web filing available
	Statement of company acting as a trustee	859J	MR06	Effective on registration	
	Particulars of alteration of a charge (particulars of a negative pledge)	859O	MR07	Effective on registration	
	Particulars of a charge where there is no instrument	859A, 859J	MR08	21 days	
	Particulars of a charge subject to which property or undertaking has been acquired where there is no instrument	859C, 859J	MR09	Effective on registration	
	Particulars for the registration of a charge to secure a series of debentures where there is no instrument	859B, 859J	MR10	21 days	
Opening of overseas branch register					
	Notice of opening of overseas branch register	130	AD06	Effective on registration	
	Notice of discontinuance of overseas branch register	135	AD07	Effective on registration	
Other appointments					
	Appointment of a manager under s. 47 of the Companies (Audit, Investigations and Community Enterprise) Act 2004 or receiver and manager under s. 18 of the Charities Act 1993 or judicial factor (Scotland)	1154	AP05	14 days	
	Change of service address for manager appointed under s. 47 of the Companies (Audit, Investigations and Community Enterprise) Act 2004 or receiver and manager under s. 18 of the Charities Act 1993 or judicial factor (Scotland)	1154	CH05	14 days	

Type	Description	CA2006 section(s)	Form code	Filing period	Web filing available
	Termination of appointment of manager under s. 47 of the Companies (Audit, Investigations and Community Enterprise) Act 2004 or receiver and manager under s. 18 of the Charities Act 1993 or judicial factor (Scotland)	1154	TM03	14 days	
People with significant control (PSC)					
	Notice of individual person with significant control (PSC)	790K, 790ZA	PSC01	As soon as possible once obligation to notify arises	Yes
	Notice of relevant legal entity (RLE) with significant control	790K, 790ZA	PSC02	As soon as possible once obligation to notify arises	Yes
	Notice of other registrable person (ORP) with significant control	790K, 790ZA	PSC03	As soon as possible once obligation to notify arises	Yes
	Change of details of individual person with significant control (PSC)	790M, 790ZA	PSC04	As soon as possible once obligation to notify arises	Yes
	Change of details of relevant legal entity (RLE) with significant control	790M, 790ZA	PSC05	As soon as possible once obligation to notify arises	Yes
	Change of details of other registrable person (ORP) with significant control	790M, 790ZA	PSC06	As soon as possible once obligation to notify arises	Yes

Type	Description	CA2006 section(s)	Form code	Filing period	Web filing available
	Notice of ceasing to be an individual person with significant control (PSC), relevant legal entity (RLE), or other registrable person (ORP)	790M, 790ZA	PSC07	As soon as possible once obligation to notify arises	Yes
	Notification of PSC statements	790M, 790ZA	PSC08	As soon as possible once obligation to notify arises	Yes
	Update to PSC statements	790M, 790ZA	PSC09	As soon as possible once obligation to notify arises	
Receiver/Manager					
	Notice of appointment of an administrative receiver, receiver or manager	859K	RM01	7 days	
	Notice of ceasing to act as an administrative receiver, receiver or manager	859K	RM02	Effective on registration	
Registrar's powers					
	Replacement of document not meeting requirements for proper delivery	1076	RP01	As specified in request from Companies House	
	Application for rectification by the Registrar of Companies	1095 and regs 4, 5 Registrar of Companies and Applications for Striking off Regulations 2009	RP02A	On application	

Type	Description	CA2006 section(s)	Form code	Filing period	Web filing available
	Application for rectification of a registered office or UK establishment address by the Registrar of Companies	1095 and regs 4, 5 Registrar of Companies and Applications for Striking off Regulations 2009	RP02B	On application	
	Notice of an objection to a request for the Registrar of Companies to rectify the Register	1095 and regs 4, 5 Registrar of Companies and Applications for Striking off Regulations 2009	RP03	Within 28 days of application	
	Second filing of a document previously delivered		RP04	Effective on registration	
	Application for removal of material about directors who have not consented to act	1095(4A) and regs 4, 5 Registrar of Companies and Applications for Striking off Regulations 2009	RP06	Effective on registration	
	Application to change a company's disputed registered office address	The Companies (Address of Registered Office) Regulations 2016	RP07	Effective on registration	
	Correction of a director's date of birth which was incorrectly stated on incorporation	167	RPCH01	Effective on registration	

Type	Description	CA2006 section(s)	Form code	Filing period	Web filing available
	Certified voluntary translation of an original document that is or has been delivered to the Registrar of Companies	1106, reg 4 Companies (Cross-Border Mergers) Regulations 2007	VT01	Effective on registration	
Re-registration					
	Application by a private company for re-registration as a public company	94, 765(4)	RR01	15 days	
	Application by a public company for re-registration as a private limited company	100	RR02	15 days	
	Notice by the company of application to the court for cancellation of resolution for re-registration	99(2)	RR03	15 days	
	Notice by the applicants of application to the court for cancellation of resolution for re-registration	99(1)	RR04	On application to court	
	Application by a private limited company for re-registration as an unlimited company	103	RR05	15 days	
	Application by an unlimited company for re-registration as a private limited company	106	RR06	15 days	
	Application by a public company for re-registration as a private unlimited company	110	RR07	15 days	
	Application by a public company for re-registration as a private limited company following a court order reducing capital	651	RR08	15 days	

Type	Description	CA2006 section(s)	Form code	Filing period	Web filing available
	Application by a public company for re-registration as a private company following cancellation of shares	664	RR09	15 days	
	Statement of capital	108	SH19	15 days	
Restoration					
	Application for administrative restoration to the register	1024	RT01	On application	
Share capital					
	Notice to non-assenting shareholders	984(3)	984	1 month, to shareholders only	
	Notice to non-assenting shareholders	980(1)	980(1)	Within 3 months after the last day the offer can be accepted, or 6 months after the date of the offer where not governed by the Takeover Code	
	Statutory declaration relating to a notice to non-assenting shareholders	980(4)(b)	980dec	When offeror gives notice under s. 979	
	Notice of application to court to cancel share warrants	s. 5(5), sch 4 SBEEA 2015	NAC01	On application	
	Return of allotment of shares	555	SH01	1 month	Yes
	Notice of consolidation, sub-division, redemption of shares or re-conversion of stock into shares	619, 621, 689	SH02	1 month	

Type	Description	CA2006 section(s)	Form code	Filing period	Web filing available
	Return of purchase of own shares	707	SH03	28 days	
	Notice of sale or transfer of treasury shares	728	SH04	28 days	
	Notice of cancellation of treasury shares	730	SH05	28 days	
	Notice of cancellation of shares	708	SH06	28 days	
	Notice of cancellation of shares held by or for a public company	663	SH07	1 month	
	Notice of name or other designation of class of shares	636	SH08	1 month	
	Return of allotment by unlimited company allotting a new class of shares	556	SH09	1 month	
	Notice of particulars of variation of rights attached to shares	637	SH10	1 month	
	Notice of new class of members	638	SH11	1 month	
	Notice of particulars of variation of class rights	640	SH12	1 month	
	Notice of name or other designation of class of members	639	SH13	1 month	
	Notice of re-denomination	625	SH14	1 month	
	Notice of reduction of capital following redenomination	627	SH15	15 days	
	Notice by the applicants of application to court for cancellation of the special resolution approving a redemption or purchase of shares out of capital	722(1)	SH16	On application to court	

Type	Description	CA2006 section(s)	Form code	Filing period	Web filing available
	Notice by the company of application to court for cancellation of the special resolution approving a redemption or purchase of shares out of capital	722(2)	SH17	On receipt of notice that an application has been made	
	Statement of capital for reduction supported by solvency statement or court order	644, 649	SH19	15 days	
	Statement of capital on cancellation of share warrants	s. 7(2), sch 4 SBEEA 2015	SH19	15 days	
	Application for trading certificate for a public company	761 & 762	SH50	On application	
Strike off and dissolution					
	Striking off application by a company	1003	DS01	On application	
	Withdrawal of striking-off application by a company	1010	DS02	On application	Yes

Statutory registers and records

The Companies Act requires the following registers to be kept by all companies:

▶ register of members;	**s.113**
▶ historic register of members;	**s.128D**
▶ register of charges – pre-6 April 2013 charges;	**s.876 or s.891**
▶ minute books of the proceedings of meetings of the shareholders and its directors, and of any sub-committees of the directors;	**ss.355,248**
▶ accounting records;	**s.386**
▶ register of directors;	**s.162**
▶ register of directors' usual residential addresses;	**s.165**
▶ copies of directors' service contracts or memorandum of terms;	**s.228**
▶ copies of any indemnity provisions for directors;	**s.237**
▶ register of secretaries;	**s.275**
▶ copies of contracts for market and off-market purchases of own shares;	**s.702**
▶ directors' and auditors' statements in relation to purchase of shares by a private company out of capital;	**s.720**
▶ although not required by the Act, if the company maintains a register of debenture holders, there are requirements laid down by the Act governing its maintenance and inspection;	**s.743**
▶ PSC Register;	**s.790M**
▶ historic PSC Register;	**s.790Z**
▶ reports into investigation of ownership of shares;	**s.805**
▶ if the company is a public company, register of interests in voting shares; and	**s.808**
▶ instruments creating charges.	**s.859Q**

Checklist

▶ Unless an election is made to use the central register to maintain the registers, where applicable, these must all be kept at the registered office or at an alternative place of inspection, details of which must be notified to Companies House on form AD02.

Procedure

None.

Notes

None.

Filing requirement

▶ Forms AD02, AD03 or AD04.

More information

 Chapter 7    Chapter 9

Treasury shares

Any company may acquire its own shares and hold these in treasury. Unlike the existing provisions relating to purchase of own shares (see page 188), shares purchased under the treasury shares provisions are not cancelled on purchase but may be retained, or sold.

s. 724 as amended by SI 2013/999

Checklist

▶ Will the shares be purchased out of distributable profit or the proceeds of a fresh issue or capital (private companies only)?

s. 724(2)

▶ Does the company have sufficient distributable profit?

s. 724(1)(b)

▶ Does the company have sufficient cash resources?

▶ Do the articles permit the purchase of its own shares by the company?

Procedure

▶ The general procedure for the purchase by a company of its own shares is set out on pages 188–193.

▶ Once the company has purchased the shares to be held in treasury, a return on form SH03 must be submitted to the Registrar, stating the number of shares and the class of shares, together with the nominal value of the shares and the date on which they were repurchased. The purchase of shares to be held in treasury by a company is subject to stamp duty, the duty being payable where the aggregate consideration exceeds £1,000 and not the nominal value at the rate of 0.5% (rounded up to the nearest £5).

s. 707

▶ If the shares are subsequently cancelled, sold or transferred, form SH04 or SH05 must be filed.

ss. 727, 728, 729

Filing requirement

▶ Copy of ordinary resolution.

▶ Form SH03.

▶ Form SH04 or SH05 within 28 days of cancellation, sale or transfer.

Notes

▶ Listed companies must comply with Chapter 13 of the Listing Rules.

▶ Shares held in treasury may be sold for cash, transferred to satisfy claims under employee share schemes or cancelled.   **s. 727**

▶ Shares held in treasury have no voting or dividend rights, but may take up rights in respect of bonus issues and may be redeemed if the shares are redeemable.   **s. 726**

▶ There is no maximum number of shares that a company can hold in treasury.   **s. 725(2), (3)**

More information

 Chapter 14    Chapter 8

Waiver of dividend

Occasionally, particularly with private family-owned companies, shareholders will elect to waive entitlement to receive dividends in respect of one or more financial years. This is commonly used where shares are held by a nominee to satisfy a minimum number of shareholder requirements in the articles and thus the nominee will elect not to receive dividends.

Checklist

▶ Waiver must pre-date date of declaration of dividend.

Procedure

▶ The shareholder will complete a formal letter of waiver under seal or witnessed and will lodge this with the company.

▶ Often waivers will be restricted to any dividends paid in respect of stated period rather than undated, as the waiver is irrevocable.

Filing requirement

None.

Notes

None.

More information

Chapter 9

Chapter 7

Appendix 1 – UK Corporate Governance Code

April 2016

Governance and the Code

1. The purpose of corporate governance is to facilitate effective, entrepreneurial and prudent management that can deliver the long-term success of the company.
2. The first version of the UK Corporate Governance Code (the Code) was produced in 1992 by the Cadbury Committee. Its paragraph 2.5 is still the classic definition of the context of the Code:

   Corporate governance is the system by which companies are directed and controlled. Boards of directors are responsible for the governance of their companies. The shareholders' role in governance is to appoint the directors and the auditors and to satisfy themselves that an appropriate governance structure is in place. The responsibilities of the board include setting the company's strategic aims, providing the leadership to put them into effect, supervising the management of the business and reporting to shareholders on their stewardship. The board's actions are subject to laws, regulations and the shareholders in general meeting.

3. Corporate governance is therefore about what the board of a company does and how it sets the values of the company. It is to be distinguished from the day to day operational management of the company by full-time executives.
4. The Code is a guide to a number of key components of effective board practice. It is based on the underlying principles of all good governance: accountability, transparency, probity and focus on the sustainable success of an entity over the longer term.
5. The Code has been enduring, but it is not immutable. Its fitness for purpose in a permanently changing economic and social business environment requires its evaluation at appropriate intervals.
6. The new Code applies to accounting periods beginning on or after 17 June 2016 and applies to all companies with a Premium listing of equity shares regardless of whether they are incorporated in the UK or elsewhere.

Preface

1. Over two decades of constructive usage of the Code have contributed to improved corporate governance in the UK. The Code is part of a framework of legislation, regulation and best practice standards which aims to deliver high quality corporate governance with in-built flexibility for companies to adapt their practices to take into account their particular circumstances. Similarly, investors must take the opportunity to consider carefully how companies have decided to implement the Code. There is always scope for improvement, both in terms of making sure that the Code remains relevant and improving the quality of reporting.

2. Boards must continue to think comprehensively about their overall tasks and the implications of these for the roles of their individual members. Absolutely key in these endeavours are the leadership of the chairman of a board, the support given to and by the CEO, and the frankness and openness of mind with which issues are discussed and tackled by all directors.

3. Essential to the effective functioning of any board is dialogue which is both constructive and challenging. The problems arising from 'groupthink' have been exposed in particular as a result of the financial crisis. One of the ways in which constructive debate can be encouraged is through having sufficient diversity on the board. This includes, but is not limited to, gender and race. Diverse board composition in these respects is not on its own a guarantee. Diversity is as much about differences of approach and experience, and it is very important in ensuring effective engagement with key stakeholders and in order to deliver the business strategy.

4. One of the key roles for the board includes establishing the culture, values and ethics of the company. It is important that the board sets the correct 'tone from the top'. The directors should lead by example and ensure that good standards of behaviour permeate throughout all levels of the organisation. This will help prevent misconduct, unethical practices and support the delivery of long-term success.

5. This update of the Code has been driven by the consequential changes required from the implementation of the European Union's Audit Regulation and Directive. Section C.3 on Audit Committees was reviewed to ensure it remained consistent and changes have only been made when necessary. It is important that companies view these changes alongside the revised Guidance on Audit Committees.

6. Following the 2014 Code amendments, which focussed on the provision by companies of information about the risks which affect longer term viability, the FRC will continue to monitor compliance with these changes. Companies should be presenting information to give a clearer and broader view of solvency, liquidity, risk management and viability. For their part, investors should assess these statements thoroughly and engage accordingly.

7. To run a corporate board successfully should not be underrated. Constraints on time and knowledge combine with the need to maintain mutual respect and openness between a cast of strong, able and busy directors dealing with each other across the different demands of executive and non-executive roles. To achieve good governance requires continuing and high quality effort.

8. Chairmen are encouraged to report personally in their annual statements how the principles relating to the role and effectiveness of the board (in Sections A and B of the Code) have been applied. Not only will this give investors a clearer picture of the steps taken by boards to operate effectively but also, by providing fuller context, it may make investors more willing to accept explanations when a company chooses to explain rather than to comply with one or more provisions.

9. While in law the company is primarily accountable to its shareholders, and the relationship between the company and its shareholders is also the main focus of the Code, companies are encouraged to recognise the contribution made by other providers of capital and to confirm the board's interest in listening to the views of such providers insofar as these are relevant to the company's overall approach to governance.

Financial Reporting Council
April 2016

Comply or Explain

1. The 'comply or explain' approach is the trademark of corporate governance in the UK. It has been in operation since the Code's beginnings and is the foundation of its flexibility. It is strongly supported by both companies and shareholders and has been widely admired and imitated internationally.

2. The Code is not a rigid set of rules. It consists of principles (main and supporting) and provisions. The Listing Rules require companies to apply the Main Principles and report to shareholders on how they have done so. The principles are the core of the Code and the way in which they are applied should be the central question for a board as it determines how it is to operate according to the Code.

3. It is recognised that an alternative to following a provision may be justified in particular circumstances if good governance can be achieved by other means. A condition of doing so is that the reasons for it should be explained clearly and carefully to shareholders,[1] who may wish to discuss the position with the company and whose voting intentions may be influenced as a result. In providing an explanation, the company should aim to illustrate how its actual practices are consistent with the principle to which the particular provision relates, contribute to good governance and promote delivery of business objectives. It should set out the background, provide a clear rationale for the action it is taking, and describe any mitigating actions taken to address any additional risk and maintain conformity with the relevant principle. Where deviation from a particular provision is intended to be limited in time, the explanation should indicate when the company expects to conform with the provision.

4. In their responses to explanations, shareholders should pay due regard to companies' individual circumstances and bear in mind in particular the size and complexity of the company and the nature of the risks and challenges it faces. While shareholders have every right to challenge companies' explanations if they are unconvincing, they should not be evaluated in a mechanistic way and departures from the Code should not be automatically treated as breaches. Shareholders should be careful to respond to the statements from companies in a manner that supports the 'comply or explain' process and bearing in mind the purpose of good corporate governance. They should put their views to the company and both parties should be prepared to discuss the position.

5. Smaller listed companies, in particular those new to listing, may judge that some of the provisions are disproportionate or less relevant in their case. Some of the provisions do not apply to companies below the FTSE 350. Such companies may nonetheless consider that it would be appropriate to adopt the approach in the Code and they are encouraged to do so. Externally managed investment companies typically have a different board structure which may affect the relevance of particular provisions; the Association of Investment Companies' Corporate Governance Code and Guide can assist them in meeting their obligations under the Code.

6. Satisfactory engagement between company boards and investors is crucial to the health of the UK's corporate governance regime. Companies and shareholders both have responsibility for ensuring that 'comply or explain' remains an effective alternative to a rules-based system. There are practical and administrative obstacles to improved interaction between boards and shareholders. But certainly there is also scope for an increase in trust which could generate a virtuous upward spiral in attitudes to the Code and in its constructive use.

The Main Principles of the Code

Section A: Leadership

Every company should be headed by an effective board which is collectively responsible for the long-term success of the company.

There should be a clear division of responsibilities at the head of the company between the running of the board and the executive responsibility for the running of the company's business. No one individual should have unfettered powers of decision.

The chairman is responsible for leadership of the board and ensuring its effectiveness on all aspects of its role.

As part of their role as members of a unitary board, non-executive directors should constructively challenge and help develop proposals on strategy.

Section B: Effectiveness

The board and its committees should have the appropriate balance of skills, experience, independence and knowledge of the company to enable them to discharge their respective duties and responsibilities effectively.

There should be a formal, rigorous and transparent procedure for the appointment of new directors to the board.

All directors should be able to allocate sufficient time to the company to discharge their responsibilities effectively.

All directors should receive induction on joining the board and should regularly update and refresh their skills and knowledge.

The board should be supplied in a timely manner with information in a form and of a quality appropriate to enable it to discharge its duties.

The board should undertake a formal and rigorous annual evaluation of its own performance and that of its committees and individual directors.

All directors should be submitted for re-election at regular intervals, subject to continued satisfactory performance.

Section C: Accountability

The board should present a fair, balanced and understandable assessment of the company's position and prospects.

The board is responsible for determining the nature and extent of the principal risks it is willing to take in achieving its strategic objectives. The board should maintain sound risk management and internal control systems.

The board should establish formal and transparent arrangements for considering how they should apply the corporate reporting, risk management and internal control principles and for maintaining an appropriate relationship with the company's auditors.

Section D: Remuneration

Executive directors' remuneration should be designed to promote the long-term success of the company. Performance-related elements should be transparent, stretching and rigorously applied.

There should be a formal and transparent procedure for developing policy on executive remuneration and for fixing the remuneration packages of individual directors. No director should be involved in deciding his or her own remuneration.

Section E: Relations with Shareholders

There should be a dialogue with shareholders based on the mutual understanding of objectives. The board as a whole has responsibility for ensuring that a satisfactory dialogue with shareholders takes place.

The board should use general meetings to communicate with investors and to encourage their participation.

Section A: Leadership

A.1: The Role of the Board

Main Principle

Every company should be headed by an effective board which is collectively responsible for the long-term success of the company.

Supporting Principles

The board's role is to provide entrepreneurial leadership of the company within a framework of prudent and effective controls which enables risk to be assessed and managed. The board should set the company's strategic aims, ensure that the necessary financial and human resources are in place for the company to meet its objectives and review management performance. The board should set the company's values and standards and ensure that its obligations to its shareholders and others are understood and met.

All directors must act in what they consider to be the best interests of the company, consistent with their statutory duties.[2]

Code Provisions

A.1.1. The board should meet sufficiently regularly to discharge its duties effectively. There should be a formal schedule of matters specifically reserved for its decision. The annual report should include a statement of how the board operates, including a high level statement of which types of decisions are to be taken by the board and which are to be delegated to management.

A.1.2. The annual report should identify the chairman, the deputy chairman (where there is one), the chief executive, the senior independent director and the chairmen and members of the board committees.[3] It should also set out the number of meetings of the board and those committees and individual attendance by directors.

A.1.3. The company should arrange appropriate insurance cover in respect of legal action against its directors.

A.2: Division of Responsibilities

Main Principle

There should be a clear division of responsibilities at the head of the company between the running of the board and the executive responsibility for the running of the company's business. No one individual should have unfettered powers of decision.

Code Provision

A.2.1 The roles of chairman and chief executive should not be exercised by the same individual. The division of responsibilities between the chairman and chief executive should be clearly established, set out in writing and agreed by the board.

A.3: The Chairman

Main Principle

The chairman is responsible for leadership of the board and ensuring its effectiveness on all aspects of its role.

Supporting Principles

The chairman is responsible for setting the board's agenda and ensuring that adequate time is available for discussion of all agenda items, in particular strategic issues. The chairman should also promote a culture of openness and debate by facilitating the effective contribution of non-executive directors in particular and ensuring constructive relations between executive and non-executive directors.

The chairman is responsible for ensuring that the directors receive accurate, timely and clear information. The chairman should ensure effective communication with shareholders.

Code Provision

A.3.1. The chairman should on appointment meet the independence criteria set out in B.1.1 below. A chief executive should not go on to be chairman of the same company. If exceptionally a board decides that a chief executive should become chairman, the board should consult major shareholders in advance and should set out its reasons to shareholders at the time of the appointment and in the next annual report.[4]

A.4: Non-executive Directors

Main Principle

As part of their role as members of a unitary board, non-executive directors should constructively challenge and help develop proposals on strategy.

Supporting Principle

Non-executive directors should scrutinise the performance of management in meeting agreed goals and objectives and monitor the reporting of performance. They should satisfy themselves on the integrity of financial information and that financial controls and systems of risk management are robust and defensible. They are responsible for determining appropriate levels of remuneration of executive directors and have a prime role in appointing and, where necessary, removing executive directors, and in succession planning.

Code Provisions

A.4.1. The board should appoint one of the independent non-executive directors to be the senior independent director to provide a sounding board for the chairman and to serve as an intermediary for the other directors when necessary. The senior independent director should be available to shareholders if they have concerns which contact through the normal channels of chairman, chief executive or other executive directors has failed to resolve or for which such contact is inappropriate.

A.4.2. The chairman should hold meetings with the non-executive directors without the executives present. Led by the senior independent director, the non-executive directors should meet without the chairman present at least annually to appraise the chairman's performance and on such other occasions as are deemed appropriate.

A.4.3. Where directors have concerns which cannot be resolved about the running of the company or a proposed action, they should ensure that their concerns are recorded in the board minutes. On resignation, a non-executive director should provide a written statement to the chairman, for circulation to the board, if they have any such concerns.

Section B: Effectiveness

B.1: The Composition of the Board

Main Principle

The board and its committees should have the appropriate balance of skills, experience, independence and knowledge of the company to enable them to discharge their respective duties and responsibilities effectively.

Supporting Principles

The board should be of sufficient size that the requirements of the business can be met and that changes to the board's composition and that of its committees can be managed without undue disruption, and should not be so large as to be unwieldy.

The board should include an appropriate combination of executive and non-executive directors (and, in particular, independent non-executive directors) such that no individual or small group of individuals can dominate the board's decision taking.

The value of ensuring that committee membership is refreshed and that undue reliance is not placed on particular individuals should be taken into account in deciding chairmanship and membership of committees.

No one other than the committee chairman and members is entitled to be present at a meeting of the nomination, audit or remuneration committee, but others may attend at the invitation of the committee.

Code Provisions

B.1.1. The board should identify in the annual report each non-executive director it considers to be independent.[5] The board should determine whether the director is independent in character and judgement and whether there are relationships or circumstances which are likely to affect, or could appear to affect, the director's judgement. The board should state its reasons if it determines that a director is independent notwithstanding the existence of relationships or circumstances which may appear relevant to its determination, including if the director:

- has been an employee of the company or group within the last five years;
- has, or has had within the last three years, a material business relationship with the company either directly, or as a partner, shareholder, director or senior employee of a body that has such a relationship with the company;
- has received or receives additional remuneration from the company apart from a director's fee, participates in the company's share option or a performance related pay scheme, or is a member of the company's pension scheme;
- has close family ties with any of the company's advisers, directors or senior employees;
- holds cross-directorships or has significant links with other directors through involvement in other companies or bodies;
- represents a significant shareholder; or
- has served on the board for more than nine years from the date of their first election.

B.1.2. Except for smaller companies,[6] at least half the board, excluding the chairman, should comprise non-executive directors determined by the board to be independent.

A smaller company should have at least two independent non-executive directors.

B.2: Appointments to the Board

Main Principle

There should be a formal, rigorous and transparent procedure for the appointment of new directors to the board.

Supporting Principles

The search for board candidates should be conducted, and appointments made, on merit, against objective criteria and with due regard for the benefits of diversity on the board, including gender.

The board should satisfy itself that plans are in place for orderly succession for appointments to the board and to senior management, so as to maintain an appropriate balance of skills and experience within the company and on the board and to ensure progressive refreshing of the board.

Code Provisions

B.2.1. There should be a nomination committee which should lead the process for board appointments and make recommendations to the board. A majority of members of the nomination committee should be independent non-executive directors. The chairman or an independent non-executive director should chair the committee, but the chairman should not chair the nomination committee when it is dealing with the appointment of a successor to the chairmanship. The nomination committee should make available its terms of reference, explaining its role and the authority delegated to it by the board.[7]

B.2.2. The nomination committee should evaluate the balance of skills, experience, independence and knowledge on the board and, in the light of this evaluation, prepare a description of the role and capabilities required for a particular appointment.

B.2.3. Non-executive directors should be appointed for specified terms subject to re-election and to statutory provisions relating to the removal of a director. Any term beyond six years for a non-executive director should be subject to particularly rigorous review, and should take into account the need for progressive refreshing of the board.

B.2.4. A separate section of the annual report should describe the work of the nomination committee,[8] including the process it has used in relation to board appointments. This section should include a description of the board's policy on diversity, including gender, any measurable objectives that it has set for implementing the policy, and progress on achieving the objectives. An explanation should be given if neither an external search consultancy nor open advertising has been used in the appointment of a chairman or a non-executive director. Where an external search consultancy has been used, it should be identified in the annual report and a statement made as to whether it has any other connection with the company.

B.3: Commitment

Main Principle

All directors should be able to allocate sufficient time to the company to discharge their responsibilities effectively.

Code Provisions

B.3.1. For the appointment of a chairman, the nomination committee should prepare a job specification, including an assessment of the time commitment expected, recognising the need for availability in the event of crises. A chairman's other significant commitments should be disclosed to the board before appointment and included in the annual report. Changes to such commitments should be reported to the board as they arise, and their impact explained in the next annual report.

B.3.2. The terms and conditions of appointment of non-executive directors should be made available for inspection.[9] The letter of appointment should set out the expected time commitment. Non-executive directors should undertake that they will have sufficient time to meet what is expected of them. Their other significant commitments should be disclosed to the board before appointment, with a broad indication of the time involved and the board should be informed of subsequent changes.

B.3.3. The board should not agree to a full time executive director taking on more than one non-executive directorship in a FTSE 100 company nor the chairmanship of such a company.

B.4: Development

Main Principle

All directors should receive induction on joining the board and should regularly update and refresh their skills and knowledge.

Supporting Principles

The chairman should ensure that the directors continually update their skills and the knowledge and familiarity with the company required to fulfil their role both on the board and on board committees. The company should provide the necessary resources for developing and updating its directors' knowledge and capabilities.

To function effectively all directors need appropriate knowledge of the company and access to its operations and staff.

Code Provisions

B.4.1. The chairman should ensure that new directors receive a full, formal and tailored induction on joining the board. As part of this, directors should avail themselves of opportunities to meet major shareholders.

B.4.2. The chairman should regularly review and agree with each director their training and development needs.

B.5: Information and Support

Main Principle

The board should be supplied in a timely manner with information in a form and of a quality appropriate to enable it to discharge its duties.

Supporting Principles

The chairman is responsible for ensuring that the directors receive accurate, timely and clear information. Management has an obligation to provide such information but directors should seek clarification or amplification where necessary.

Under the direction of the chairman, the company secretary's responsibilities include ensuring good information flows within the board and its committees and between senior management and non-executive directors, as well as facilitating induction and assisting with professional development as required.

The company secretary should be responsible for advising the board through the chairman on all governance matters.

Code Provisions

B.5.1. The board should ensure that directors, especially non-executive directors, have

access to independent professional advice at the company's expense where they judge it necessary to discharge their responsibilities as directors. Committees should be provided with sufficient resources to undertake their duties.
B.5.2. All directors should have access to the advice and services of the company secretary, who is responsible to the board for ensuring that board procedures are complied with. Both the appointment and removal of the company secretary should be a matter for the board as a whole.

B.6: Evaluation

Main Principle

The board should undertake a formal and rigorous annual evaluation of its own performance and that of its committees and individual directors.

Supporting Principles

Evaluation of the board should consider the balance of skills, experience, independence and knowledge of the company on the board, its diversity, including gender, how the board works together as a unit, and other factors relevant to its effectiveness.

The chairman should act on the results of the performance evaluation by recognising the strengths and addressing the weaknesses of the board and, where appropriate, proposing new members be appointed to the board or seeking the resignation of directors.

Individual evaluation should aim to show whether each director continues to contribute effectively and to demonstrate commitment to the role (including commitment of time for board and committee meetings and any other duties).

Code Provisions

B.6.1. The board should state in the annual report how performance evaluation of the board, its committees and its individual directors has been conducted.
B.6.2. Evaluation of the board of FTSE 350 companies should be externally facilitated at least every three years. The external facilitator should be identified in the annual report and a statement made as to whether they have any other connection with the company.
B.6.3. The non-executive directors, led by the senior independent director, should be responsible for performance evaluation of the chairman, taking into account the views of executive directors.

B.7: Re-election

Main Principle

All directors should be submitted for re-election at regular intervals, subject to continued satisfactory performance.

Code Provisions

B.7.1. All directors of FTSE 350 companies should be subject to annual election by shareholders. All other directors should be subject to election by shareholders at the first annual general meeting after their appointment, and to re-election thereafter at intervals of no more than three years. Non-executive directors who have served longer than nine years should be subject to annual re-election. The names of directors submitted for election or re-election should be accompanied by sufficient biographical details and any other relevant information to enable shareholders to take an informed decision on their election.
B.7.2. The board should set out to shareholders in the papers accompanying a resolution to elect a non-executive director why they believe an individual should be elected. The

chairman should confirm to shareholders when proposing re-election that, following formal performance evaluation, the individual's performance continues to be effective and to demonstrate commitment to the role.

Section C: Accountability

C.1: Financial and Business Reporting

Main Principle
The board should present a fair, balanced and understandable assessment of the company's position and prospects.

Supporting Principles
The board's responsibility to present a fair, balanced and understandable assessment extends to interim and other price-sensitive public reports and reports to regulators as well as to information required to be presented by statutory requirements.

The board should establish arrangements that will enable it to ensure that the information presented is fair, balanced and understandable.

Code Provisions
C.1.1. The directors should explain in the annual report their responsibility for preparing the annual report and accounts, and state that they consider the annual report and accounts, taken as a whole, is fair, balanced and understandable and provides the information necessary for shareholders to assess the company's position and performance, business model and strategy. There should be a statement by the auditor about their reporting responsibilities.[10]

C.1.2. The directors should include in the annual report an explanation of the basis on which the company generates or preserves value over the longer term (the business model) and the strategy for delivering the objectives of the company.[11]

C.1.3. In annual and half-yearly financial statements, the directors should state whether they considered it appropriate to adopt the going concern basis of accounting in preparing them, and identify any material uncertainties to the company's ability to continue to do so over a period of at least twelve months from the date of approval of the financial statements.[12]

C.2: Risk Management and Internal Control

Main Principle
The board is responsible for determining the nature and extent of the principal risks it is willing to take in achieving its strategic objectives. The board should maintain sound risk management and internal control systems.

Code Provisions
C.2.1. The directors should confirm in the annual report that they have carried out a robust assessment of the principal risks facing the company, including those that would threaten its business model, future performance, solvency or liquidity. The directors should describe those risks and explain how they are being managed or mitigated.

C.2.2. Taking account of the company's current position and principal risks, the directors should explain in the annual report how they have assessed the prospects of the company, over what period they have done so and why they consider that period to be appropriate. The directors should state whether they have a reasonable expectation that the company will be able to continue in operation and meet its liabilities as they fall due over the period of their assessment, drawing attention to any qualifications or assumptions as necessary.[13]

C.2.3. The board should monitor the company's risk management and internal control systems and, at least annually, carry out a review of their effectiveness, and report on that review in the annual report.[14] The monitoring and review should cover all material controls, including financial, operational and compliance controls.

C.3: Audit Committee and Auditors[15]

Main Principle

The board should establish formal and transparent arrangements for considering how they should apply the corporate reporting and risk management and internal control principles and for maintaining an appropriate relationship with the company's auditors.

Code Provisions

C.3.1. The board should establish an audit committee of at least three, or in the case of smaller companies[16] two, independent non-executive directors. In smaller companies the company chairman may be a member of, but not chair, the committee in addition to the independent non-executive directors, provided he or she was considered independent on appointment as chairman. The board should satisfy itself that at least one member of the audit committee has recent and relevant financial experience.[16] The audit committee as a whole shall have competence relevant to the sector in which the company operates.[17]

C.3.2. The main role and responsibilities of the audit committee should be set out in written terms of reference[18] and should include:

- to monitor the integrity of the financial statements of the company and any formal announcements relating to the company's financial performance, reviewing significant financial reporting judgements contained in them;
- to review the company's internal financial controls and, unless expressly addressed by a separate board risk committee composed of independent directors, or by the board itself, to review the company's internal control and risk management systems;
- to monitor and review the effectiveness of the company's internal audit function;
- to make recommendations to the board, for it to put to the shareholders for their approval in general meeting, in relation to the appointment, reappointment and removal of the external auditor and to approve the remuneration and terms of engagement of the external auditor;
- to review and monitor the external auditor's independence and objectivity and the effectiveness of the audit process, taking into consideration relevant UK professional and regulatory requirements;
- to develop and implement policy on the engagement of the external auditor to supply non-audit services, taking into account relevant ethical guidance regarding the provision of non-audit services by the external audit firm; and to report to the board, identifying any matters in respect of which it considers that action or improvement is needed and making recommendations as to the steps to be taken; and
- to report to the board on how it has discharged its responsibilities.

C.3.3. The terms of reference of the audit committee, including its role and the authority delegated to it by the board, should be made available.[19]

C.3.4. Where requested by the board, the audit committee should provide advice on whether the annual report and accounts, taken as a whole, is fair, balanced and understandable and provides the information necessary for shareholders to assess the company's position and performance, business model and strategy.

C.3.5. The audit committee should review arrangements by which staff of the company may, in confidence, raise concerns about possible improprieties in matters of financial reporting or other matters. The audit committee's objective should be to ensure that arrangements are in place for the proportionate and independent investigation of such matters and for appropriate follow-up action.

C.3.6. The audit committee should monitor and review the effectiveness of the internal audit activities. Where there is no internal audit function, the audit committee should consider annually whether there is a need for an internal audit function and make a recommendation to the board, and the reasons for the absence of such a function should be explained in the relevant section of the annual report.

C.3.7. The audit committee should have primary responsibility for making a recommendation on the appointment, reappointment and removal of the external auditors.[20] If the board does not accept the audit committee's recommendation, it should include in the annual report, and in any papers recommending appointment or reappointment, a statement from the audit committee explaining the recommendation and should set out reasons why the board has taken a different position.

C.3.8. A separate section of the annual report should describe the work of the committee in discharging its responsibilities.[21] The report should include:

▶ the significant issues that the committee considered in relation to the financial statements, and how these issues were addressed;

▶ an explanation of how it has assessed the effectiveness of the external audit process and the approach taken to the appointment or reappointment of the external auditor, information on the length of tenure of the current audit firm, when a tender was last conducted and advance notice of any retendering plans;[22] and

▶ if the external auditor provides non-audit services, an explanation of how auditor objectivity and independence are safeguarded.

Section D: Remuneration

D.1: The Level and Components of Remuneration

Main Principle

Executive directors' remuneration should be designed to promote the long-term success of the company. Performance-related elements should be transparent, stretching and rigorously applied.

Supporting Principles

The remuneration committee should judge where to position their company relative to other companies. But they should use such comparisons with caution, in view of the risk of an upward ratchet of remuneration levels with no corresponding improvement in corporate and individual performance, and should avoid paying more than is necessary.

They should also be sensitive to pay and employment conditions elsewhere in the group, especially when determining annual salary increases.

Code Provisions

D.1.1. In designing schemes of performance-related remuneration for executive directors, the remuneration committee should follow the provisions in Schedule A to this Code. Schemes should include provisions that would enable the company to recover sums paid or withhold the payment of any sum, and specify the circumstances in which it would be appropriate to do so.

D.1.2. Where a company releases an executive director to serve as a non-executive director elsewhere, the remuneration report[23] should include a statement as to whether or not the director will retain such earnings and, if so, what the remuneration is.

D.1.3. Levels of remuneration for non-executive directors should reflect the time commitment and responsibilities of the role. Remuneration for non-executive directors should not include share options or other performance-related elements. If, exceptionally, options are granted, shareholder approval should be sought in advance and any shares acquired by exercise of the options should be held until at least one year after the non-executive director leaves the board. Holding of share options could be relevant to the determination of a non-executive director's independence (as set out in provision B.1.1).

D.1.4. The remuneration committee should carefully consider what compensation commitments (including pension contributions and all other elements) their directors' terms of appointment would entail in the event of early termination. The aim should be to avoid rewarding poor performance. They should take a robust line on reducing compensation to reflect departing directors' obligations to mitigate loss.

D.1.5. Notice or contract periods should be set at one year or less. If it is necessary to offer longer notice or contract periods to new directors recruited from outside, such periods should reduce to one year or less after the initial period.

D.2: Procedure

Main Principle

There should be a formal and transparent procedure for developing policy on executive remuneration and for fixing the remuneration packages of individual directors. No director should be involved in deciding his or her own remuneration.

Supporting Principles

The remuneration committee should take care to recognise and manage conflicts of interest when receiving views from executive directors or senior management, or consulting the chief executive about its proposals. The remuneration committee should also be responsible for appointing any consultants in respect of executive director remuneration.

The chairman of the board should ensure that the committee chairman maintains contact as required with its principal shareholders about remuneration.

Code Provisions

D.2.1. The board should establish a remuneration committee of at least three, or in the case of smaller companies[24] two, independent non-executive directors. In addition the company chairman may also be a member of, but not chair, the committee if he or she was considered independent on appointment as chairman. The remuneration committee should make available its terms of reference, explaining its role and the authority delegated to it by the board.[25] Where remuneration consultants are appointed, they should be identified in the annual report and a statement made as to whether they have any other connection with the company.

D.2.2. The remuneration committee should have delegated responsibility for setting remuneration for all executive directors and the chairman, including pension rights and any compensation payments. The committee should also recommend and monitor the level and structure of remuneration for senior management. The definition of 'senior management' for this purpose should be determined by the board but should normally include the first layer of management below board level.

D.2.3. The board itself or, where required by the Articles of Association, the shareholders should determine the remuneration of the non-executive directors within the limits set in the

Articles of Association. Where permitted by the Articles, the board may however delegate this responsibility to a committee, which might include the chief executive.

D.2.4. Shareholders should be invited specifically to approve all new long-term incentive schemes (as defined in the Listing Rules[26]) and significant changes to existing schemes, save in the circumstances permitted by the Listing Rules.

Section E: Relations with Shareholders

E.1: Dialogue with Shareholders

Main Principle

There should be a dialogue with shareholders based on the mutual understanding of objectives. The board as a whole has responsibility for ensuring that a satisfactory dialogue with shareholders takes place.[27]

Supporting Principles

While recognising that most shareholder contact is with the chief executive and finance director, the chairman should ensure that all directors are made aware of their major shareholders' issues and concerns.

The board should keep in touch with shareholder opinion in whatever ways are most practical and efficient.

Code Provisions

E.1.1. The chairman should ensure that the views of shareholders are communicated to the board as a whole. The chairman should discuss governance and strategy with major shareholders. Non-executive directors should be offered the opportunity to attend scheduled meetings with major shareholders and should expect to attend meetings if requested by major shareholders. The senior independent director should attend sufficient meetings with a range of major shareholders to listen to their views in order to help develop a balanced understanding of the issues and concerns of major shareholders.

E.1.2. The board should state in the annual report the steps they have taken to ensure that the members of the board, and in particular the non-executive directors, develop an understanding of the views of major shareholders about the company, for example through direct face-to-face contact, analysts' or brokers' briefings and surveys of shareholder opinion.

E.2: Constructive Use of General Meetings

Main Principle

The board should use general meetings to communicate with investors and to encourage their participation.

Code Provisions

E.2.1. At any general meeting, the company should propose a separate resolution on each substantially separate issue, and should in particular propose a resolution at the AGM relating to the report and accounts. For each resolution, proxy appointment forms should provide shareholders with the option to direct their proxy to vote either for or against the resolution or to withhold their vote. The proxy form and any announcement of the results of a vote should make it clear that a 'vote withheld' is not a vote in law and will not be counted in the calculation of the proportion of the votes for and against the resolution.

E.2.2. The company should ensure that all valid proxy appointments received for general meetings are properly recorded and counted. For each resolution, where a vote has been taken on a show of hands, the company should ensure that the following information is given at the meeting and made available as soon as reasonably practicable on a website which is maintained by or on behalf of the company:

- the number of shares in respect of which proxy appointments have been validly made;
- the number of votes for the resolution;
- the number of votes against the resolution; and
- the number of shares in respect of which the vote was directed to be withheld.

When, in the opinion of the board, a significant proportion of votes have been cast against a resolution at any general meeting, the company should explain when announcing the results of voting what actions it intends to take to understand the reasons behind the vote result.

E.2.3. The chairman should arrange for the chairmen of the audit, remuneration and nomination committees to be available to answer questions at the AGM and for all directors to attend.

E.2.4. The company should arrange for the Notice of the AGM and related papers to be sent to shareholders at least 20 working days before the meeting. For other general meetings this should be at least 14 working days in advance.

Schedule A: The design of performance-related remuneration for executive directors

Balance

The remuneration committee should determine an appropriate balance between fixed and performance-related, immediate and deferred remuneration. Performance conditions, including non-financial metrics where appropriate, should be relevant, stretching and designed to promote the long-term success of the company. Remuneration incentives should be compatible with risk policies and systems. Upper limits should be set and disclosed.

The remuneration committee should consider whether the directors should be eligible for annual bonuses and/or benefits under long-term incentive schemes.

Share-based remuneration

Traditional share option schemes should be weighed against other kinds of long-term incentive scheme. Executive share options should not be offered at a discount save as permitted by the relevant provisions of the Listing Rules.

Any new long-term incentive schemes which are proposed should be approved by shareholders and should preferably replace any existing schemes or, at least, form part of a well-considered overall plan incorporating existing schemes. The total rewards potentially available should not be excessive.

For share-based remuneration the remuneration committee should consider requiring directors to hold a minimum number of shares and to hold shares for a further period after vesting or exercise, including for a period after leaving the company, subject to the need to finance any costs of acquisition and associated tax liabilities. In normal circumstances, shares granted or other forms of deferred remuneration should not vest or be paid, and options should not be exercisable, in less than three years. Longer periods may be appropriate. Grants under executive share option and other long-term incentive schemes should normally be phased rather than awarded in one large block.

Pensions

In general, only basic salary should be pensionable. The remuneration committee should consider the pension consequences and associated costs to the company of basic salary increases and any other changes in pensionable remuneration, especially for directors close to retirement.

Schedule B: Disclosure of corporate governance arrangements

Corporate governance disclosure requirements are set out in three places:

- FCA Disclosure and Transparency Rules ('DTR') sub-chapters 7.1 and 7.2, which set out certain mandatory disclosures;
- FCA Listing Rules ('LR') 9.8.6 R, 9.8.7 R, and 9.8.7A R, which includes the 'comply or explain' requirement; and
- The UK Corporate Governance Code ('the Code') – in addition to providing an explanation where they choose not to comply with a provision, companies must disclose specified information in order to comply with certain provisions.

These requirements are summarised below, with the full text contained in the relevant chapters of the FCA Handbook.

The DTR sub-chapters 7.1 and 7.2 apply to issuers whose securities are admitted to trading on a regulated market (this includes all issuers with a Premium or Standard listing). The LR 9.8.6 R, 9.8.7 R and 9.8.7A R and the Code apply to issuers of Premium listed equity shares only.

There is some overlap between the mandatory disclosures required under the DTR and those expected under the Code. Areas of overlap are summarised in the Appendix to this Schedule. In respect of disclosures relating to the audit committee and the composition and operation of the board and its committees, compliance with the relevant provisions of the Code will result in compliance with the relevant Rules.

Disclosure and Transparency Rules

DTR sub-chapter 7.1 concerns audit committees or bodies carrying out equivalent functions.

DTR 7.1.1 R, 7.1.1A R and 7.1.3 R set out requirements relating to the composition and functions of the committee or equivalent body:

- DTR 7.1.1 R states that an issuer must have a body or bodies responsible for performing the functions set out in DTR 7.1.3 R.
- DTR 7.1.1A R requires that a majority of the members of the relevant body must be independent, at least one member must have competence in accounting or auditing, or both, and that members of the relevant body as a whole must have competence relevant to the sector in which the issuer is operating.
- DTR 7.1.2 G states that the requirements for independence and competence in accounting and/or auditing may be satisfied by the same members or by different members of the relevant body.
- DTR 7.1.3 R states that an issuer must ensure that, as a minimum, the relevant body must:
  1. monitor the financial reporting process and submit recommendations or proposal to ensure its integrity;
  2. monitor the effectiveness of the issuer's internal quality control and risk management systems and, where applicable, its internal audit, regarding the financial reporting of the issuer, without breaching its independence;
  3. monitor the statutory audit of the annual and consolidated financial statements, in particular, its performance, taking into account any findings and conclusions by the competent authority under article 26(6) of the Audit Regulation;
  4. review and monitor the independence of the statutory auditor, in accordance with articles 22, 22a, 22b, 24a and 24b of the Audit Directive and article 6 of the Audit

Regulation, and in particular the appropriateness of the provision of non-audit services to the issuer in accordance with article 5 of the Audit Regulation;

5. inform the administrative or supervisory body of the issuer of the outcome of the statutory audit and explain how the statutory audit contributed to the integrity of financial reporting and what the role of the relevant body was in that process; and

6. except when article 16(8) of the Audit Regulation is applied, be responsible for the procedure for the selection of statutory auditor(s) and recommend the statutory auditor(s) to be appointed in accordance with article 16 of the Audit Regulation.

DTR 7.1.5 R sets out what disclosure is required. Specifically:

▶ DTR 7.1.5 R states that the issuer must make a statement available to the public disclosing which body carries out the functions required by DTR 7.1.3 R and how it is composed.

▶ DTR 7.1.6 G states that this can be included in the corporate governance statement required under sub-chapter DTR 7.2 (see below).

▶ DTR 7.1.7 G states that compliance with the relevant provisions of the Code (as set out in the Appendix to this Schedule) will result in compliance with DTR 7.1.1 R to 7.1.5 R.

Sub-chapter 7.2 concerns corporate governance statements. Issuers are required to produce a corporate governance statement that must be either included in the directors' report (DTR 7.2.1 R); or set out in a separate report published together with the annual report; or set out in a document on the issuer's website, in which case there must be a cross-reference in the directors' report (DTR 7.2.9 R).

DTR 7.2.2 R requires that the corporate governance statement must contain a reference to the corporate governance code to which the company is subject (for companies with a Premium listing this is the Code). DTR 7.2.3 R requires that, where that it departs from that code, the company must explain which parts of the code it departs from and the reasons for doing so. DTR 7.2.4 G states that compliance with LR 9.8.6 R (6) (the 'comply or explain' rule in relation to the Code) will also satisfy these requirements.

DTR 7.2.5 R, DTR 7.2.6 R, DTR 7.2.7 R and DTR 7.2.10 R set out certain information that must be disclosed in the corporate governance statement:

▶ DTR 7.2.5 R states that the corporate governance statement must contain a description of the main features of the company's internal control and risk management systems in relation to the financial reporting process. DTR 7.2.10 R states that an issuer which is required to prepare a group directors' report within the meaning of Section 415(2) of the Companies Act 2006 must include in that report a description of the main features of the group's internal control and risk management systems in relation to the financial reporting process for the undertakings included in the consolidation, taken as a whole.

▶ DTR 7.2.6 R states that the corporate governance statement must contain the information required by paragraph 13(2)(c), (d), (f), (h) and (i) of Schedule 7 to the Large and Medium-sized Companies and Groups (Accounts and Reports) Regulations 2008 (SI 2008/410) where the issuer is subject to the requirements of that paragraph.

▶ DTR 7.2.7 R states that the corporate governance statement must contain a description of the composition and operation of the issuer's administrative, management and supervisory bodies and their committees. DTR 7.2.8 G states that compliance with the relevant provisions of the Code (as set out in the Appendix to this Schedule) will satisfy these requirements.

Listing Rules

LR 9.8.6 R (for UK incorporated companies) and LR 9.8.7 R (for overseas incorporated companies) state that in the case of a company that has a Premium listing of equity shares, the following items must be included in its annual report and accounts:

▶ a statement of how the listed company has applied the Main Principles set out in the Code, in a manner that would enable shareholders to evaluate how the principles have been applied; and

▶ a statement as to whether the listed company has:

▷ complied throughout the accounting period with all relevant provisions set out in the Code; or

▷ not complied throughout the accounting period with all relevant provisions set out in the Code, and if so, setting out:

– those provisions, if any, it has not complied with;

– in the case of provisions whose requirements are of a continuing nature, the period within which, if any, it did not comply with some or all of those provisions; and

– the company's reasons for non-compliance.

LR 9.8.6 R (3) requires statements by the directors on:

a) the appropriateness of adopting the going concern basis of accounting (containing the information set out in provision C.1.3 of the Code); and

b) their assessment of the prospects of the company (containing the information set out in provision C.2.2 of the Code);

prepared in accordance with the 'Guidance on Risk Management, Internal Control and Related Financial and Business Reporting' published by the Financial Reporting Council in September 2014.

The UK Corporate Governance Code

In addition to the 'comply or explain' requirement in the LR, the Code includes specific requirements for disclosure which must be provided in order to comply. These are summarised below.

The annual report should include:

▶ a statement of how the board operates, including a high level statement of which types of decisions are to be taken by the board and which are to be delegated to management (A.1.1);

▶ the names of the chairman, the deputy chairman (where there is one), the chief executive, the senior independent director and the chairmen and members of the board committees (A.1.2);

▶ the number of meetings of the board and those committees and individual attendance by directors (A.1.2);

▶ where a chief executive is appointed chairman, the reasons for their appointment (this only needs to be done in the annual report following the appointment) (A.3.1);

▶ the names of the non-executive directors whom the board determines to be independent, with reasons where necessary (B.1.1);

▶ a separate section describing the work of the nomination committee, including the process it has used in relation to board appointments; a description of the board's policy on diversity, including gender; any measurable objectives that it has set for implementing the policy, and progress on achieving the objectives. An explanation should be given if neither external search consultancy nor open advertising has been used in the appointment of a chairman or a non-executive director. Where an external search consultancy has been used it should be identified and a statement made as to whether it has any other connection with the company (B.2.4);

▶ the impact of any changes to the other significant commitments of the chairman during the year should explained (B.3.1);

▶ a statement of how performance evaluation of the board, its committees and its directors has been conducted (B.6.1). Where an external facilitator has been used, they should be identified and a statement made as to whether they have any other connection to the company (B.6.2);

- an explanation from the directors of their responsibility for preparing the accounts and a statement that they consider that the annual report and accounts, taken as a whole, is fair, balanced and understandable and provides the information necessary for shareholders to assess the company's position and performance, business model and strategy. There should also be a statement by the auditor about their reporting responsibilities (C.1.1);
- an explanation from the directors of the basis on which the company generates or preserves value over the longer term (the business model) and the strategy for delivering the objectives of the company (C.1.2);
- a statement from the directors whether they considered it appropriate to adopt the going concern basis of accounting in preparing them, and identify any material uncertainties to the company's ability to continue to do so over a period of at least twelve months from the date of approval of the financial statements (C.1.3);
- confirmation by the directors that they have carried out a robust assessment of the principal risks facing the company, including those that would threaten its business model, future performance, solvency or liquidity. The directors should describe the risks and explain how they are being managed or mitigated (C.2.1);
- a statement from the directors explaining how they have assessed the prospects of the company (taking account of the company's current position and principal risks), over what period they have done so and why they consider that period to be appropriate. The directors should state whether they have a reasonable expectation that the company will be able to continue in operation and meet its liabilities as they fall due over the period of their assessment, drawing attention to any qualifications or assumptions as necessary (C.2.2);
- a report on the board's review of the effectiveness of the company's risk management and internal controls systems (C.2.3);
- where there is no internal audit function, the reasons for the absence of such a function (C.3.6);
- where the board does not accept the audit committee's recommendation on the appointment, reappointment or removal of an external auditor, a statement from the audit committee explaining the recommendation and the reasons why the board has taken a different position (C.3.7);
- a separate section describing the work of the audit committee in discharging its responsibilities, including: the significant issues that it considered in relation to the financial statements, and how these issues were addressed; an explanation of how it has assessed the effectiveness of the external audit process and the approach taken to the appointment or reappointment of the external auditor, including the length of tenure of the current audit firm, when a tender was last conducted and advance notice of any retendering plans; and, if the external auditor provides non-audit services, an explanation of how auditor objectivity and independence is safeguarded (C.3.8);
- a description of the work of the remuneration committee as required under the Large and Medium-Sized Companies and Groups (Accounts and Reports) Regulations 2013, including, where an executive director serves as a nonexecutive director elsewhere, whether or not the director will retain such earnings and, if so, what the remuneration is (D.1.2);
- where remuneration consultants are appointed they should be identified and a statement made as to whether they have any other connection with the company (D.2.1); and
- the steps the board has taken to ensure that members of the board, and in particular the non-executive directors, develop an understanding of the views of major shareholders about their company (E.1.2).

The following information should be made available (which may be met by placing the information on a website that is maintained by or on behalf of the company):

- the terms of reference of the nomination, audit and remuneration committees, explaining their role and the authority delegated to them by the board (B.2.1, C.3.3 and D.2.1); and
- the terms and conditions of appointment of non-executive directors (B.3.2) (see footnote 9).

The board should set out to shareholders in the papers accompanying a resolution to elect or re-elect directors:

- sufficient biographical details to enable shareholders to take an informed decision on their election or re-election (B.7.1);
- why they believe an individual should be elected to a non-executive role (B.7.2); and
- on re-election of a non-executive director, confirmation from the chairman that, following formal performance evaluation, the individual's performance continues to be effective and to demonstrate commitment to the role (B.7.2).

The board should set out to shareholders in the papers recommending appointment or reappointment of an external auditor:

- if the board does not accept the audit committee's recommendation, a statement from the audit committee explaining the recommendation and from the board setting out reasons why they have taken a different position (C.3.7).

Additional guidance

The FRC publishes guidance on the strategic report, risk management, internal control, business and financial reporting and audit committees, which relate to Section C of the Code. These guidance notes are available on the FRC website.

Notes

1   References to shareholders in this section also apply to intermediaries and agents employed to assist shareholders in scrutinising governance arrangements.
2   For directors of UK incorporated companies, these duties are set out in the Sections 170 to 177 of the Companies Act 2006.
3   Provisions A.1.1 and A.1.2 overlap with FCA Rule DTR 7.2.7 R; Provision A.1.2 also overlaps with DTR 7.1.5R (see Schedule B).
4   Compliance or otherwise with this provision need only be reported for the year in which the appointment is made.
5   A.3.1 states that the chairman should, on appointment, meet the independence criteria set out in this provision, but thereafter the test of independence is not appropriate in relation to the chairman.
6   A smaller company is one that is below the FTSE 350 throughout the year immediately prior to the reporting year.
7   The requirement to make the information available would be met by including the information on a website that is maintained by or on behalf of the company.
8   This provision overlaps with FCA Rule DTR 7.2.7 R (see Schedule B).
9   The terms and conditions of appointment of non-executive directors should be made available for inspection by any person at the company's registered office during normal business hours and at the AGM (for 15 minutes prior to the meeting and during the meeting).
10 This requirement may be met by the disclosures about the audit scope and responsibilities of the auditor included, or referred to, in the auditor's report pursuant

to the requirements of ISA (UK) 700 'Forming an Opinion and Reporting on Financial Statements' – Paragraphs 38–40. Copies are available from the FRC website.

11 Section 414C(8) (a) and (b) of the Companies Act 2006 requires a description of a company's business model and strategy as part of the Strategic Report that forms part of the annual report. Guidance as to the matters that should be considered in an explanation of the business model and strategy is provided in the FRC's 'Guidance on the Strategic Report'. Copies are available from the FRC website.

12 This provision overlaps with FCA Rule LR 9.8.6 R (3) (see Schedule B). Additional information relating to C.1.3 and C.2 can be found in 'Guidance on Risk Management, Internal Control and Related Financial and Business Reporting'. Copies are available from the FRC website.

13 This provision overlaps with FCA Rule LR 9.8.6 (3) R (see Schedule B).

14 In addition, FCA Rule DTR 7.2.5 R requires companies to describe the main features of the internal control and risk management systems in relation to the financial reporting process.

15 'Guidance on Audit Committees' suggests means of applying this part of the Code. Copies are available from the FRC website.

16 See footnote 6.

17 This provision overlaps with FCA Rule DTR 7.1.1A R (see Schedule B).

18 This provision overlaps with FCA Rule DTR 7.1.3 R (see Schedule B).

19 See footnote 7.

20 This overlaps with Part 3 of the Statutory Audit Services for Large Companies Market Investigation (Mandatory Use of Competitive Tender Processes and Audit Committee Responsibilities) Order 2014 and the requirements of Chapter 2 of Part 16 of the Companies Act 2006 as inserted by the Statutory Auditors and Third Country Auditors Regulations 2016 on the appointment of auditors to public companies that are Public Interest Entities.

21 This provision overlaps with FCA Rules DTR 7.1.5 R and 7.2.7 R (see Schedule B).

22 This overlaps with Part 4 of The Statutory Audit Services for Large Companies Market Investigation (Mandatory Use of Competitive Tender Processes and Audit Committee Responsibilities) Order 2014.

23 As required for UK incorporated companies under the Large and Medium-Sized Companies and Groups (Accounts and Reports) Regulations 2013.

24 See footnote 6.

25 This provision overlaps with FCA Rule DTR 7.2.7 R (see Schedule B).

26 Listing Rules LR 9.4. Copies are available from the FCA website.

27 Nothing in these principles or provisions should be taken to override the general requirements of law to treat shareholders equally in access to information.

Appendix

Overlap between the Disclosure and Transparency Rules and the UK Corporate Governance Code

Disclosure and transparency rules	UK Corporate Governance Code
DTR 7.1.1 R and 7.1.1 AR Sets out minimum requirements on composition of the audit committee or equivalent body.	**Provision C.3.1** Sets out recommended composition of the audit committee.
DTR 7.1.3 R Sets out minimum functions of the audit committee or equivalent body.	**Provision C.3.2** Sets out the recommended minimum terms of reference for the audit committee.
DTR 7.1.5 R The composition and function of the audit committee or equivalent body/bodies must be disclosed in the annual report. *DTR 7.1.7 G states that compliance with Code provisions A.1.2, C.3.1, C.3.2, C.3.3. and C.3.8 will result in compliance with DTR 7.1.1 R to DTR 7.1.5 R.*	This requirement overlaps with a number of different Code provisions: A.1.2: the annual report should identify members of the board and board committees. C.3.1: sets out the recommended minimum terms of reference for the audit committee. C.3.2: sets out the recommended minimum terms of reference for the audit committee. C.3.3: the terms of reference of the audit committee, including its role and the authority delegated to it by the board, should be made available. C.3.8: the annual report should describe the work of the audit committee.
DTR 7.2.5 R The corporate governance statement must contain a description of the main features of the issuer's internal control and risk management systems in relation to the financial reporting process. *While this requirement differs from the requirement in the Code, it is envisaged that both could be met by a single internal control statement.*	**Provision C.2.1** The directors should confirm that they have carried out a robust assessment of the principal risks facing the company – including those that would threaten its business model, future performance, solvency or liquidity. The directors should describe those risks and explain how they are being managed or mitigated. **Provision C.2.3** The board should monitor the company's risk management and internal control systems and, at least annually, carry out a review of their effectiveness, and report on that review in the annual report. The monitoring and review should cover all material controls, including financial, operational and compliance controls.

DTR 7.2.7 R The corporate governance statement must contain a description of the composition and operation of the issuer's administrative, management and supervisory bodies and their committees. *DTR 7.2.8 R states that compliance with Code provisions A.1.1, A.1.2, B.2.4, C.3.3, C.3.8 and D.2.1 will result in compliance with DTR 7.2.7 R.*	This requirement overlaps with a number of different Code provisions: A.1.1: the annual report should include a statement of how the board operates. A.1.2: the annual report should identify members of the board and board committees. B.2.4: the annual report should describe the work of the nomination committee. C.3.3: the terms of reference of the audit committee, including its role and the authority delegated to it by the board, should be made available. C.3.8: the annual report should describe the work of the audit committee. D.2.1: a description of the work of the remuneration committee should be made available. [Note: in order to comply with DTR 7.2.7 R, this information will need to be included in the corporate governance statement.]

Appendix 2 – Stewardship Code

Financial Reporting Council September 2012

Contents

Stewardship and the Code

1. Stewardship aims to promote the long term success of companies in such a way that the
    ultimate providers of capital also prosper. Effective stewardship benefits companies,
    investors and the economy as a whole.
2. In publicly listed companies responsibility for stewardship is shared. The primary
    responsibility rests with the board of the company, which oversees the actions of its
    management. Investors in the company also play an important role in holding the board
    to account for the fulfilment of its responsibilities.
3. The UK Corporate Governance Code identifies the principles that underlie an effective
    board. The UK Stewardship Code sets out the principles of effective stewardship by
    investors. In so doing, the Code assists institutional investors better to exercise their
    stewardship responsibilities, which in turn gives force to the 'comply or explain' system.
4. For investors, stewardship is more than just voting. Activities may include monitoring
    and engaging with companies on matters such as strategy, performance, risk, capital
    structure, and corporate governance, including culture and remuneration. Engagement
    is purposeful dialogue with companies on these matters as well as on issues that are the
    immediate subject of votes at general meetings.
5. Institutional investors' activities include decision-making on matters such as allocating
    assets, awarding investment mandates, designing investment strategies, and buying or
    selling specific securities. The division of duties within and between institutions may
    span a spectrum, such that some may be considered asset owners and others asset
    managers.
6. Broadly speaking, asset owners include pension funds, insurance companies,
    investment trusts and other collective investment vehicles. As the providers of capital,
    they set the tone for stewardship and may influence behavioural changes that lead to
    better stewardship by asset managers and companies. Asset managers, with day-to-day

responsibility for managing investments, are well positioned to influence companies' long-term performance through stewardship.

7.   Compliance with the Code does not constitute an invitation to manage the affairs of a company or preclude a decision to sell a holding, where this is considered in the best interest of clients or beneficiaries.

Application of the Code

1.   The UK Stewardship Code traces its origins to 'The Responsibilities of Institutional Shareholders and Agents: Statement of Principles,' first published in 2002 by the Institutional Shareholders Committee (ISC), and which the ISC converted to a code in 2009. Following the 2009 Walker Review of governance in financial institutions, the FRC was invited to take responsibility for the Code. In 2010, the FRC published the first version of the UK Stewardship Code, which closely mirrored the ISC code. This edition of the Code does not change the spirit of the 2010 Code.

2.   The Code is directed in the first instance to institutional investors, by which is meant asset owners and asset managers with equity holdings in UK listed companies. Institutional investors may choose to outsource to external service providers some of the activities associated with stewardship. However, they cannot delegate their responsibility for stewardship. They remain responsible for ensuring those activities are carried out in a manner consistent with their own approach to stewardship. Accordingly, the Code also applies, by extension, to service providers, such as proxy advisers and investment consultants.

3.   The FRC expects signatories of the Code to publish on their website, or if they do not have a website in another accessible form, a statement that:

   ▶   describes how the signatory has applied each of the seven principles of the Code and discloses the specific information requested in the guidance to the principles; or
   ▶   if one or more of the principles have not been applied or the specific information requested in the guidance has not been disclosed, explains why the signatory has not complied with those elements of the Code.

4.   Disclosures under the Code should improve the functioning of the market for investment mandates. Asset owners should be better equipped to evaluate asset managers, and asset managers should be better informed, enabling them to tailor their services to meet asset owners' requirements.

5.   In particular the disclosures should, with respect to conflicts of interest, address the priority given to client interests in decision-making; with respect to collective engagement, describe the circumstances under which the signatory would join forces with other institutional investors to ensure that boards acknowledge and respond to their concerns on critical issues and at critical times; and, with respect to proxy voting agencies, how the signatory uses their advice.

6.   The statement of how the Code has been applied should be aligned with the signatory's role in the investment chain.

7.   Asset owners' commitment to the Code may include engaging directly with companies or indirectly through the mandates given to asset managers. They should clearly communicate their policies on stewardship to their managers. Since asset owners are the primary audience of asset managers' public statements as well as client reports on stewardship, asset owners should seek to hold their managers to account for their stewardship activities. In so doing, they better fulfil their duty to their beneficiaries to exercise stewardship over their assets.

8.   An asset manager should disclose how it delivers stewardship responsibilities on

behalf of its clients. Following the publication in 2011 of the Stewardship Supplement to Technical Release AAF 01/06, asset managers are encouraged to have the policies described in their stewardship statements independently verified. Where appropriate, asset owners should also consider having their policy statements independently verified.

9. Overseas investors who follow other national or international codes that have similar objectives should not feel the application of the Code duplicates or confuses their responsibilities. Disclosures made in respect of those standards can also be used to demonstrate the extent to which they have complied with the Code. In a similar spirit, UK institutions that apply the Code should use their best efforts to apply its principles to overseas equity holdings.

10. Institutional investors with several types of funds or products need to make only one statement, but are encouraged to explain which of their funds or products are covered by the approach described in their statements. Where institutions apply a stewardship approach to other asset classes, they are encouraged to disclose this.

11. The FRC encourages service providers to disclose how they carry out the wishes of their clients with respect to each principle of the Code that is relevant to their activities.

12. Signatories are encouraged to review their policy statements annually, and update them where necessary to reflect changes in actual practice.

13. This statement should be easy to find on the signatory's website, or if they do not have a website in another accessible form, and should indicate when the statement was last reviewed. It should include contact details of an individual who can be contacted for further information and by those interested in collective engagement. The FRC hosts on its website the statements of signatories without their own website.

14. The FRC retains on its website a list of asset owners, asset managers and service providers that have published a statement on their compliance or otherwise with the Code, and requests that signatories notify the FRC when they have done so, and when the statement is updated.

15. The FRC regularly monitors the take-up and application of the Code. It expects the content of the Code to evolve over time to reflect developments in good stewardship practice, the structure and operation of the market, and the broader regulatory framework. Unless circumstances change, the FRC does not envisage proposing further changes to the Code until 2014 at the earliest.

Financial Reporting Council
September 2012

Comply or Explain

1. As with the UK Corporate Governance Code, the UK Stewardship Code should be applied on a 'comply or explain' basis.

2. The Code is not a rigid set of rules. It consists of principles and guidance. The principles are the core of the Code and the way in which they are applied should be the central question for the institutional investor as it determines how to operate according to the Code. The guidance recommends how the principle might be applied.

3. Those signatories that choose not to comply with one of the principles, or not to follow the guidance, should deliver meaningful explanations that enable the reader to understand their approach to stewardship. In providing an explanation, the signatory should aim to illustrate how its actual practices contribute to good stewardship and promote the delivery of the institution's or its clients' investment objectives. They should provide a clear rationale for their approach.

4. The Financial Services Authority requires any firm authorised to manage funds, which is not a venture capital firm, and which manages investments for professional clients that

are not natural persons, to disclose 'the nature of its commitment' to the Code or 'where it does not commit to the Code, its alternative investment strategy' (under Conduct of Business Rule 2.2.3).

5. The FRC recognises that not all parts of the Code are relevant to all signatories. For example, smaller institutions may judge that some of its principles and guidance are disproportionate in their case. In these circumstances, they should take advantage of the 'comply or explain' approach and set out why this is the case.

6. In their responses to explanations, clients and beneficiaries should pay due regard to the signatory's individual circumstances and bear in mind in particular the size and complexity of the signatory, the nature of the risks and challenges it faces, and the investment objectives of the signatory or its clients.

7. While clients and beneficiaries have every right to challenge a signatory's explanations if they are unconvincing, they should not evaluate explanations in a mechanistic way. Departures from the Code should not be automatically treated as breaches. A signatory's clients and beneficiaries should be careful to respond to the statements from the signatory in a manner that supports the 'comply or explain' process and bears in mind the purpose of good stewardship. They should put their views to the signatory and both parties should be prepared to discuss the position.

The Principles of the Code

So as to protect and enhance the value that accrues to the ultimate beneficiary, institutional investors should:

1. publicly disclose their policy on how they will discharge their stewardship responsibilities;
2. have a robust policy on managing conflicts of interest in relation to stewardship which should be publicly disclosed;
3. monitor their investee companies;
4. establish clear guidelines on when and how they will escalate their stewardship activities;
5. be willing to act collectively with other investors where appropriate;
6. have a clear policy on voting and disclosure of voting activity; and
7. report periodically on their stewardship and voting activities.

The UK Stewardship Code

Principle 1: Institutional investors should publicly disclose their policy on how they will discharge their stewardship responsibilities.

Guidance

Stewardship activities include monitoring and engaging with companies on matters such as strategy, performance, risk, capital structure, and corporate governance, including culture and remuneration. Engagement is purposeful dialogue with companies on those matters as well as on issues that are the immediate subject of votes at general meetings.

The policy should disclose how the institutional investor applies stewardship with the aim of enhancing and protecting the value for the ultimate beneficiary or client.

The statement should reflect the institutional investor's activities within the investment chain, as well as the responsibilities that arise from those activities. In particular, the stewardship responsibilities of those whose primary activities are related to asset ownership may be different from those whose primary activities are related to asset management or other investment-related services.

Where activities are outsourced, the statement should explain how this is compatible with the proper exercise of the institutional investor's stewardship responsibilities and what steps the investor has taken to ensure that they are carried out in a manner consistent with the approach to stewardship set out in the statement.

The disclosure should describe arrangements for integrating stewardship within the wider investment process.

Principle 2: Institutional investors should have a robust policy on managing conflicts of interest in relation to stewardship which should be publicly disclosed.

Guidance

An institutional investor's duty is to act in the interests of its clients and/or beneficiaries.

Conflicts of interest will inevitably arise from time to time, which may include when voting on matters affecting a parent company or client.

Institutional investors should put in place, maintain and publicly disclose a policy for identifying and managing conflicts of interest with the aim of taking all reasonable steps to put the interests of their client or beneficiary first. The policy should also address how matters are handled when the interests of clients or beneficiaries diverge from each other.

Principle 3: Institutional investors should monitor their investee companies.

Guidance

Effective monitoring is an essential component of stewardship. It should take place regularly and be checked periodically for effectiveness.

When monitoring companies, institutional investors should seek to:

- keep abreast of the company's performance;
- keep abreast of developments, both internal and external to the company, that drive the company's value and risks;
- satisfy themselves that the company's leadership is effective;
- satisfy themselves that the company's board and committees adhere to the spirit of the UK Corporate Governance Code, including through meetings with the chairman and other board members;
- consider the quality of the company's reporting; and
- attend the General Meetings of companies in which they have a major holding, where appropriate and practicable.

Institutional investors should consider carefully explanations given for departure from the UK Corporate Governance Code and make reasoned judgements in each case. They should give a timely explanation to the company, in writing where appropriate, and be prepared to enter a dialogue if they do not accept the company's position.

Institutional investors should endeavour to identify at an early stage issues that may result in a significant loss in investment value. If they have concerns, they should seek to ensure that the appropriate members of the investee company's board or management are made aware.

Institutional investors may or may not wish to be made insiders. An institutional investor who may be willing to become an insider should indicate in its stewardship statement the willingness to do so, and the mechanism by which this could be done.

Institutional investors will expect investee companies and their advisers to ensure that information that could affect their ability to deal in the shares of the company concerned is not conveyed to them without their prior agreement.

Principle 4: Institutional investors should establish clear guidelines on when and how they will escalate their stewardship activities.

Guidance

Institutional investors should set out the circumstances in which they will actively intervene and regularly assess the outcomes of doing so. Intervention should be considered regardless of whether an active or passive investment policy is followed. In addition, being underweight is not, of itself, a reason for not intervening. Instances when institutional investors may want to intervene include, but are not limited to, when they have concerns about the company's strategy, performance, governance, remuneration or approach to risks, including those that may arise from social and environmental matters.

Initial discussions should take place on a confidential basis. However, if companies do not respond constructively when institutional investors intervene, then institutional investors should consider whether to escalate their action, for example, by:

- holding additional meetings with management specifically to discuss concerns;
- expressing concerns through the company's advisers;
- meeting with the chairman or other board members;
- intervening jointly with other institutions on particular issues;
- making a public statement in advance of General Meetings;
- submitting resolutions and speaking at General Meetings; and
- requisitioning a General Meeting, in some cases proposing to change board membership.

Principle 5: Institutional investors should be willing to act collectively with other investors where appropriate.

Guidance

At times collaboration with other investors may be the most effective manner in which to engage.

Collective engagement may be most appropriate at times of significant corporate or wider economic stress, or when the risks posed threaten to destroy significant value.

Institutional investors should disclose their policy on collective engagement, which should indicate their readiness to work with other investors through formal and informal groups when this is necessary to achieve their objectives and ensure companies are aware of concerns. The disclosure should also indicate the kinds of circumstances in which the institutional investor would consider participating in collective engagement.

Principle 6: Institutional investors should have a clear policy on voting and disclosure of voting activity.

Guidance

Institutional investors should seek to vote all shares held. They should not automatically support the board.

If they have been unable to reach a satisfactory outcome through active dialogue then they should register an abstention or vote against the resolution. In both instances, it is good practice to inform the company in advance of their intention and the reasons why.

Institutional investors should disclose publicly voting records.

Institutional investors should disclose the use made, if any, of proxy voting or other voting advisory services. They should describe the scope of such services, identify the providers and disclose the extent to which they follow, rely upon or use recommendations made by such services.

Institutional investors should disclose their approach to stock lending and recalling lent stock.

Principle 7: Institutional investors should report periodically on their stewardship and voting activities.

Guidance

Institutional investors should maintain a clear record of their stewardship activities.

Asset managers should regularly account to their clients or beneficiaries as to how they have discharged their responsibilities. Such reports will be likely to comprise qualitative as well as quantitative information. The particular information reported and the format used, should be a matter for agreement between agents and their principals.

Asset owners should report at least annually to those to whom they are accountable on their stewardship policy and its execution.

Transparency is an important feature of effective stewardship. Institutional investors should not, however, be expected to make disclosures that might be counterproductive. Confidentiality in specific situations may well be crucial to achieving a positive outcome.

Asset managers that sign up to this Code should obtain an independent opinion on their engagement and voting processes having regard to an international standard or a UK framework such as AAF 01/06. The existence of such assurance reporting should be publicly disclosed. If requested, clients should be provided access to such assurance reports.

Web directory

Government sites

Charity Commission
www.gov.uk/government/organisations/charity-commission

Companies House
www.gov.uk/government/organisations/companies-house

Competition and Markets Authority
www.gov.uk/government/organisations/competition-and-markets-authority

Department for Business, Energy and Industrial Strategy
www.gov.uk/government/organisations/department-for-business-energy-and-industrial-strategy

HM Land Registry
www.gov.uk/government/organisations/land-registry

HM Revenue & Customs
www.gov.uk/government/organisations/hm-revenue-customs

Insolvency Service
www.gov.uk/government/organisations/insolvency-service

Legislation
www.legislation.gov.uk

Patent/Trademark Office
www.gov.uk/government/organisations/intellectual-property-office

Public Service Information
www.gov.uk

Professional bodies

Association of Chartered Certified Accountants	www.acca.org.uk
Chamber of Commerce	www.britishchambers.org.uk
Chartered Institute of Building	www.ciob.org
Chartered Institute of Management Accountants	www.cimaglobal.com
Chartered Institute of Marketing	www.cim.co.uk
Confederation of British Industry	www.cbi.org.uk
Institute of Chartered Accountants in England and Wales	www.icaew.com

Institute of Chartered Accountants in Ireland	www.charteredaccountants.ie
Institute of Chartered Accountants in Scotland	www.icas.com
Institute of Chartered Secretaries and Administrators	www.icsa.org.uk
Institute of Directors	www.iod.com
The Law Society	www.lawsociety.org.uk
The Law Society of Scotland	www.lawscot.org.uk
Trade Union Congress	www.tuc.org.uk

Other

European Business Registry	www.ebr.org
European Patent Office	www.epo.org
Nominet UK	www.nominet.uk

Index